Schistosomiasis Control in China

# Challenges
in Public Health

Editor: Prof. Dr. Oliver Razum, Bielefeld

Formerly/früher: Medizin in Entwicklungsländern
Herausgegeben von
Prof. Dr. Hans Jochen Diesfeld, Heidelberg

Volume 65

Zu Qualitätssicherung und Peer Review
der vorliegenden Publikation

Die Qualität der in dieser Reihe
erscheinenden Arbeiten wird
vor der Publikation durch den
Herausgeber der Reihe geprüft.

Notes on the quality assurance
and peer review of this publication

Prior to publication, the
quality of the work published
in this series is reviewed
by the editor of the series.

Pauline Grys

Schistosomiasis Control in China

Diagnostics and Control Strategies Leading to Success

Bibliographic Information published by the Deutsche Nationalbibliothek
The Deutsche Nationalbibliothek lists this publication in the Deutsche Nationalbibliografie; detailed bibliographic data is available in the internet at http://dnb.d-nb.de.

Library of Congress Cataloging-in-Publication Data
Names: Grys, Pauline, 1976- author.
Title: Schistosomiasis control in China : diagnostics and control strategies leading to success / Pauline Grys.
Other titles: Challenges in public health ; v. 65. 1863-768X
Description: Frankfurt am Main ; New York : Peter Lang, 2016. |
Series: Challenges in public health, ISSN 1863-768X ; volume 65 |
Includes bibliographical references.
Identifiers: LCCN 2016034372| ISBN 9783631667323 |
ISBN 9783653063066 (E-Book)
Subjects: | MESH: Schistosomiasis—diagnosis | Schistosomiasis—prevention & control | Disease Eradication—methods | China
Classification: LCC RC182.S24 | NLM WC 810 | DDC 616.9/63—dc23 LC record available at https://lccn.loc.gov/2016034372

ISSN 1863-768X
ISBN 978-3-631-66732-3 (Print)
E-ISBN 978-3-653-06306-6 (E-PDF)
E-ISBN 978-3-631-69746-7 (EPUB)
E-ISBN 978-3-631-69747-4 (MOBI)
DOI 10.3726/b10466

© Peter Lang GmbH
Internationaler Verlag der Wissenschaften
Frankfurt am Main 2016
All rights reserved.
PL Academic Research is an Imprint of Peter Lang GmbH.

Peter Lang – Frankfurt am Main · Bern · Bruxelles · New York · Oxford · Warszawa · Wien

All parts of this publication are protected by copyright. Any utilisation outside the strict limits of the copyright law, without the permission of the publisher, is forbidden and liable to prosecution. This applies in particular to reproductions, translations, microfilming, and storage and processing in electronic retrieval systems.

This publication has been peer reviewed.
www.peterlang.com

To the people of Wuhan,
who generously shared their wealth of
knowledge and experience with me

Preface

Science is perceived as a sequence of new results, which contribute to the progress of knowledge. This apparently linear process relies, however, also on non-linear, but essential events. This book provides an eloquent example of this process by researching in a perfect inter-disciplinary approach, how one of the most important parasitic diseases – schistosomiasis – may be successfully controlled. This work also examines how progress in schistosomiasis control leads the adaption of the required tools and affects necessary manpower. This research was done in the particular context of the Chinese national schistosomiasis control program, which has been a steady and continuous government-driven activity. This book illustrates that a research approach to co-operate between the "West" and the "East" may particularly benefit from having knowledge of language and life habits.

This research was performed in China, in co-operation with research as well as implementation institutions. Co-operation of "the West" with China is normally based on English communication, just as how we used to co-operate with our Chinese partners: thirty years ago, during our first collaborative visit to Wuhan (China), communication by itself was a challenge, since in the academic environment English-speaking colleagues were still rare; the young generation was not yet trained sufficiently – in fact there was still a complete lack of English teachers – and the English-speaking older generation was scarce. Today, English is common in academia, but with health workers in the endemic countryside, who implement schistosomiasis control, communication remains sometimes difficult for Germans and other Western scientists.

Pauline Grys, who studied Sinology, communicated in Chinese with people at all levels of schistosomiasis control. The basic level is represented by the villagers, who live in an endemic area, in villages, as farmers or fishermen. They are exposed to infection and receive health education as well as medical services. The most relevant aspect of the research was the author´s ability to read and understand the documents and files collected by the control authorities. This book is quite unique in that it opens up the wealth of documentation in the schistosomiasis control stations to interested people in our part of the world.

The studies in this book have become possible only through a lengthy collaboration based on patience and trust and, most relevantly, reliable dedication to common goals. The first contact with our academic partners in Wuhan dates back 30 years ago, up until spring 1986. One of us (AR) had obtained a grant from the Volkswagen Foundation to collaborate with the Department of Parasitology of the Tongji Medical College (TMC) in Wuhan. Whilst preparations for a laboratory workshop in Wuhan were in progress, the provincial governments of Baden-Württemberg (Germany) and of the Hubei Province (China) planned for a visit of a delegation from Baden-Württemberg in order to discuss common research interests with the TMC. HJD was appointed as member of that delegation to represent the discipline of tropical medicine. To our surprise, when AR informed his Institute Director HJD about the timing of the workshop in Wuhan, we discovered independent travel, but at the same time to the TMC in Wuhan.

These parallel events were transformed into a coherent plan for research on schistosomiasis control, which developed into a true win-win cooperation between the partners at TMC working in the endemic area with schistosomiasis patients and us in Heidelberg with active research in parasite immunology. Scientifically, this became a most productive enterprise, when looking at joint publications and joint grants. By organization, this cooperation was actively maintained by Prof Li Yonglong (LYL) at TMC and AR in Heidelberg. In the late nineties, cooperation was extended to the Schistosomiasis Control Institute in Wuhan. In contrast to the German situation, where co-operations are more a matter of individual scientists rather than that of an institute or even the University, co-operation in China was initiated through the top directors and then down the institution to scientists. Combining these managerial traditions was a challenge, but once all "hierarchical levels" had agreed, the basis was solid to engage in joint activities where each partner played synergistic roles on the basis or mutual competence and trust.

Mutual understanding of structures and tools of work was, however, not necessarily evident. Thus, schistosomiasis control in China had been discussed over and over in Western countries, just as schistosomiasis control in the Western hemisphere, which in this context includes Africa, was discussed in China. Both sides used similar words, but were less clear about the different meanings. In fact, misunderstandings were frequent, since schistosomiasis control in the Chinese context acts in positive synergy with agricultural development, whereas agricultural development in Africa frequently results in the spread of schistosomiasis and, thus, counteracts some control elements. This represents a most important conceptual difference. A more explanatory description of this contradiction can be found in the introductory chapter of this book. Pauline Grys has the merit to have made understandable for us non-Chinese-speaking scientists the details of Chinese schistosomiasis control actions, the structure of this successful control system, as well as to allow us to understand the complex interaction of the necessary workforce.

Immunological knowledge, on the other side, is needed not only to develop and apply sero-diagnostic tests, but also to correctly interpret the tests' results. Unease had been expressed for a long time by the practitioners of schistosomiasis control in that immunologically positive tests were not necessarily a proof of an active infection with the parasites. Of course, specific anti-parasite antibodies are formed after infection with schistosomes (as with any other pathogen), these are detected by a sero-diagnostic test in the patient's serum and the positive test is then taken as an indication to administer the anti-schistosomal drug (praziquantel) which kills the schistosome worms. However, the antibodies against schistosomes may persist in the patient serum with the consequence being that subsequent tests may yield positive results in the absence of worms. Now, re-infections are more or less likely as long as the complicated life cycle of schistosomes, which includes snails as vectors of the parasite, persists. The fact that this happens is an unfortunate truth as long as the parasite life cycle has not been effectively interrupted, e.g. by repeated drug administrations. Thus, in a schistosome control program, a positive serologic test may not only simply reflect persisting antibodies, called an "immunologic scar", but may also result from new infections of a previously treated patient.

This book describes unique research to prove not only the existence of such an immunological scar, but also to estimate its potential duration of persistence, and this based on the retrospective analysis of individual test results and treatment outcomes of several hundred individuals in a schistosomiasis endemic village. This meant, first, allowing access to a foreign scientist to the detailed control records of the schistosomiasis control institute. This is significant as such documents are not determined for outsiders; AR was granted – in 1986 – only a view into the room with the boxes of such records, used for reporting purposes only but not for epidemiological research. Such research was deemed as a priority in times when the development of biomedical and molecular science became strongly favored in China. These files, however offered the chance to investigate the "immunologic scar", and this was undertaken by Pauline Grys. In cooperation with her partners at the Schistosomiasis Control institute in Wuhan, Pauline Grys was able to identify among the coded patients, who was treated with praziquantel on which diagnostic basis and at which times. She was able to track the immune response in routine serologic tests of individuals for a period of up to 8 years together with schistosome egg excretion, and in relation to demographic characteristics. Not only does this book provide evidence for the reality of the so far elusive "immunological scar"; the curious reader may also learn also how long it persists.

China has long performed one of the most efficient schistosomiasis controls among endemic countries worldwide. This system is based on a solid personal structure, the details of which are, however, relatively poorly understood outside of China. For Africa, where many endemic areas still have a very much higher schistosomiasis prevalence, the costs for an individual to be treated in a mass campaign has been estimated at around 1 Euro including drug delivery. Pauline Grys, who is also an economist, set out with her co-operators to estimate the costs in the current Chinese situation of comparatively low endemicity, i.e. the situation of successful schistosomiasis control. It turns out that the costs per patient rise considerably as patient numbers drop: the infrastructure for control needs to be maintained in order to prevent resurgence of the disease. This is an inconvenient truth, but this book provides the convincing evidence.

This book offers an unusually detailed view into Chinese schistosomiasis control. It also illustrates the potential value of data files, originally compiled for reporting purposes only, but which represent a valuable source for public health research. Pauline Grys was the right person in the right place and at the right time to dig successfully in to this data mine. We hope that the results of this collaborative research will raise the curiosity of other public health researchers and practitioners.

April 2016

Prof. Dr. Andreas Ruppel (Bammental)
Prof. Dr. Hans Jochen Diesfeld (Starnberg)

Acknowledgements

This book is based on a dissertation that I completed as a requirement for obtaining my doctoral degree at the Medical Faculty at Heidelberg University. I would like to express my sincere gratitude to the many people who, through their constant support, advice and encouragement contributed to making this research possible.

First of all I would like to thank my supervisor, Prof. Dr. Andreas Ruppel, who opened the door for me to the fascinating world of schistosomes. I am deeply grateful for his confidence in me and his full support throughout this entire research project. Without his mentorship and continuous guidance, this research would not have been possible. Equally, I would like to express my gratitude to my Chinese co-supervisor Prof. Yonglong Li. I am thankful for his willingness to take me on as his student and for always taking his time to meet with me in his office to converse, discuss and reflect on the research progress while enjoying a nice cup of tea together.

This research is based on a longstanding partnership and fruitful cooperation between the Heidelberg Institute of Public Health and the Department of Parasitology at the Tongji Medical College of Huazhong University of Science and Technology in Wuhan. I would like to thank the Head of the Department of Parasitology, Dr. Wenqi Liu, and all team members for their unconditional support of my research, for providing me with a workplace and for assisting in every possible way during my frequent visits to Wuhan, allowing them to always be very enjoyable and successful.

This research would not have been possible without the solid assistance and co-operation of the Wuhan Center for Disease Prevention and Control (Wuhan CDC). I gratefully acknowledge the huge support given by all staff of the *Institute for Schistosomiasis Control* at the Wuhan CDC, in particular the Head of the Institute, Mr. Mingxing Xu, and Mrs. Yang Yan. I am very thankful for their continuous support of my work, for their willingness to share their data, knowledge and experience about schistosomiasis control activities, for investing lots of time and patience in answering my many questions and for paving the way for me in so many ways during my field visits to endemic areas and data collection. I am also thankful for the provision and permission of the use of the photographs of Figures 11 and 14 for this publication.

My special thanks go to all my interview partners in the schistosomiasis control stations, hospitals and endemic villages who have so openly shared their views, opinions and experiences with me. Thank you also to Mrs Manting Wang for supporting me with the translations of questionnaires.

I would like to express my heartfelt appreciation to the many colleagues and friends at the Heidelberg Institute of Public Health – Shafiu Mohammed, Shelby Yamamoto, Yan Ding, Peter Dambach, Ahmad Azam Malik, Revati Phalkey, Budi Aji, Aminul Haque, Andreas Deckert, Amal Shafik – who have always encouraged me and kept me motivated over the past years. I also wish to thank my colleagues at the Teaching Unit, Olaf Horstick, Katharina Sommer, Anke Nitschke-Edert and Nandita Rothermund for their concern and support, especially during the last months of my dissertation.

I would like to express my gratitude to the Athenaeum-Stiftung (Heinz-Götze Memorial Fellowship Program) for granting me a six month scholarship and to the Heidelberg Graduate Academy for financial support for one field research trip to Wuhan. I thank Prof. Hans Jochen Diesfeld for his suggestion and encouragement to publish my research as a book and Prof. Oliver Razum for the opportunity to do so within this publication series.

Finally, my biggest thanks go to my family. I am grateful to my parents for supporting all of my life choices, as challenging as this might have been for them at times. I am grateful for their love and support and for not giving up hope. And I thank my grandmother Christine Schwierz, who never ceased to let me know how very proud she was of me.

Contents

Preface vii

Acknowledgements xi

List of Abbreviations xvii

List of Tables xix

List of Figures xxi

1 Introduction 1
  1.1 Aspects of schistosomiasis 1
    1.1.1 Schistosome species 1
    1.1.2 Life cycle 2
    1.1.3 Transmission factors 3
    1.1.4 Clinical stages and symptoms 6
    1.1.5 Diagnostics 7
    1.1.6 Treatment 14
    1.1.7 Epidemiology, economic burden and control 16
  1.2 Schistosomiasis japonica in China 19
    1.2.1 Significance of schistosomiasis in China –
          a historical review 19
    1.2.2 Control strategies 23
    1.2.3 National criteria for control and elimination 25
  1.3 Study rationale 26

2 Methods and materials 29
  2.1 Study setting 29
  2.2 Schistosomiasis control efforts in Wuhan – System structure 31
  2.3 Health Workforce 33
  2.4 Diagnostics 37
    2.4.1 Indirect Haemagglutination Assay 38
    2.4.2 Kato-Katz thick smear test 40
    2.4.3 Database description 41

2.5 Ethical Considerations 44
2.6 Study limitations 45

3 Results 47
3.1 Description of schistosomiasis control system in Wuhan 47
    3.1.1 Historical background 47
    3.1.2 Structure of the system 48
        3.1.2.1 Surveillance sites 48
        3.1.2.2 Institutions and control measures 49
        3.1.2.3 Surveillance and control work activities 52
        3.1.2.4 Endemic situation 55
    3.1.3 Operation of the system 58
        3.1.3.1 Surveillance 58
        3.1.3.2 Response 60
        3.1.3.3 Resources 60
3.2 Health workforce for schistosomiasis control in Wuhan 64
    3.2.1 Availability and distribution of human resources 64
    3.2.2 Work load 72
    3.2.3 Control activities 75
    3.2.4 Community participation and
           community health education 79
3.3 Schistosomiasis surveillance in Xiang Lu village 80
    3.3.1 Description of study population 80
    3.3.2 Serological and parasitological prevalence 84
        3.3.2.1 IHA titer and KK test results 87
        3.3.2.2 Age and sex-specific serological prevalence 90
        3.3.2.3 Titer value-specific serological prevalence 94
    3.3.3 Sero-conversion and sero-reversion 96
        3.3.3.1 Sero-conversion and titer values 99
        3.3.3.2 Age and sex-specific sero-conversion rates 100
        3.3.3.3 Sero-reversion and post-treatment titer values 102
        3.3.3.4 Sero-reversion and pre-treatment titer values 104
        3.3.3.5 Age and sex-specific sero-reversion rates 106
    3.3.4 Individual titer courses over 6–8 consecutive periods 111

4 Discussion 115
4.1 Human Resources in schistosomiasis control in Wuhan 115
    4.1.1 Availability and distribution of human resources 115
    4.1.2 Workload and activities 117

4.2 Diagnostics 119
   4.2.1 Study population 119
   4.2.2 Serological and parasitological prevalence 120
      4.2.2.1 Agreement between IHA und KK 121
      4.2.2.2 Age and sex specific serological prevalence 122
      4.2.2.3 Age specific serological prevalence and
              titer values 123
   4.2.3 Sero-conversions and sero-reversions 123
      4.2.3.1 Dependencies in data 124
      4.2.3.2 Sero-conversion and -reversion and titer-values 126
   4.2.4 Serological non-reverters 128
   4.2.5 Determination of the "serological scar" 129
4.3 Conclusion 131

5 References 135

6 Annexes 153

List of Abbreviations

AM	Artemether
ARTs	Artemisinin derivatives
AS	Artesunate
CAA	Circulating anodic antigen
CCA	Circulating cathodic antigen
CCP	Chinese Communist Party
CDC	Centre of Disease Prevention and Control
COPT	Circumoval precipitation test
DALY	Disability-adjusted life years
DW	Disability weight
ELISA	Enzyme-linked immunosorbet assay
EPG	Eggs per gram
GBD	Global Burden of Disease
IHA	Indirect haemagglutination assay
KK	Kato-Katz-Test
LTA	Low transmission area(s)
MHA	Miracidial hatching assay
NPV	Negative predictive value
NTP	Non-transmission period
PRC	People's Republic of China
PPV	Positive predictive value
PZQ	Praziquantel
SC	Sero-conversion
SEA	Soluble egg antigen
S. haematobium	*Schistosoma haematobium*
S. intercalatum	*Schistosoma intercalatum*
S. japonicum	*Schistosoma japonicum*
S. mansoni	*Schistosoma mansoni*
S. mekongi	*Schistosoma mekongi*
SR	Sero-reversion
TP	Transmission period
WBLP	World Bank Loan Project
WHO	World Health Organization

List of Tables

Table 1:	Characteristics of human schistosome species	4
Table 2:	Parasite species and clinical symptoms of the two chronic forms of schistosomiasis infections	6
Table 3:	Categories of diagnostic methods for schistosome infections	8
Table 4:	Reviewed aspects of schistosomiasis control in Wuhan	32
Table 5:	Screening information	42
Table 6:	Schistosomiasis control status of Wuhan endemic city districts, towns and villages in 2008	56
Table 7:	Wuhan endemic situation overview in 2009	57
Table 8:	Funding of integrated state and province level control activities in Wuhan in 2009	61
Table 9:	Funding of integrated city level control activities in Wuhan in 2009	63
Table 10:	Summary of respondents and their work facilities per district	68
Table 11:	Respondents' sex distribution per human resource category	70
Table 12:	Respondents' work experience in schistosomiasis prevention and control	71
Table 13:	Respondents' view on schistosomiasis related workload	72
Table 14:	Respondents' view on employment for work load in schistosomiasis control	73
Table 15:	Respondents' view on achievement of further decrease of schistosomiasis infection rates	75
Table 16:	Non-clinical staff and self-reported estimation of work time invested in control activities	76
Table 17:	Clinical staff and self-reported estimation of work time invested in control activities	78
Table 18:	Respondents' contact to different groups of community members	79
Table 19:	Overview and structure of the dataset (*2003–2010*)	81
Table 20:	Occupation of study population in 2006	82
Table 21:	Educational background of study population in 2006	83
Table 22:	Serological prevalence of schistosomiasis japonica in Xiang Lu village (2003–2010)	84

Table 23:	Parasitological prevalence of schistosomiasis japonica in Xiang Lu village (2003–2010) as tested by KK	85
Table 24:	Association between IHA titer and KK test result per year and titer	87
Table 25:	Association of titer values and positive KK test result in univariate analysis	89
Table 26:	Age specific coverage of population by IHA tests and serological prevalence per year	91
Table 27:	Serological prevalence according to titer values (2005–2010)	94
Table 28:	Occupation of study population	97
Table 29:	Number of available IHA test results according to age and sex	97
Table 30:	Sero-conversion with respect to titer values	99
Table 31:	Age and sex-specific sero-conversion (2005–2010)	100
Table 32:	Age and titer value-specific sero-conversion (2005–2010)	101
Table 33:	Sero-reversion rates one or two years after IHA positive testing	103
Table 34:	Development of titers one year after treatment	103
Table 35:	Frequency of sero-reversion one year after treatment per pre-treatment titer value	104
Table 36:	Overview of IHA titer values for 2 consecutive years	105
Table 37:	Age and sex specific sero-reversion rates one year after treatment	107
Table 38:	Test results of people with 6 or more consecutive tests	111
Table 39:	Number of tests included into analysis of SR per time category	124
Table 40:	Number of time categories covered by test results from individual persons	124
Table 41:	Number of non-reverters with respect to their belonging to different categories	125

List of Figures

Figure 1:	Global distribution of schistosomiasis	2
Figure 2:	Schistosomiasis life cycle	3
Figure 3:	Status of schistosomiasis endemic countries	17
Figure 4:	Schistosomiasis regional distribution before the 1950s in China	21
Figure 5:	Schistosomiasis regional distribution according to the 3rd nationwide cluster sampling survey in 2004	22
Figure 6:	Map of Wuhan	30
Figure 7:	Overview of institutions responsible for schistosomiasis control at each administrative level and their respective documents and guidelines	33
Figure 8:	Xiang Lu village street and surrounding area	37
Figure 9:	IHA test produced and used in Wuhan City and staff performing IHA	39
Figure 10:	CDC staff preparing stool samples for Kato-Katz tests in Xiang Lu village	41
Figure 11:	Examples of control measures in Wuhan	50
Figure 12:	Hierarchical structure of schistosomiasis control institutions in Wuhan City	51
Figure 13:	Collection of *Oncomelania hupensis* snails in a schistosomiasis endemic area and microscopic examination for infections in the CDC laboratory	53
Figure 14:	Distribution of praziquantel to chronic patients and treatment of a patient with advanced schistosomiasis in hospital	55
Figure 15:	Mapping of endemic villages in Jiangxia district according to their control status	56
Figure 16:	Decision tree to determine human schistosome infections	58
Figure 17:	Distribution of health personnel in schistosomiasis control in Wuhan in 2008	65
Figure 18:	Distribution of technical and non-technical staff at each administrative level of the schistosomiasis control system in Wuhan in 2008	66
Figure 19:	Distribution of health personnel according to their educational background at each administrative level of employment facility in 2008	67

Figure 20:	Age structure of total registered population of Xiang Lu Village in 2006	83
Figure 21:	Age structure population of Xiang Lu village in 2006 of people tested at least one time between 2003–2010	84
Figure 22:	Serological and parasitological prevalence of schistosomiasis per year in Xiang Lu village (2003–2010)	86
Figure 23:	Frequency of agreement between IHA titer and positive KK test per year	89
Figure 24:	Age specific serological prevalence per year and accumulated for all years 2003–2010	93
Figure 25:	Age and sex specific serological prevalence accumulated for all years 2003–2010	93
Figure 26:	IHA Titer level-specific serological prevalence per year (2005–2010)	95
Figure 27:	Age-specific serologic prevalence per titer	96
Figure 28:	Sero-conversion and sero-reversion rates	99
Figure 29:	Sex-specific sero-conversion accumulated for all years (2005–2010)	101
Figure 30:	Age-specific sero-conversion to different titer levels (2005–2010)	102
Figure 31:	Age specific sero-reversion rates one year after treatment per year and accumulated for all years 2005–2010	110
Figure 32:	Age and sex-specific sero-reversion rates one year after treatment accumulated for all years 2005–2010	110
Figure 33:	Individual patient patterns of changes in IHA titers over ≥ 6 consecutive years	112

List of Annexes

Annex 1A: IHA test results of 163 individual persons who were tested IHA negative in 2003 and followed for up to 8 consecutive years until 2010 153

Annex 1B: IHA test results of 23 individual persons who were tested IHA positive in 2003 and followed for up to 8 consecutive years until 2010 154

Annex 2A: IHA test results of 293 individual persons who were not tested in 2003, but tested IHA negative in 2004 and followed for up to 7 consecutive years until 2010 155

Annex 2B: IHA test results of 48 individual persons who were not tested in 2003, but tested IHA positive in 2004 and followed for up to 7 consecutive years until 2010 156

Annex 3A: IHA test results of 185 individual persons who were not tested in 2003 and 2004, but tested IHA negative in 2005 and followed for up to 6 consecutive years until 2010 157

Annex 3B: IHA test results of 155 individual persons who were not tested in 2003 and 2004, but tested IHA positive in 2005 and followed for up to 6 consecutive years until 2010 158

Annex 4: Questionnaire for the heads of 12 district level control stations 159

Annex 5: Questionnaire for non-clinical staff 163

1 Introduction

Schistosomiasis is one of the most widespread parasitic diseases worldwide and continues to remain a major public health challenge in many tropical and subtropical regions in the world. The disease affects almost 240 million people worldwide, with over 61 million people being reported to have received treatment for schistosomiasis in 2014 alone (WHO 2016).

Schistosomiasis is caused by parasitic worms, digenic blood trematodes of the genus *Schistosoma*. Named after the German pathologist Theodor Bilharz, who first identified the worms in 1851, the disease is also known as bilharziasis. This chapter provides an overview of the various biological, pathological, clinical, immunological and socio-economical aspects of schistosomiasis, before taking a closer look at the particular case of schistosomiasis japonica in the People's Republic of China.

1.1 Aspects of schistosomiasis

1.1.1 Schistosome species

There are five principal species of the genus *Schistosoma* known to infect man. Three species, *S. mansoni*, *S. haematobium* and *S. japonicum* are responsible for the majority of schistosomiasis infections, whilst the other two species, *S. intercalatum* and *S. mekongi* parasitize humans to a much lesser extent. Figure 1 shows their geographical distribution.

S. mansoni is widespread in much of sub-Saharan Africa. It also is found in northeast Brazil, Surinam, Venezuela, the Caribbean, lower and middle Egypt and the Arabic peninsula. *S. haematobium* occurs predominantly in sub-Saharan Africa, the Nile valley in Egypt and Sudan, the Maghreb and the Arabic peninsula. *S. japonicum* is limited to areas along the central lakes and rivers in China and the Philippines (Mindanao, Leyte, and some other islands), and to two isolated areas in Indonesia. *S. mekongi* is prevalent only in the central Mekong Basin, in Laos and Cambodia. *S. intercalatum* has been reported sporadically in pockets in Western and Central Africa.

Figure 1: Global distribution of schistosomiasis (modified after Gryseels et al., 2006)

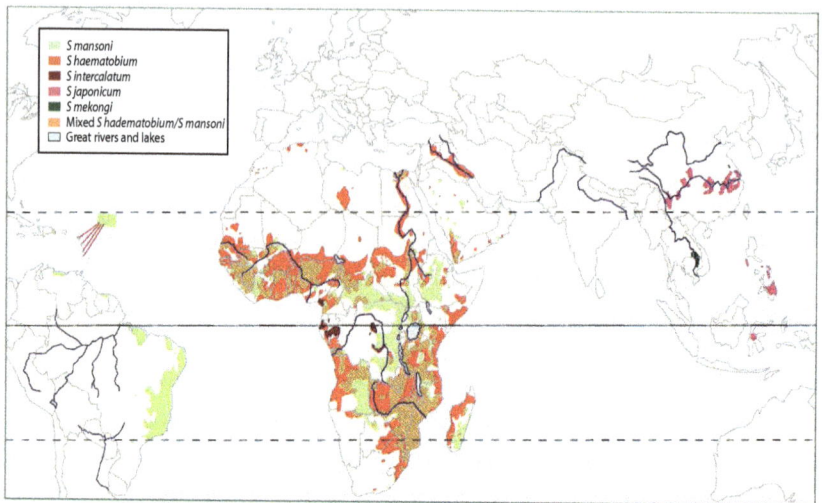

1.1.2 Life cycle

The life cycle of the five schistosome species include the human and, in the case of *S. japonicum*, also animal final hosts and different intermediate host snails. All five species are contracted in the same way, through direct contact with fresh water (e.g., when wading, swimming, or bathing) infested with the free-living form of the parasite known as cercariae. The life cycles of the human schistosomes, as seen in Figure 2, are largely similar.

Eggs are excreted with faeces or urine (1) and, in areas with poor sanitation, contaminate fresh-water sources. Under optimal conditions, the eggs hatch and release miracidia (2). Freshwater snails become infected with the miracidium (3), which multiplies inside the snail and matures into multiple cercariae (5) that the snails release into the water. The cercariae, which survive outside a host for up to 48 hours, quickly penetrate intact skin. Once inside the human body, the worms penetrate the wall of the nearest vein and travel to the liver where they grow and sexually mature (8, 9). Mature males pair with female worms and migrate either to the intestinal veins or those of the bladder where egg production occurs. Most eggs leave the blood stream and body through the intestines or bladder. Some of the eggs, however, are not excreted and can become lodged in the tissues. The pathology associated with schistosomiasis is caused by the cellular infiltration resulting from antigens secreted by trapped eggs. It is the presence of these eggs rather than the worms themselves that causes the disease (CDC 2009).

Figure 2: Schistosomiasis life cycle (CDC 2009)

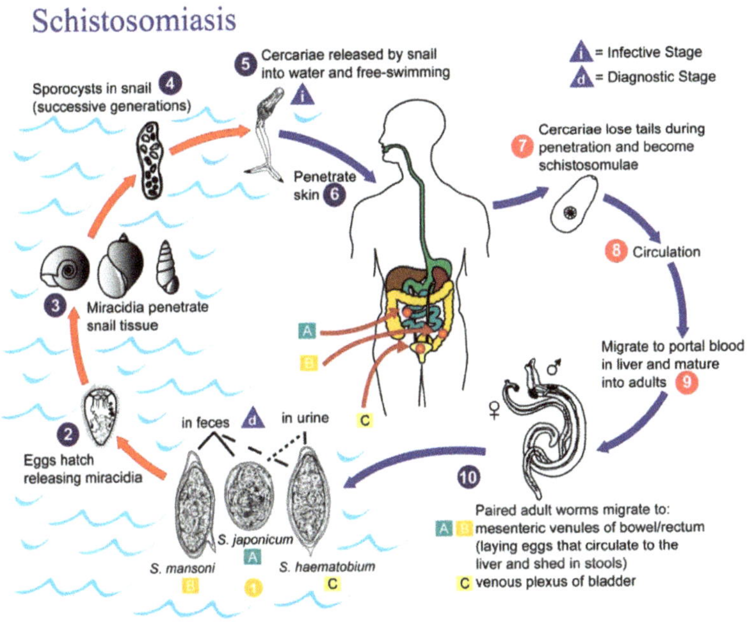

Schistosomiasis

- 5 Cercariae released by snail into water and free-swimming
- i = Infective Stage
- d = Diagnostic Stage
- 4 Sporocysts in snail (successive generations)
- 6 Penetrate skin
- 7 Cercariae lose tails during penetration and become schistosomulae
- 3 Miracidia penetrate snail tissue
- 8 Circulation
- 2 Eggs hatch releasing miracidia
- d in feces
- c in urine
- 9 Migrate to portal blood in liver and mature into adults
- S. mansoni
- S. japonicum
- S. haematobium
- 10 Paired adult worms migrate to:
  - A B mesenteric venules of bowel/rectum (laying eggs that circulate to the liver and shed in stools)
  - C venous plexus of bladder

1.1.3 Transmission factors

Transmission of schistosome infections is influenced by several factors, such as the presence of the intermediate hosts, i.e. specific snails. The definite host primarily maintains transmission through contamination of fresh water and contact of hosts with infested waters. Table 1 lists some of the relevant characteristics of the five human schistosome species.

Species-specific aspects:

Looking at all schistosome species, there are three characteristics of relevance unique to *S. japonicum* worth mentioning. For one, *S. japonicum* is a zoonosis. The same parasite can infect both humans and animals. More than 40 mammal species can act as a definite parasite host. In China, bovines, especially water buffaloes, play a major role in the transmission of the disease by contributing considerably in the deposition of *S. japonicum* eggs into the environment and contaminating fresh waters (Guo et al. 2001; Shi *et al.* 1990). Their daily total egg output, is significantly higher than that of human individuals (Gray *et al.* 2009; Guo *et al.* 2006) and attributes to as much as 75 % of human infections. Secondly, *S. japonicum* is the most pathogenic of the *Schistosoma* species. With an egg production of up to 3.500 eggs per day, the egg load is around 10 times higher than that of, for example, *S. mansoni*. And thirdly, the life cycle of the intermediate host, which is the amphibic snail *Oncomelania hupensis*, differs from vector snails in Africa. While the latter are aquatic and almost always rely on permanent waters, *Oncomelania hupensis* is amphibious, lives on land near water and requires alternating dry and flooding seasons for reproduction (Richter & Ruppel 2010).

All these biological and environmental factors influence the transmission of the disease and, therefore, also influence the strategy and the choice of control measures to fight the parasite and with it the disease.

Table 1: Characteristics of human schistosome species (modified after Richter and Ruppel, 2010)

	S. mansoni	S. japonicum	S. haematobium	S. intercalatum	S. mekongi
Schistosome worms					
Life span of adult worms (years)	5- more than 30	Max. more than 40	3–10	3–10 (?)	4 – ?
Number of eggs shed per worm pair per day	250–400	1.500–3.500	200–1.000	160–400	ca. 1.000 (?)
Intermediate parasite host					
Snail genus	Biomphalaria	Oncomelania	Bulinus		Neotricula
Snail lifestyle	Aquatic	Amphibious	Aquatic	Aquatic	Amphibious
Definite hosts					
	Humans, occasionally apes and rodents	Humans and more than 40 other mammal species	Humans, occasionally monkeys	Humans, occasionally rodents	Humans, dogs

Environmental factors:

The natural habitat of the snail intermediate host plays a major role in the transmission of schistosomiasis. The level of transmission varies widely according to the physical characteristics of the surface water, ranging from stagnant to flowing and from small streams to the largest lakes of Africa and Asia (WHO 1993).

Natural environmental changes, induced for example by floods, may affect the natural habitat of intermediate snails and influence schistosomiasis transmission (Wu et al. 2008; Yang 2006). Man-made changes to environments may enhance the transmission of schistosomiasis or even introduce schistosomiasis to a formally non-endemic area, by creating new snail habitats. In the same way, environmental management can serve as an effective control measure against the spread of schistosomaisis by destroying existing snail habitats.

There are many examples from all over the world on how the development of man-made water resources, namely the construction of damns for water regulation, affects schistosomiasis transmission as a result (Li et al. 2007; Liang et al. 2007; Ofoezie & Asaolu 1997; Steinmann et al. 2006; Wu et al. 2008; Yang 2006; Zhu et al. 2008). Equally, the link between irrigation developments and an increase in schistosomiasis is well documented (TDR, 1995). There are many examples of how irrigation led to the increase of schistosomiasis as a result, such as the Oyan reservoir in Nigeria (Ofoezie & Asaolu 1997; Ofoezie et al. 1991), the Volta region in Ghana after the creation of Lake Volta (Klumpp & Chu 1977; Paperna 1970) or the Nile region in Egypt (Michelson et al. 1993; Watts & El Katsha 1997).

Human infections:

Schistosomiasis is strongly associated with poverty (King 2010; King & Bertino 2008). Snail-bearing water must be contaminated by human sewage for the snails to acquire their infection. Then, in turn, people must come into contact with the same snail-infested water in order to become infected. Consequently, mainly rural population groups with low living standards and poor hygienic conditions are affected.

Social and economic context and determinants play a major role in schistosomiasis transmission (Huang & Manderson 2005). In less-developed communities that have only limited water resources, exposure of infection is often unavoidable. At highest risk of becoming infected are people with regular contact to contaminated waters, namely children playing and bathing and people working near or in contaminated waters, such as fishermen or farmers, or women washing clothes. Males are frequently more affected than females (Huang & Manderson 2005; WHO 2013) Health education has already for a long time been recognized as crucial in helping people at risk of infection to understand their role in the cause and prevention of schistosomiasis (WHO 1990).

1.1.4 Clinical stages and symptoms

The clinical manifestations of schistosomiasis can be divided into acute schistosomiasis and chronic schistosomiasis. Acute schistosomiasis occurs 3–10 weeks after infection and is an immunological response to the infection ('serum sickness'), probably relating to the onset of egg production. Usually the acute phase of schistosomiasis is asymptomatic. However, clinical signs of varying intensity may occur, the most common ones being dry cough, weakness, headache, abdominal symptoms, and urticarial or angioedema (Jaureguiberry et al. 2010). If there is no treatment, the infection progresses to the chronic phase (King & Dangerfield-Cha 2008).

There are two major forms of chronic schistosomiasis infections – intestinal and urogenital (Table 2): In intestinal schistosomiasis infections the highest affected organs are the large intestine and the liver and spleen, in urogenital schistosomiasis the genito-urinary tract.

Table 2: Parasite species and clinical symptoms of the two chronic forms of schistosomiasis infections (WHO 2013)

Chronic schistosomiasis		
	Causal schistosome species	Clinical symptoms
Intestinal schistosomiasis	S. mansoni S. japonicum S. mekongi S. intercalatum and related S. guineensis	Abdominal pain, diarrhoea and blood in the stool; liver enlargement is common in advanced cases, frequently associated with an accumulation of fluid in the peritoneal cavity and hypertension of the abdominal blood vessels; in such cases there may also be enlargement of the spleen

Chronic schistosomiasis		
	Causal schistosome species	Clinical symptoms
Urogenital schistosomiasis	S. haematobium	Haematuria (blood in urine); common findings in advanced cases are fibrosis of the bladder and ureter, kidney damage; bladder cancer and female genital schistosomiasis may also be a possible late-stage complication

The chronic phase can be divided into early and late stages. In China a further distinction is made between chronic schistosomiasis and a third phase named late stage schistosomiasis. The latter is an extreme form of chronic schistosomiasis and is associated with portal hypertension, splenomegaly, ascites, and gastro-oesophageal variceal bleeding, or with severe growth retardation or granulomatous disease of the large intestine (Jia et al. 2011).

1.1.5 Diagnostics

Diagnosis is central to all aspects of schistosomiasis. Diagnosis in non-endemic countries, for example Germany, is predominantly a matter of travel medicine. This book deals, however, only with diagnosis in endemic areas. Determination of target populations for chemotherapy in the endemic communities and / or assessment of morbidity all build on the results of diagnostic tests (Zhou et al. 2007b). Diagnostic needs in highly endemic areas differ from those in low endemic areas. Therefore, with falling endemicity levels, the diagnostic approach needs to be adapted accordingly and changed as further progress is made towards control and ultimate elimination of the disease (Bergquist et al. 2009).

There are many different diagnostic methods used to detect schistosome infections. Direct diagnostic methods detect ova, schistosome antigens or DNA in urine, stool, tissue or blood, whilst indirect methods rely on clinical, biochemical or immunological disease markers including antibody detection (Mott & Dixon 1987). An overview of available diagnostics for schistosomiasis as of 2012 is reproduced in the following table 3 (McCarthy et al. 2012):

Table 3: Categories of diagnostic methods for schistosome infections (McCarthy et al. 2012)

	Schistosomiasis		
	Schistosoma mansoni	*Schistosoma haematobium*	*Schistosoma japonicum*
Parasitological diagnosis	Stool Kato-Katz	Urine filtration	Stool Kato-Katz
Antibody detection	✓	✓	✓
Antigen detection	+	+/−	N/A
PCR		----Experimental----	
Assessment of infection intensity	Stool Kato-Katz	Urinary egg count	Stool Kato-Katz
Assessment of drug efficacy	Clearance of eggs from stool	Clearance of eggs from urine	Clearance of eggs from stool
Mapping/elimination	Seroepidemiology	Seroepidemiology	Seroepidemiology

✓, Available or method of choice; N/A, not available; +/−, acceptable but not ideal.
doi:10.1371/journal.pntd.0001601.t005

There are considerable differences in terms of sensitivity and specificity, ease of use and cost of different tests available. And even more importantly, a given test may perform differently with changing factors, such as different *Schistosoma* species or different infection intensities. Characteristics, advantages and shortcomings of different tests are dealt with in more detail below.

Parasitological methods:

Examination of stool/urine for ova is the primary method of diagnosis for suspected schistosome infections. However, this method is not suitable for diagnosis during the early stages of acute schistosomiasis, as detection of eggs is possible only 5–10 weeks after infection (Ruppel *et al.* 1985). Ova production begins when worms reach their mature form and migrate to their final destination. *S. mansoni*, *S. japonicum*, *S. mekongi*, and *S. intercalatum* reside in the mesenteric venous plexus of infected hosts and eggs are shed in faeces; *S. haematobium* adult worms are found in the venous plexus of the lower urinary tract and eggs are shed in urine.

The most widely used direct parasitological stool examination in the field is the Kato-Katz (KK) thick smear test (Katz *et al.* 1972), which also is recommended by the World Health Organization (WHO) for surveillance and epidemiological field survey of intestinal schistosome infections (Montresor *et al.* 1998). It has a very high specificity, is simple to perform, requires, except for a microscope, only basic single-use equipment and basic chemicals, and it is relatively cheap. The number of eggs can be counted which makes KK the best quantitative test allowing the estimation of infection intensity.

However, this method is very labor-intensive and time consuming. Results depend upon the number of stool samples tested (Ruppel *et al.* 1990) and, moreover, the rate of egg excretion varies considerably depending on intensity or duration of infection. In particular low infection intensities which are common in low transmission areas (LTA) or after deworming (Booth *et al.* 2003) can present a problem for microscopic testing (Idris *et al.* 2003). With the KK technique, the examined amount of stool is relatively small; the most common size equals 41.7 mg of stool. Given the dilution factor of human excreta, the fact that about half of all parasite eggs never leave the host and/or the day to day fluctuation in egg excretion, the number of eggs found in faeces with this method can differ considerably (Corachan 2002; Engels *et al.* 1996). If only a single KK slide is prepared from a single stool specimen, sensitivity has been proven to be reduced, particularly in light infections (Lin *et al.* 2008a). This can result in underestimation of prevalence of infection and confound evaluation and assessment of infection status (Booth *et al.* 2003; De Jonge *et al.* 1990a; De Jonge *et al.* 1990b; Gold *et al.* 1969). Many studies have demonstrated that sensitivity can be improved and to which degree by either examining multiple Kato-Katz thick smears produced from a single stool sample, or by examining multiple stool samples (Deelder *et al.* 1976; Knopp *et al.* 2008; Ruppel *et al.* 1990; Steinmann 2008).

However, very often examining multiple Kato-Katz smears or even obtaining repeated stool samples from the same individuals at different days is unrealistic when operating in the field. Not only does it represent a logistical challenge to obtain repeated stool samples from the same individuals, it also requires increased time and human resource investment for preparation and examination, which are often unavailable.

Another parasitological method for the detection of active schistosomiasis is the Miracidial Hatching Assay (MHA), which is particularly sensitive for detecting vital eggs. However, this method is relatively time consuming and costly. Also, the result of the hatching test depends upon factors such as temperature, light and water quality (Ye *et al.* 1997), which makes it difficult to standardize. In China, a variation of the MHA, the "nylon bag" method, is sometimes used. Here, a large stool sample of about 30g is flushed with water through a mesh container into a nylon bag with a dense mesh of 300 holes per square inch. The content of the bag is transferred into a bottle and filled with fresh non-chlorinated water with a pH ranging from 7.4 to 7.6. The bottle is kept at between 24–30 °C and in strong light. It is checked for swimming miracidia at regular intervals of 4, 8, 12 and 24 hours. The release of actively swimming larvae, which are readily visible to the naked eye or with a magnifying glass, demonstrate egg viability. If no miracidia can be detected after 24 hours, the person is considered negative for infection (Yu *et al.* 2007).

Yu *et al.* (2007) compared the Kato-Katz method using duplicate faecal smears and the "nylon bag" hatching test to detect *S. japonicum* infection in endemic areas in China. The study concluded that seven Kato-Katz thick smears are equivalent to the performed hatching method. However, despite the improved test sensitivity for intestinal schistosomiasis, the hatching test technique is considered less practical and more difficult for preparation and examination in the field. Therefore, Yu *et al.* question, whether the added time and cost required justify its wider use.

Immunological methods:

There are two main principles of immunodiagnostic tests used for the diagnosis of schistosomiasis in field situations, the detection of either antibodies (indirect method) or of circulation antigens (direct method) in serum. The detection of DNA (Pontes *et al.* 2002) is not practical for endemic areas. Therefore, these recently advocated tests would not be considered here.

Indirect immunological tests:

Antibody assays can differ in several aspects. Firstly, the antigen used can originate from different stages of the schistosome lifecycle, namely worms, cercariae or eggs. Secondly, there are different forms of antigen purity which are used: crude preparations, purified antigen mixtures and recombinant peptides of proteins. Finally, there are several different assay systems used.

Nowadays, for the detection of serum antibodies in schistosome infections in men, the indirect haemagglutination assay (IHA), the circumoval precipitin test (COPT) and the enzyme-linked immunosorbet assay (ELISA) are among the assays for large scale use.

COPT and IHA had already been developed and applied in the 1960s and since then have undergone a series of modifications with the aim to standardize the two testing systems including antigen preparation and testing protocols (Wu 2002).

The indirect haemagglutination assay (IHA) is an extensively employed method for community screening for schistosomiasis, especially in China. In a laboratory comparison with worm and egg antigens and schistosomiasis mansoni, haematobia, and japonica, a commercial Chinese IHA based on soluble extracts of schistosome eggs performed comparatively best (Gui *et al.* 1991). This type of IHA has been investigated in several field studies (Yu *et al.* 2007; Zhou *et al.* 2008; Zhou *et al.* 2007b). Zhou *et al.* (2011) compared eight such studies with regard to key characteristics. The reference gold standard for six of those studies was KK examination using a range of 3–14 slides. Among them, Yu *et al.* (2007) used the most comprehensive gold standard, duplicate KK slides from seven different stool samples. The other two studies used MHA as gold standard. Comparison of results showed that the sensitivity of the IHA method varied from 69.7 % to 100 %, and specificity ranged from 35.7 % to 93.6 %. With repeated chemotherapy in the endemic areas, the PPV of the IHA method was low. Most of the eight studies reported PPVs less than 37 %.

COPT is time-consuming and relatively complicated to perform, which limits its wide application in the field. Zhou *et al.* (2011) summarized the findings of COPT performance from several studies conducted in China. Accordingly, sensitivity was high between 94.1 %-98.6 %, whilst the false-positive rate was very low at 2.5 %-3.6 %. However, due to repeated chemotherapy in endemic areas a drop in sensitivity to 72.2 %-85.8 % could be observed. In addition, whereas the negative predictive value (NPV) was high with over 87 %, the positive predictive value (PPV) of COPT tests was low, ranging between 31.7 % and 74.9 % (Zhou *et al.* 2011).

The enzyme-linked immunosorbent assay (ELISA) is a test that determines serum antibodies by color change of a substrate. Here, antibodies bind to specific known antigens. An antigen-antibody complex is formed and recognized by a second enzyme-linked antibody against human immunoglobulins. A substance containing the enzymes substrate is added and the subsequent reaction produces a detectable signal, i.e. a color change of the substrate. ELISA methods for diagnosis of schistosome infection differ according to the choice of assay designs and the antigens used. Most commonly applied is the ELISA test with soluble egg antigen (SEA), which first emerged in the late 1970s. Antigens and test systems were already compared in a WHO-coordinated evaluation 30 years ago (Mott & Dixon 1982). The test was regarded optimal for field use, reliable, sensitive and specific (Wu 2002). In a study conducted by Zhou *et al.* (2007b) in two Chinese villages, ELISA and IHA were compared to the KK gold standard. Sensitivity of ELISA was found to be slightly higher than that of IHA, but the specificity was lower with 38 % compared to 56 % and 67 % in the two respective villages.

Another study conducted by Lin *et al.* (2008a) compared ELISA and KK for two consecutive years in a population with relatively high prevalence but low infection intensity. Using KK as the gold standard, ELISA showed sensitivities of 79 % and 87 %, specificities of 39 % and 54 %, positive predictive values of 21 % and 25 % and negative predictive values of 93 % and 94 %. The correlation between antibody levels and infection intensity was found to be poor. Furthermore, when studying changes in ELISA results from one year to the next, ELISA showed limited ability to detect new infections and to differentiate between active and past infections. The authors suggested that ELISA alone must be used with caution for both individual level diagnosis and for population-based targeting (Lin *et al.* 2008b).

There are several shortcomings common for most antibody detection assays. A frequently raised concern is that there is the possibility of cross-reaction with other infections which may lead to false positive results (Alarcon de Noya *et al.* 1996). However, a sero-epidemiological study in Oman excluded the presence of cross reacting antibodies at least for intestinal parasitic worms (Idris *et al.* 2003). Similarly, a review on sero-diagnosis pointed out that the low sensitivity of the KK Test, if this test is used as gold standard for serology, suggests "wrong" positive ELISA values, thus decreasing formal specificity (Doenhoff *et al.* 2004). Also, specific antibodies may persist even after cure ("immunological scar"). In these patients, the antibody detection assay might give a false positive result, because it is unable to distinguish past infections from active infections (Ruppel *et al.* 1991).

Efforts have been made to overcome the latter shortcoming through the development of antigen tests to detect active infections based on the presence of schistosomal antigens.

Direct immunological tests:

Detection of antigens secreted from the parasite proves the presence of the parasite directly and not through an indirect, e.g. antibody-based test. The presence of schistosome antigens in serum or urine of infected subjects was demonstrated over fifty years ago (Deelder et al. 1976; Gold et al. 1969). Since then, many studies have been carried out to investigate major schistosome antigens suitable for development of immunodiagnostic assays (Li et al. 2003; Mott et al. 1987).

Research in this context has mainly been focused on two circulating antigens, named according to their electrophoretic migratory behavior, the circulating anodic antigen (CAA) and circulating cathodic antigen (CCA). The presence of CAA has even been detected in Egyptian mummies (Deelder et al. 1990). First explorations of detecting the CAA for immunodiagnosis of *S. japonicum* infection in China were already initiated in the early 1980s (Qian & Deelder 1983).

Detection of CAA presence in the serum is generally a good diagnostic indicator of active schistosome infection. The CAA used in a study of de Jonge et al. (1988) reaches a sensitivity of 75–93 % and a specificity of 100 % (De Jonge et al. 1988; De Jonge et al. 1990c). Another study by Al-Sherbiny et al. (1999) used CAA and CCA to test sera and urine samples of patients with confirmed *S. haematobium* infections. With serum samples, sensitivity reached 55 % (CAA) and with urine samples 78 % (CCA). This diagnostic procedure has also been used to monitor the success of chemotherapy in humans, especially using praziquantel. The CAA was shown to have completely cleared from the circulation of patients infected with *S. mansoni* and *S. haematobium* already one month after praziquantel treatment (Kumar 1999). The key problem with tests based on CAA or CCA was already raised long ago: the detection limit is not better than egg detection with low level infections, as shown in experimental animals infected with various doses of cercaria (Deelder et al. 1976).

Indirect methods using clinical, subclinical or biochemical morbidity markers:

Current clinical methods for diagnosing schistosome infections include, for example, ultrasonography, liver biopsy, and measurement of biochemical markers or histological examination.

Ultrasonography is a safe, rapid and non-invasive technique for morbidity assessment in schistosomiasis. This technique allows direct visualization of the organ-specific schistosomiasis-associated changes seen in the liver and urinary bladder, as well as additional disease complications such as portal hypertension and hydronephrosis (Carlton *et al.* 2010; Guangjin *et al.* 2002; Hatz *et al.* 1992; Hsiang *et al.* 2010). Standard protocols for ultrasound examination and the quantification of morbidity in *S. haematobium* and *S. mansoni* infections have been developed by expert meetings sponsored by WHO (Richter *et al.* 2000). However, this method requires well-trained staff.

Another way of assessing morbidity may be simply to ask subjects about the presence of the signs and symptoms of morbidity associated with schistosomiasis (Moestue *et al.* 2003; Partnership for Child Development 1999; Vennervald & Dunne 2004). A multi-country study conducted from 1990–1992 used questionnaires as a means of identifying communities with a high risk of urinary schistosomiasis (UNDP/World Bank/WHO 1995). The diagnostic questionnaire approach is based on self-reporting red (bloody) urines. It worked well, showing high test efficiency in five of the 7 countries examined. Lengeler and colleagues achieved similar positive and encouraging results (Lengeler *et al.* 2002). The questionnaires were well accepted, highly reliable, and of low cost and, therefore, proved to be a feasible and cost-effective primary screening method for *S. haematobium* infections especially in resource poor countries, where large scale testing is too costly.

Questionnaire-based screening for *S. japonicum* in schoolchildren was also developed in China, showing a high sensitivity and specificity (Tan *et al.* 2004; Zhou *et al.* 1998). High-risk schoolchildren were identified by only three simple yes/no questions concerning frequent water contact, frequent weakness, and frequent diarrhea (Zhou *et al.* 1998), thus making this approach also applicable in China.

1.1.6 Treatment

Until now, there is no vaccine for schistosomiasis available, but internationally, many efforts have been and still are made to develop one (Bergquist & Colley 1998; Bergquist *et al.* 2008; Bethony *et al.* 2008; Capron *et al.* 2002;

Doenhoff 1998; McManus & Loukas 2008; Wu *et al.* 2005). Difficulties finding schistosoma antigens suitable for use in a vaccine and questions about the size of the market for a potential vaccine have previously hindered development, and it is unlikely that a vaccine will become available in the near future (James *et al.* 2005).

For schistosomiasis treatment, three drugs have recently been used to treat schistosomiasis, which differ in their effects on schistosome species. While metrifonate targets *S. haematobium* and oxamniquine targets *S. mansoni*, the drug praziquantel (PZQ) works against all human schistosome species. Metrifonate and oxamniquine are no longer used.

PZQ was developed in the laboratories for parasitological research of the German companies Bayer AG and Merck KGaA located in Elberfeld and Darmstadt in the mid-1970s. In 1979, praziquantel was approved for humans and became generally available for individual selective and mass treatment during the 1980s. PZQ is included in the "Model List of Essential Medicines" published by the WHO. Due to its broad spectrum against several trematodes beyond schistosomes, its efficacy after a single oral dose, the rare, temporary and relatively minor side-effects reported with this drug, and its present low cost or even free donations by Bayer AG, PZQ is the official WHO-recommended anti-schistosomal drug for use in preventive chemotherapy (WHO 2006).

WHO has advocated for increased access to praziquantel and resources for implementation. At least 28 countries were able to implement preventive chemotherapy for schistosomiasis in 2010. The number of people treated for schistosomiasis increased from 12.4 million in 2006 to 33.5 million in 2010 (WHO 2013).

Although PZQ has been used to treat schistosomiasis for almost 30 years, its mechanism of action still remains unknown (Aragon *et al.* 2009; Pica-Mattoccia *et al.* 2008). Treatment with PZQ is effective at killing adult worms in the body. However, it does not prevent new infections. For this reason, repeated treatments are often necessary. Also, in recent years, potential development of resistance to PZQ emerges as a concern (Alonso *et al.* 2006; Appleton & Mbaye 2001; Botros *et al.* 2005; Doenhoff *et al.* 2008; Fallon 1998; King *et al.* 2000; Kusel & Hagan 1999; Melman *et al.* 2009; Seto *et al.* 2011b).

Thus, the search for alternative drugs is considered a necessity. Potential candidates are artemether (AM) and artesunate (AS), artemisinin derivatives (ARTs) with anti-schistosomal potential (Caffrey & Secor 2011; Liu et al. 2011; Utzinger et al. 2001; Utzinger et al. 2007).

1.1.7 Epidemiology, economic burden and control

Schistosomiasis is one of the most widespread parasitic diseases, being only second after malaria in socioeconomic and public health importance for tropical and subtropical areas. An estimated 779 million people are at risk of infection with more than 200 million people being infected worldwide (Steinmann et al. 2006). Of those infected with schistosomiasis, about 120 million people are estimated to be symptomatic. Around 20 million of those develop severe disease.

Although the total number of infected persons and people at risk of infection worldwide did not change considerably over the past 30 years, their global distribution has changed and there is a growing discrepancy between sub-Saharan Africa and the rest of the world in terms of transmission and control (Engels et al. 2002). Whereas about 90 % of the total population requiring preventive chemotherapy for schistosomiasis live within the WHO African Region, the number for the WHO Region of the Americas and the WHO Western Pacific region (including China) is only 3,02 % and 0,56 %, respectively (WHO 2010).

Untreated cases of schistosomiasis result in substantial morbidity and even mortality. Particularly with untreated schistosomiasis japonica morbidity and associated mortality are high, probably due to the considerably higher rate of "egg production" by *S. japonicum* (Ross et al. 2001). Even though the more pathogenic type of schistosomiasis, caused by *S. japonicum*, is found in Asia, most of the severe cases occur in Africa. As many as 280,000 deaths per year are attributed to *S. haematobium* and *S. mansoni* infections in sub-Saharan Africa alone (van der Werf et al. 2003). This is mainly due to insufficient control measures, related to both transmission and morbidity control. Figure 3 gives an overview of the status of schistosomiasis endemic countries worldwide.

Schistosomiasis is endemic in 78 countries and territories. Active transmission is reported from 67 countries and territories. Of these, 43 are in Africa (WHO 2016). Sub-Saharan Africa alone accounts for about 89 % of the global burden with a prevalence of 166 million and high morbidity (Molyneux *et al.* 2005; van der Werf *et al.* 2003).

Figure 3: Status of schistosomiasis endemic countries (WHO 2014)

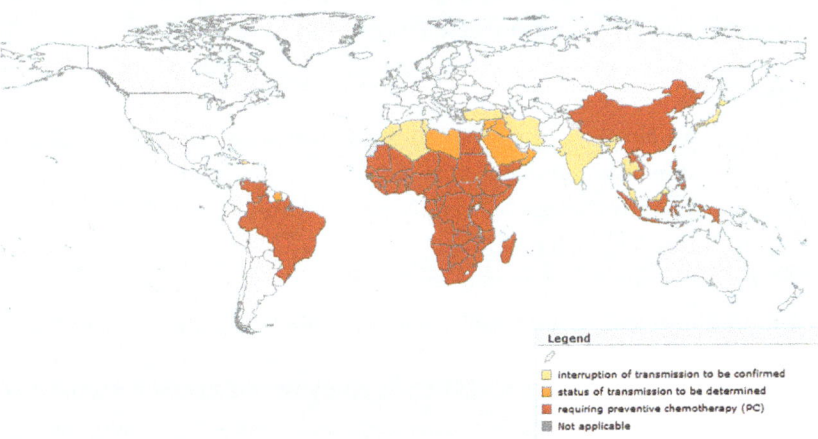

There are several factors that can influence the development and the level of morbidity in humans, such as the degree and length of exposure, the intensity of infection, co-infections, among others (Vennervald & Dunne 2004). It is very difficult to measure or even to estimate the burden of disease resulting from human schistosomiasis. Many researchers have tried to answer the question of how debilitating it is for an average person to have schistosomiasis and how to reach accurate disability estimates. The Global Burden of Disease (GBD) study conducted by WHO and the World Bank assigns disability weight (DW) to individual diseases on a scale from 0 (no disability) to 1 (death). In the case of schistosomiasis, a disability weight of 0.005 was assigned for school-aged children, and of 0.006 for those older than 14 years (Mathers *et al.* 2007). The global burden of schistosomiasis, expressed in 'disability-adjusted life years' (DALYs) lost annually due to the disease, is estimated at 4.5 million (WHO 2002).

However, several authors argue that the burden of schistosomiasis, presented in form of DW or as DALY rankings, has been significantly underestimated because the disease has many non-specific symptoms and signs and a number of under-acknowledged subclinical morbidities that affect patients on a daily basis (Jia et al. 2011; King 2008; King et al. 2005). In particular, complications such as diarrhea, anemia, epilepsy and cognitive impairment are proven to have causative links with schistosomiasis, but had been disaggregated from schistosomiasis in the GBD system.

With *S. japonicum*, even though nowadays most of the infected people are regarded as asymptomatic, there is still a substantial morbidity with impact on the growth of children, quality of life and working capacity (King & Dangerfield-Cha 2008).

A disability analysis reported by Finkelstein and colleagues has taken these complications into account and estimated an aggregate disability impact of 9.8 % for children and of 18.6 % for adults having schistosomiasis japonica (Finkelstein et al. 2008). A study on the disability weight of chronic schistosomiasis japonica also suggested serious underestimation of the real burden in endemic populations. The authors estimated an overall disability weight of 0.191, while age-specific weights ranged from 0.095 among those aged 5–14 years to 0.246 among those aged > 60 years (Jia et al. 2007). In another study, the age-specific DW of advanced schistosomiasis japonica was estimated based on patients' self-rated health scores on the visual analogue scale of the questionnaire. For advanced *S. japonicum*, the overall DW was 0.447, and age-specific DWs ranged from 0.378 among individuals aged 30–44 years to 0.510 among the elderly aged ≥ 60 years (Jia et al. 2011). All these findings support the claim of serious underestimation of the burden of schistosomiasis as calculated for the GBD and the call for revision of the GBD.

In large parts of sub-Saharan Africa control programmes are very limited or non-existent. However, it is equally noteworthy that due to a consequence of effective control programs based on chemical molluscicides, mass or selective chemotherapy and sanitary measures, the prevalences of human schistosomiasis have decreased considerably in other parts of the world, namely in American and Asian endemic areas. Countries such as Brazil, China, Dominican Republic, Egypt, Laos, and Saudi Arabia, are being considered low transmission areas (LTA) (WHO 2001). In particular in China, achievement of LTA status is a result of many decades of rigorous implementation of control activities.

The particular case of Schistosomiasis japonica control in China will be discussed in the following.

1.2 Schistosomiasis japonica in China

China's achievements in the fight against schistosomiasis are worldwide acknowledged (Collins *et al.* 2012; Utzinger *et al.* 2005; Wang *et al.* 2008; Zhou *et al.* 2005b). In fact, schistosomiasis control in China enjoyed a status in health policy during the past 60 years that is rather unique in the world. Without this prominent status, China would not have been able to reach visible signs of success and would not stand where it is today in the fight to control schistosomiasis. To understand this special character, it is necessary to take a closer look at China's recent history.

1.2.1 Significance of schistosomiasis in China – a historical review

Archaeological findings confirmed the presence of *S. japonicum* in China over a very long time. Schistosome eggs were identified in a corpse which was exhumed in Hubei province, dating back to the Western Han dynasty more than 2000 years ago (Wei *et al.* 1980). The first reported clinical case in modern medicine in China was made in Hunan province by the American physician O.T. Logan in 1905 (Logan 1905 in: Ross *et al.* 2001). However, for many years following this discovery until the end of the first half of the 20th century, schistosomiasis received little or almost no attention in China. Some fragmentary surveys were conducted (Mao 1948) and research on the disease was done by the in 1915 newly founded Peking Union Medical College and sporadic reviews and control activities organized by the newly founded Ministry of Public Health (Gross 2010).

This changed in 1949, when Mao Zedong and the Chinese Communist Party (CCP) took over power and the People's Republic of China (PRC) was founded. The new leaders were facing multiple problems, especially in the health sector. Epidemic and endemic diseases were wide spread, life expectancy low, infant mortality high, and most people outside the cities had never even seen a physician. Facing all these challenges, it is rather unique that the CCP concentrated one of its first efforts in health on the fight against schistosomiasis, a still rather unknown rural disease that generally takes decades to kill off its victims.

The motivation behind this was primarily a political one. The new leaders soon were made aware of the great threat and the crucial impact that schistosomiasis had on two significant areas: military security and economic development. In the early 1950s, the CCP tried to take firm control of the countryside to consolidate its power. In addition, the newly founded state also participated in the Korean War where an estimated 400,000 troops died. Therefore, military fitness and the procurement of a steady supply of healthy recruits were of high priority. However, thousands of soldiers and potential recruits were or became unfit for military service due to schistosome infections. Of equal importance was the severe impact of the disease on agricultural productivity in rice-growing regions of China where schistosomiasis was prevalent and due to which the working capacity of a large proportion of the rural population was lost (Gross 2010). All this contributed to the launch of probably the longest health campaign in PRC history. A national schistosomiasis control program was established in the mid-1950s and has been implemented ever since.

The total Chinese population at the time of the start of the control program in the mid-1950s was approximately 600 million (United Nations. Department of Economic and Social Affairs 2013). Large-scale epidemiological surveys carried out in China at that time revealed that schistosomiasis was highly endemic in the Yangtze River basin in the southern part of China, namely in 373 counties of the provinces Anhui, Fujian, Guangdong, Hubei, Hunan, Jiangsu, Jiangxi, Sichuan, Yunnan and Zhejiang provinces, the Guangxi autonomous region and Shanghai municipality (Figure 4). An estimated 100 million people were at risk of schistosomiasis and about 11.6 million infected with *S. japonicum*. Mortality due to advanced schistosomiasis was high with an estimated case fatality rate of 1 %. A total area of around 14,000 km² was identified as being infested by the intermediate host snail *Oncomelania* and therefore considered as potential transmission area (Guo et al. 2005). In addition, an estimated five million cattle were at risk of *S. japonicum* infection and an estimated 1.2 million cattle were infected.

Fifty years later, China's population has more than doubled to a total of 1.3 billion people (United Nations, 2012). However, by then the number of *S. japonicum*-infected people had decreased by over 90 % to an estimated 843,000 in 2003. The number of patients with acute schistosomiasis was reduced from over 10,000 cases annually in the 1950s of the control programme to 1114 cases in 2003 (Zhou et al. 2005b). In addition, intermediate host snails were found on a total surface area of only 3.500 km². This translates to a decrease of 75 % compared to the surface area of 14,000 km² at the early stage of the national control programme in the 1950s and is accompanied with an almost equally high decrease of the total endemic area, as seen in Figure 5.

Figure 4: Schistosomiasis regional distribution before the 1950s in China (Jiang et al. 2002)

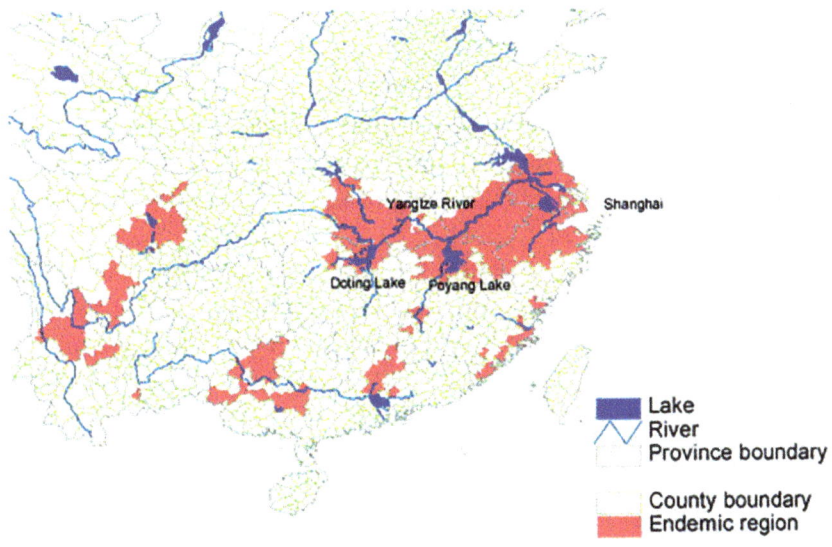

Figure 5: Schistosomiasis regional distribution according to the 3rd nationwide cluster sampling survey in 2004 (Zhou et al. 2007a)

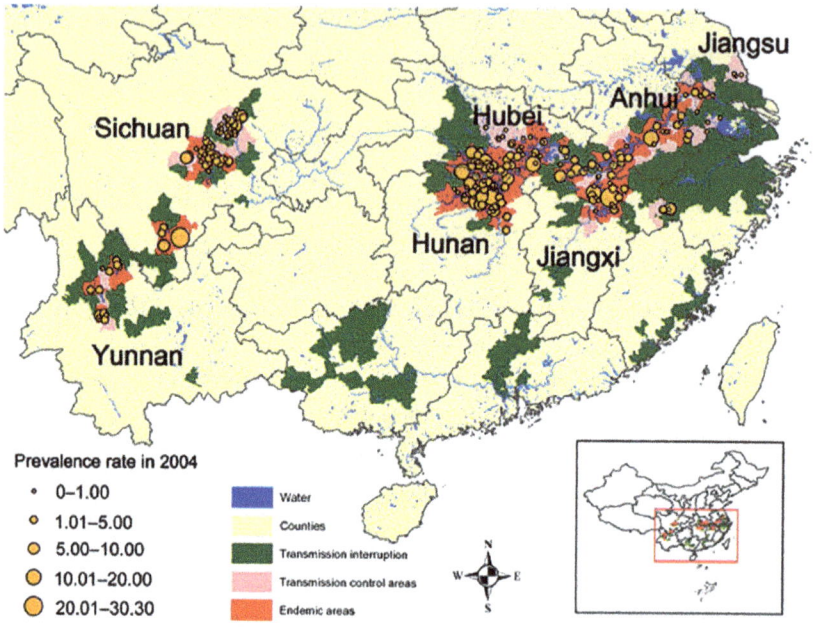

Schistosomiasis is a regionally endemic disease and depends heavily on *Oncomelania* snail distribution. Based upon the epidemiological pattern of schistosomiasis and ecological characteristics of the snail vectors, in China, a distinction is made between 3 types of endemic areas, i.e. marshland and lake regions, hilly and mountainous regions and plain regions with waterway networks (Guo *et al.* 2005).

The marshland and lake regions cover the area on the banks of the Yangtze River and surrounding lakes in the provinces Hunan, Hubei, Jiangxi, Jiangsu and Anhui province. Hilly and mountainous regions are mainly found in Sichuan and Yunnan provinces, where population density is quite low but the snail habitats are extensive. Plain regions are mainly densely populated areas with rich network of water sources in the Yangtze delta (Mao & Shao 1982).

According to the 3rd nationwide cluster sampling survey, the large majority of snail-infested areas are located in the lake regions, i.e. 3615.1 km^2

(95.5 %), whereas only 4.3 km² (0.1 %) were found in the plain regions with water-way networks, and the remaining 167.4 km² (4.4 %) were in the mountainous regions of Sichuan and Yunnan provinces (Zhou et al. 2007a).

The success in schistosomiasis control over the past 60 years was mainly due to the longstanding political commitment of all Chinese leaders up to today as well as the establishment and strict implementation of a control strategy. This strategy has moved through different stages over the past 6 decades. It was influenced by international "trends" in schistosomiasis control, but clear national adaptations to the changing economic, epidemiological and socio-political conditions were observable nonetheless (Wang et al. 2008).

1.2.2 Control strategies

The schistosomiasis control programme in PRC for the past 60 years can be divided into three main phases. Each of these phases took place in distinct policy-making environments (Collins et al. 2012)

In the first phase (1950s- early 1980s) control efforts focused on transmission control through snail elimination. This was in line with the global control strategy promoted at that time by the WHO, when the control of molluscan intermediate hosts was considered the single most important method of preventing bilharziasis (WHO 1953). At that time, chemotherapy was still highly problematic, based on toxic drugs (e.g. stibophen) and praziquantel was to be discovered only some 30 years later.

With the discovery and launch of the drug praeziquantel in the mid-1980s, the WHO recommended schistosomiasis control strategies for humans by focusing on the large-scale population-based and repeated chemotherapy (WHO 1983). China imported this global strategy in the second phase (mid 1980s-2003) by shifting their control measures to morbidity control based on chemotherapy, but at the same time keeping some emphasis on snail control and treatment of animals. A large scale ten-year long World Bank Loan Project (WBLP), implemented from 1992–2001 in the 8 provinces where *S. japonicum* remained endemic when the project started, further enhanced this strategy. A final evaluation in 2002 showed that infection rates in humans and livestock had decreased by 55 % and 50 %, respectively. The number of acute infections and of individuals with advanced disease had also significantly decreased (Xianyi *et al.* 2005). However, a very recent study comes to the conclusion that the WBLP strategy had a good short-term impact on schistosomiasis control, but its long-term impact is not ideal. Morbidity of schistosomiasis was successfully reduced to a low level. But continuing the strategy cannot contribute further to China's schistosomiasis control because it fails to reach transmission control or to eliminate the infection (Zhang *et al.* 2012). This is in line with the viewpoint of many other authors who acknowledge that large-scale application of chemotherapy is effective in reducing prevalence and morbidity. But at the same time they emphasize that transmission control cannot be achieved based on praziquantel alone (Chen 2005; King 2009; Utzinger *et al.* 2003; Zhao *et al.* 2005).

After the end of the WBLP, a re-emergence of schistosomiasis was noted in certain areas in China (Liang *et al.* 2006; Zhao *et al.* 2005). Fuelled by the potential re-emergence, the government renewed its dedication to the fight of schistosomiasis by classifying it, together with HIV/AIDS, tuberculosis and hepatitis B as a priority in the control of communicable diseases in 2004 (Wang *et al.* 2008). In order to reach the goal set by the government, namely reduction of infection prevalence among humans in all endemic counties to <5 % by 2008, and then to below 1 % by 2015, the implementation of new control strategies was considered necessary (Wang *et al.* 2009b).

This resulted in the initiation of the third phase of integrated schistosomiasis control activities in 2004, which continues until today and shows very promising results. Wang and colleagues conducted a study using two intervention and two control villages in lake regions of China, all previously subjected to annual praziquantel treatment. As interventions they carried out a number of newly introduced control measures promoted as the new national strategy, such as implementing an intensive health education programme, removing cattle from snail-infested grassland, providing farmers with mechanized farm equipment and improving sanitation by providing tap water and building lavatories. After three transmission seasons, the prevalence of *S. japonicum* in humans was reduced to <1 % and a significant reduction in the number of infected *O. hupensis* snails in the sampling sites became apparent (Wang *et al.* 2009b).

Given these positive and promising results, elimination of schistsomiasis in some areas in China seems possible. However, there is also doubt on the generalizability of this national integrated strategy to control and eventually interrupt the transmission of *S. japonicum*. Mainly because the studies mentioned above were conducted in lake regions of China, whereas in hilly and mountainous regions of Sichuan and Yunnan the transmission ecology is quite different (Seto *et al.* 2011a). Furthermore, other factors which are not considered in the national strategy, such as non-bovine animal hosts or human movements may pose great obstacles towards transmission interruption of the parasite and need to be assessed (Zhou *et al.* 2012).

1.2.3 National criteria for control and elimination

China's national criteria for morbidity control, transmission control, transmission interruption and elimination of schistosomiasis as stated in the document "Criteria for control and elimination of Schistosomiasis" (GB15976-2006) are as follows:

Morbidity control:

1) The prevalence rate in residents is less than 5 %.
2) The prevalence rate in domestic animals is less than 5 %.
3) No occurrence of outbreaks of acute schistosomiasis. In an administrative village or unit, within 2 weeks, fewer than 10 acute schistosomiasis cases, including clinical or parasitological confirmed cases occur, or fewer than 5 acute cases occur within one week in the same place.
4) Data and files reflecting the changes in human and snail infections at administrative village level are available.

Transmission control:

1) The prevalence rate in residents is less than 1 %.
2) The prevalence rate in domestic animals is less than 1 %.
3) No acute schistosomiasis cases due to locally acquired infection are found.
4) No infected *Oncomelania* snails are found for two successive years.
5) Data and files reflecting the changes in human and snail infections at administrative village level are available.

Transmission interruption:

1) No human schistosomiasis case with locally acquired infection is found for five successive years.
2) No schistosomiasis case in domestic animals with local infection is found for five successive years.
3) No infected *Oncomelania* snails are found after careful surveys for two successive years.
4) Data and files reflecting the changes in human and snail infections at administrative village level are available.

Elimination:

No new infection in men or domestic animals is detected for five consecutive years after reaching the criteria for transmission interruption.

Today, China has achieved interruption of transmission in 5 out of 12 endemic provinces and has controlled transmission in 5 others. The long-term goal is nationwide transmission interruption for all endemic sites and eventually, the ultimate goal is elimination of schistosomiasis.

Against this background, this book aims to make a contribution to the scientific discourse on schistosomiasis control in general , particularly highlighting China as a prime example.

1.3 Study rationale

In diseases targeted for elimination, the closer one is to the goal, the greater the focus needs to be laid on the completeness and accuracy of reporting disease occurrence. This often requires substantially intensive monitoring methods (King 2009). In China, where an efficient national control program is well established (Engels *et al.* 2005; Utzinger *et al.* 2003; Zhou *et al.* 2005a) further progress on effective schistosomiasis control depends on additional factors such as the performance of stakeholders at the grass roots level, the availability of human resources and of public health infrastructure in the communities, the adaptation of effective surveillance systems, and the rigorous implementation of sustained control measures in the endemic villages. However, detailed knowledge on the surveillance and control processes on grass root level in China is very limited in the international scientific community, particularly due to a lack of insight resulting from language barriers.

This book presents a scientific investigation into the practical implementation of the Chinese national control strategy at the grass root level, using the example of the city of Wuhan.

One main focus lies on the investigation of the human resource investment needed and available for schistosomiasis control activities. Given the present situation of very low endemicity (low infection rates and low infection intensity), how many human resources does it take to sustain the success in China to control the disease at the present level, or to even improve the situation if aiming at elimination? And is this investment necessary? The city of Wuhan in the province of Hubei, Central China is taken as an example representative for the still endemic areas.

The second main focus of this study lies on the role of diagnosis as a means of case detection for effective surveillance. The national schistosomiasis control program in China advocates 'selective' chemotherapy with praziquantel as the main strategy. Determination of target populations for chemotherapy in the endemic communities and / or assessment of morbidity all build on the results of diagnostic tests (Zhou *et al.* 2007b). Therefore, diagnosis is a key component for treatment. Several studies have compared different available diagnostic methods and tests with respect to applicability in the field and sensitivity of results (Balen *et al.* 2007; Noya *et al.* 2002; Yu *et al.* 2007). However, results of these diagnostic tests are often presented as aggregate data for whole villages or communities at risk. Few studies investigate disease patterns within single individuals of the respective communities tested. The research presented here aims to close this knowledge gap through analyzing results from individual people and yearly trends of serological and parasitological testing of patients, in order to understand the on-going situation of schistosomiasis infections in a low transmission area.

The following research questions are addressed:

1. What is the structure and what are the different components of schistosomiasis control in Wuhan?

2. What is the distribution of human resources available for schistosomiasis control among all administrative levels and institutions and how is the work for different surveillance, control and treatment activities distributed in Wuhan city?
3. What information do diagnostic tests performed for surveillance purposes give about the form and actual extent of the disease?
4. What ability do serologic surveys have to detect short-term or temporary changes in the level of schistosomiasis transmission?

2 Methods and materials

This chapter presents an overview of the methodological approaches used to answer the above stated research questions. In total three different topics are addressed: a) the description of the control system (research question 1), b) the analysis of the workforce (research question 2) and c) the assessment of diagnostic tests carried out in the field (research questions 3 and 4). These three topics are approached separately using different methods and tools and are therefore discussed individually here.

2.1 Study setting

The study was conducted in Wuhan city, the capital of Hubei province, located in central China (Figure 6). At the time of the beginning of the national control program, Hubei province occupied second place for prevalence rates and first place for areas of snail habitats among all schistosomiasis endemic provinces (Zhou *et al.*, 2005). Today, Hubei is still among the top five provinces most affected by schistosomiasis.

Wuhan is situated east of the *Jianghan Plain,* at the junction of the Yangtse River and its tributary, the Han River. Most of the city is not higher than 50 meters above sea level with low and smooth terrain on the plain, and a great number of lakes and pools. Nearly 200 lakes of various sizes make up 26 % of Wuhan's entire territory. Enough rainfall, seasonal water fluctuations and floods, as well as a favourable climate, offer a suitable environment for *Oncomelania* snail breeding. Wuhan municipality falls into the category of marshland and lake endemic areas, where, influenced by the Yangtze River, snails spread out in vast areas (for definition see introduction page 22). Schistosomiasis transmission occurs between March and September.

Within China's structure of administrative divisions, Wuhan holds the status of a *sub-provincial city*[1]. As such, it is an administrative unit comprising of not only the main central urban area (Wuhan City Proper), but

---

1   A sub-provincial city is ruled by a province, but administered independently in regard to economy and law. Its status is below that of municipalities (highest

also its much larger surrounding rural area, including many smaller cities, towns and villages. Wuhan's entire municipal jurisdiction occupies a land area of roughly 8,500 km² with a total of 8.35 million people, out of which 2.93 million are agricultural population (2009).

Wuhan is subdivided into thirteen city districts (Figure 6) and one Economic Development District. The latter refers to three state-level development zones: Wuhan Economic and Technological Development Zone (Zhuankou Development Zone), East Lake Hi-Tech Development Zone (Optical Valley of China) and Wuhan Wujiashan Economic and Technological Development Zone. Geographically the development Zones are spread out over several city districts.

Figure 6: Map of Wuhan

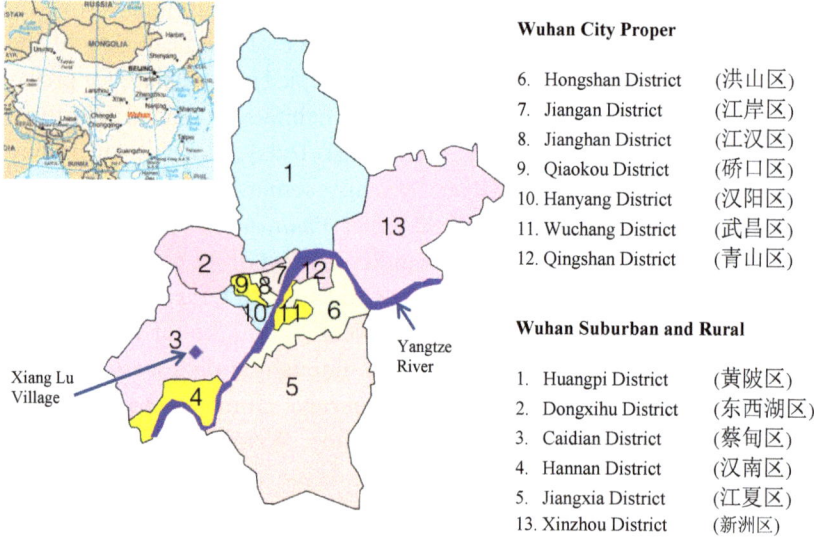

About 4.78 million people reside in the seven urban districts (Wuhan city proper) with an area of 890 km². The average population density is

---

level classification for cities in China; i.e. Beijing, Tianjin, Shanghai and Chongqing), but above regular prefecture level cities, which are completely ruled by their provinces.

30

8,800 persons/ km². In contrast, the six surrounding suburban and rural districts comprise of an area of 7,600 km², with a population of 3.57 million, the average population density being 470 persons/ km² (Su 2010).

Economically, Wuhan has experienced rapid growth in recent years, with an annual GDP growth rate exceeding 12 % over the past 7 years. In 2009, the ratio of economic value for the primary (agriculture, mining), secondary (industry, construction) and tertiary (services) sectors was 3:46:50. Farming constitutes the main part of Wuhan's agriculture, with major farm products being grain, cotton crops, tea, fruits, vegetables, slaughtered hogs and poultry, eggs, milk and fish.

Meteorologically, the city falls under the sub-tropical humid monsoon climate, with abundant rainfall and four distinctive seasons; spring and autumn are generally mild, whilst winters are cold and dry, and summers hot and humid. In the past thirty years, the average annual rainfall was 1,269 mm, mainly from June until August; annual temperature was 15.8℃-17.5℃ with an average temperature in July of 37℃.The annual frost free period lasts between 211 and 272 days.

2.2 Schistosomiasis control efforts in Wuhan – System structure

To investigate schistosomiasis control efforts in Wuhan, descriptive qualitative and quantitative approaches were used. Qualitative approaches included key informant interviews, observations and document review. Quantitative approaches included secondary surveillance data and financial data collected and made available by the CDC Wuhan.

The objectives of the schistosomiasis control system, i.e. the relevance of schistosomiasis in China and the historical development of the system, have already been addressed in the introduction chapter. With this information, several aspects of the organizational and operational structure of schistosomiasis control in Wuhan were reviewed. Table 4 summarizes all aspects and the respective data sources as well as the various interview tools used for analysis.

Table 4: Reviewed aspects of schistosomiasis control in Wuhan

System	Aspects	Data sources
Background	Schistosomiasis control in Wuhan, current endemic situation and control measures	Key informant interviews, surveillance data provided by CDC Wuhan
Organizational structure of the system	Institutions and key stakeholders involved; operational and decision-making processes from national level to village level	Key informant interviews, review of public health policy documents
Operation of the system	a) Surveillance: case definition, case detection, case registration / notification, data management, data analysis, data interpretation, data dissemination b) Response: feedback within the system, dissemination of information to the community c) Resources used to operate system: Funding sources Investment in human resources	Observations during field visits, technical guidelines published at different levels (state, province, city), key informant interviews, surveillance data provided by CDC Wuhan (2003–2010), Chinese publications about schistosomiasis control in Wuhan City Interviews with key informants, internal financial documents, questionnaires among health workers

Background information about the structure and procedures of control activities on city, district, town and village level was obtained through literature and document review (English and Chinese), observations, and through a number of informal interviews and discussions with key informants employed in schistosomiasis control. These included the head of the institute of schistosomiasis control of the CDC Wuhan, directors and members from district schistosomiasis control stations, members of field control staff and doctors from township hospitals. The interviews covered topics of schistosomiasis control history, control methods, the surveillance system, patients' treatment as well as future challenges.

The hierarchy of administration of schistosomiasis control is shown in Figure 7, which include internal guidelines published on various levels.

These documents were kindly made available at Wuhan CDC in order to be used in this study.

Figure 7: Overview of institutions responsible for schistosomiasis control at each administrative level and their respective documents and guidelines

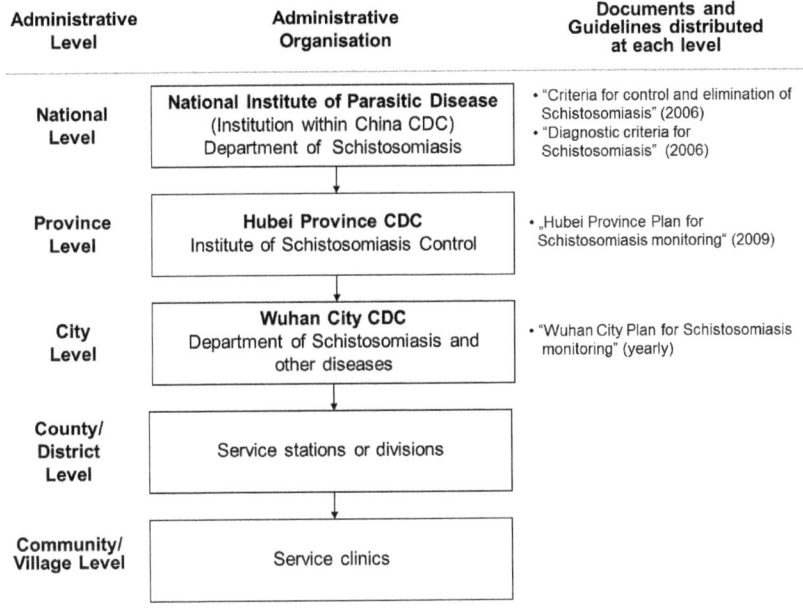

During field visits additional access to internal surveillance documents was granted. Information on financial aspects of schistosomiasis control in Wuhan was obtained during several personal meetings with respective authorities. Due to the sensitive nature, this information was granted only in form of estimates, but allowed to be used.

The two aspects of human resources and the quality and meaningfulness of diagnostic tests used in schistosomiasis control were reviewed separately in-depth.

2.3 Health Workforce

A cross-sectional study using questionnaires was conducted to investigate the current state of human resource availability for schistosomiasis control activities carried out in Wuhan City and to assess their respective workload. Human resources for schistosomiasis control include trained health professionals (doctors, nurses, laboratory and other health-related technical assistants), as well as non-health professionals (managers, economists, accountants and all other administrative supporting workers), working in hospitals and control departments or control institutes. In addition, also those people who volunteer and support control activities in villages and communities are included.

The workforce available for schistosomiasis control was investigated regarding the following aspects:

1. Distribution (geographical distribution among the endemic districts, facility level distribution, gender and age distribution, etc.)
2. Composition (types of health workers)
3. Performance (work activities, workload).

The first data collection phase took place in 2008. A baseline study was conducted by Wuhan CDC to collect information about the current state of human resources engaging in schistosomiasis control in Wuhan. The data was made available for this study. General administrative data for 2008 on health workers at city, district and town level was obtained from schistosomiasis control offices in 1(out of 14) city districts where schistosomiasis is endemic and provided for preliminary analysis. Information asked for and used for this preliminary analysis included age, gender, educational background, occupation and place of work of health workers in schistosomiasis control.

In a second data collection phase in 2010, a study was conducted among all health workers identified in phase 1 to gain a deeper understanding of health worker composition, areas of performance as well as health workers' private opinions on schistosomiasis work-related issues. Three different sets of questionnaires were developed and translated into Chinese.

The sets of questionnaires differ mainly in targeted personnel of specific different work places, namely hospitals and schistosomiasis control departments and institutes that were identified and explained in detail in the first part of the results section. One questionnaire targeted the leader of city level CDC as well as heads of district level control stations of endemic districts in Wuhan (Annex 5). A second questionnaire targeted non-clinical staff (Annex 6) and a third one targeted clinical staff (Annex 7).

In our understanding, clinical staff comprises all personnel working in so-called schistosomiasis hospitals. It can include both technical staff (such as doctors or nurses) and non-technical staff (such as managers or support workers). Equally, non-clincial staff comprise of all personnel working at departments or institutes of schistosomiasis control. Non-clinical staff can also include both technical and non-technical personnel. The differentiation between clinical and non-clinical staff takes into consideration the interaction between both groups and in some cases also the overlap in work activities performed. Therefore, there are some overlaps between the three sets of questionnaires, which consist of two or three parts A, B and C. Several questions are asked in all of the questionnaires, while others are modified and adapted to the respective target group of each questionnaire.

Part A is identical in all three sets of questionnaires. This section deals with questions about respondents' general background, i.e. year of birth, sex, place of birth, educational background, the name and level (city, district or town level) of their respective work facility, their employment status (full time, part time) and monthly income. Part B consists of several questions related to respondents' work in the field of schistosomiasis. Part C includes questions on respondents' contact with community workers in their work. To assess the workforce in schistosomiasis control, the "formal" workforce does not represent the entire picture. A lot of work is carried out on community level by the so-called "informal" workforce, for example villagers and volunteers, who are not officially employed but nevertheless contribute considerably to schistosomiasis control activities. Unfortunately, it was not logistically possible to include the informal health workers' side in the assessment carried out in this research. Therefore, in order to indirectly include this unquestionably important workforce, non-clinical and clinical staff was asked questions relating to their contact with community workers in part C.

Leaders of control stations are decision makers supervising and managing health staff in their respective districts and institutions. At the same time, however, they themselves are members of the health workforce. Therefore, the questionnaire includes questions addressing the schistosomiasis control station leaders as both health workers and supervisors of subordinate health workers. In their function of leaders in charge of health personnel, respondents were asked to give their personal opinion on several given statements regarding regulations, workload and sufficiency in human resources available for schistosomiasis control.

The three sets of questionnaires were introduced and explained in detail by a CDC staff at a meeting between the directors of district control stations of the twelve schistosomiasis endemic district and CDC officials in June 2011. All directors and further authorities were asked for their support for dissemination of the questionnaires among all health workers in their respective districts. This request was granted. The mode of distribution was electronically (Word file) or, if requested by respondents, in hard copies. All questionnaires were self-administered, and returned electronically to the CDC Wuhan main office. Respondents received ID numbers for further processing of data. Detected inconsistencies and irregularities were discussed with partners at CDC, sometimes re-investigated, and at times resulted in exclusion of responses from analysis. Reasons for exclusion of a response were either that the specific question was not answered or the answer was unclear. Microsoft Excel was used for data analysis.

In total, questionnaires were distributed to all 516 health personnel identified in the first data collection phase. Out of these, 216 questionnaires were returned electronically, of which 12 questionnaires were from the leaders of city and district level control offices, 100 questionnaires from non-clinical staff and 104 from clinical staff. Univariate and multivariate analysis was performed for quantitative and qualitative variables. All 216 questionnaires were analysed according to the responses of respective variables. Differences in answers by clinical and non-clinical staff were examined with the Wilcoxon rank-sum (Mann-Whitney) test. Differences by facility level of employment of respondents were examined using Kruskal-Wallis equality-of-populations rank test.

Information obtained through the questionnaires was triangulated with information obtained through interviews and observations to provide an overall picture of the situation of health worker in schistosomiasis control in Wuhan.

2.4 Diagnostics

For investigation of diagnostic tests performed for surveillance purposes in Wuhan, this study used surveillance data collected in the village of Xiang Lu (香炉). The village is part of *Tonghu (桐湖)* township which is located in *Caidian District* (Figure 6 area 3). Xiang Lu was chosen as the site for this study as since 2004 the village is one of thirty national surveillance sites for schistosomiasis in China. Therefore, collected data is relatively complete and the quality relatively high compared to other surveillance sites. Results are reported straight to province level authorities and entered into the national statistics on schistosomiasis control.

Figure 8: Xiang Lu village street and surrounding area

In 2009 the village was constituted of 329 households with a total registered population of 1,217. The number of the resident population, however, was only 692. The reason for this is because very often citizens work outside of the village for an extended period of time. De facto, they do not really live in the village, but are still registered there. The average GDP per person was 8,000 Yuan, the average yearly net income per person in 2009 was 3,000 Yuan. The village has an agriculture-based economy, with rice as the main crop. It includes 300 hectares of arable land, with 120 hectares being paddy field area. With formerly (in the 1980s) a total area of 1,769,000 m² being snail infested, in 2009 the snail infested areas was only 174,733 m², with additional 133,400 m² identified as susceptible to snail infestation.

Xiang Lu has the category 3 status "morbidity control" (definition: see chapter 1.2.3). It is one of 17 % of all endemic villages in this category (see Table 6) and is therefore among one of the villages in Wuhan most affected by schistosomiasis.

The design for this study is a population-based, retrospective longitudinal analysis, using annual survey data for the years 2003–2010 made available by the Caidian district schistosomiasis control office, Wuhan. All district offices of schistosomiasis endemic areas are required to monitor prevalence and incidence of disease, the number of acute and advanced cases and hectares of snail-infested areas each year. The data collected includes the numbers of people screened, of individuals diagnosed as positive and of patients who received treatment. Data from all districts was collected by the schistosomiasis office at the city level, which then presented the aggregate data to the higher authority, i.e. the Hubei province schistosomiasis office.

Villagers were tested for schistosomiasis infections once a year after the transmission season (May-September). In early October, health workers visited the village, went door to door and carried out preliminary serological tests on all residents present at the time of visits. Collected blood samples were sent to be analysed in a laboratory in the city. All people tested serologically positive were required to provide a stool sample, which was collected by health workers in the villages and analysed in a laboratory of the nearby *Tonghu* town.

2.4.1 Indirect Haemagglutination Assay

The Indirect Haemagglutination Assay (IHA) detects schistosome-specific serum antibodies (Figure 9) and was used for preliminary serological testing on all villagers present on the day of testing. It has been technically well established and routinely used for decades for schistosomiasis control in Wuhan (and China). This test was part of a laboratory evaluation in Heidelberg, where all scientific details can be found (Gui *et al.* 1991). For the scope of this study, the official instructions by the Chinese authorities have been translated.

Figure 9: IHA test produced and used in Wuhan City (left); Staff performing IHA (right)

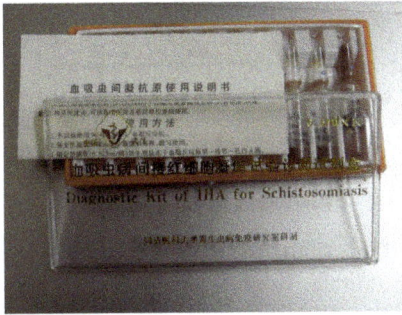 

The IHA was conducted as described in the national guidelines *Diagnostic Criteria for Schistosomiasis* (WS 261–2006) (Ministry of Health 2006b). The production of and instructions for performing an IHA test stated in these guidelines are as follows:

> "a) Antigen: Sheep red blood cells (SRBC) are used as carrier of antigen. Soluble schistosome egg antigen (SEA) is used to sensitize sheep SRBC after previous purification over SephadexG100. Before sensitization, SRBC are soaked with 2.5 % glutaraldehyde, and then tanned with 1:5000 tannic acid. The sensitized SRBC are mixed with PBS (pH7.2) which contains 10 % glucose and 1 % normal rabbit serum to maintain them in suspension, then aliquoted and sealed in ampoules following lyophilization. The final concentration of SEA for coating should be determined for each batch of antigen, and should be between 1:1280 to 1:2560. The antigen can be replaced by a mixture of SEA and adult worm antigen (Kikuchi *et al.*); also one may use human 'O' group instead of SRBC.
> b) Method: microtiter plates with 96 wells are used for conducting the test. SRBC are given to all wells. Then, serial dilutions are done, whereby serum is added to the first well and the same quantity of reagent is taken from one well to the next. The first well remains with the same volume as was put in and two-fold dilutions are obtained. Hemagglutination is expressed as titer. A titer is the inverse of the last dilution that is positive, e.g. 1:40.
> c) Reading / Test interpretation: If sufficient antibody is present in a serum to crosslink SRBC, these will agglutinate and form a mat at the bottom of the well. If insufficient antibody is present, the cells will roll down to the bottom of the wells to form a red pellet or "button" at the bottom of the well.

Negative wells (no red cell agglutination) have an intact button at the bottom of the well.

Positive wells (red cell agglutination) are graded:
++++ Red cells settle as a fine carpet, and ragged edges can be seen.
+++ Red cells settle as a fine carpet, and fill the bottom of the wells.
++ Red cells settle as a fine carpet, but the area is smaller than '+++'.
+ Most red cells are settled at the bottom of the well, and appear as a button with slightly agglutinated red cells around, and blurred edges can be seen around the point of the button.

Response criteria: if the red blood cells agglutinate at the serum dilution of 1:10, then the test is interpreted as showing a positive reaction." (End of translation).

However, in the field a test with titers of ≥ 5 is already considered positive and patients will be treated with Praziquantel.

2.4.2 Kato-Katz thick smear test

The Kato-Katz (KK) test was originally developed for African schistosomiasis and a field application can be found in Ruppel *et al.* (1990). In recent years, the test became routine in China and is now the standard method for the detection and quantification of egg burden in China. The test is simple to perform, requires, except for a microscope, only basic single-use equipment (Kato-set, containing template with hole, nylon screen, plastic spatula, gloves, microscope slides and cover slips) and basic consumables (cellophane as cover slip, soaked in Glycerol-malachitegreen solution) and is relatively cheap.

The KK test was conducted (see Figure 10) as described in the national guidelines on *Diagnostic Criteria for Schistosomiasis* (WS 261–2006) (Ministry of Health 2006b) and also in the national guidelines on *Criteria for control and elimination of Schistosomiasis* (GB15976-2006) (Ministry of Health 2006a). The instructions for performing a KK test as stated in the guidelines are translated as follows:

"Procedure in detail: Put a piece of nylon (80 meshes/25.4 mm~100 meshes/25.4 mm) on the faecal sample, slightly press the nylon on the top with a soft plastic spatula, so that some of the faeces filter through and appear on the surface of the nylon. Scrape with the flat spatula across the upper surface to collect the filtered faeces and fill these into the whole of the provided template (3 cm×4cm×5cm, the centre hole diameter is 3.5 mm, the volume is 41.7mg after being scraped flat) which have been placed on the centre of a microscope slide. Lift the template carefully, so that the cylinder of faeces is left on the microscope slide. Cover the faecal material with the pre-soaked glycerin-cellophane strip (30 mm×30mm). Invert the microscope slide and firmly press the faecal sample under the cellophane strip on a smooth and hard surface such as rubber or another microscope slide, so that the material will be spread evenly. Place the slide overnight at room temperature (25 °C) and relative humidity of 75 %, then examine under the microscope. Each stool sample should be read in three smears. The smear should be examined in a systematic manner, and the eggs of each parasite species reported. Multiply the number of counted eggs by 24 to obtain the number of the eggs per gram faeces." (End of translation).

Figure 10: CDC staff preparing stool samples for Kato-Katz tests in Xiang Lu village

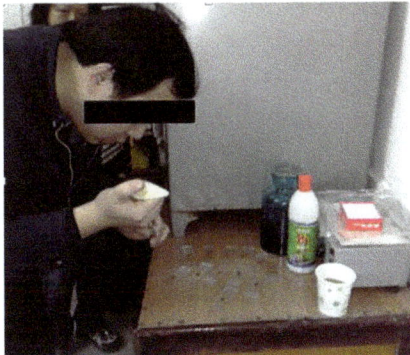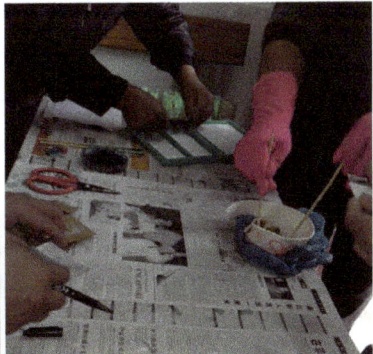

One stool specimen was obtained from each IHA-positive individual, from which three smear slides (in 2003 only 2 smear slides, Table 5) were prepared. Slides were examined by experienced laboratory technicians under a light microscope.

Test interpretation: Test positivity is defined by detection of eggs. Conversely, test negativity is defined by non-detection of eggs. People with at least one egg-positive slide were considered infected. The number of eggs was counted on each slide and the arithmetic mean value was calculated for each person. One egg detected on one slide of three calculates to 8 eggs per gram (EPG).

2.4.3 Database description

For this study, surveillance data for the endemic village Xiang Lu for the years 2003–2010 were obtained and analyzed. Collected information regarding population screenings includes the following (Table 5):

Table 5: Screening information

Year	IHA test results	IHA Titer	KK test results	MHA results	Kato-Katz results	KK egg counts	Treatment with PZQ (40mg/kg)
2003	+	−	+	+	2 smears	+	−
2004	+	−	+	−	3 smears	−	−
2005	+	+	+	−	3 smears	+	+
2006	+	+	+	+	3 smears	−	+
2007	+	+	+	−	3 smears	+	+
2008	+	+	+	−	3 smears	+	+
2009	+	+	+	−	3 smears	−	+
2010	+	+	+	−	3 smears	+	+

+ data available
− data not available

The KK tests were also read for possible co-infections with other parasites (roundworm, hookworm and whipworm). This data were not used any further in this study. In addition, the following demographic data for the entire population of the village was made available: name, birth date, sex, education and occupation of each individual person tested each year. The variables analysed included IHA test results, IHA titers, KK test results, KK egg counts and birth year, sex, educational background, occupation as demographic variables. Raw surveillance data was provided by the CDC Wuhan in the form of Excel sheets for each individual year.

The study population consisted of 1,217 people, according to the official village registry established in the year 2006. The demographic structure of the village and composition of the population of the village was different between 2003 to 2005. The registry list had not been updated since 2006, e.g. by adding newborns to the list or removing deceased villagers from the list. Therefore, the list used for this analysis did not change from 2006 until 2010. Between 2003 and 2005 all villagers were identified who were also included in the registry of 2006. Test results for all years were matched to the respective individual patients. Patients received ID numbers for further processing of data. Detected inconsistencies and irregularities were discussed in person during repeated visits and clarified directly with Wuhan CDC staff.

STATA 9 software package was used for analysis of surveillance data. All available data from the study population (1,217 people) was used for analysis. Based on the IHA results, the serologic profile of individual people was studied. The individual IHA test results of some patients included in this analysis are shown in Annex 1, 2 and 3: Annex 1 consists of two tree diagrams, representing all IHA test outcomes of those patients, who came for testing in 2003 and following them for up to 8 consecutive years until 2010; Graph a) of Annex 1 follows only those people, whose first IHA test in 2003 was positive (23 people), while graph b) of Annex 1 follows only those people, whose first IHA test in 2003 was negative (163 people).

Similarly, Annex 2 consists of two tree diagrams representing all IHA test outcomes for people who were not tested in 2003, but came for their first testing in 2004, and follows them for up to 7 consecutive years until 2010; Graph a) follows only those people, whose first IHA test in 2004 was positive (48 persons), while graph b) follows only those people, whose first IHA test in 2004 was negative (293 persons). Following this structure, Annex 3 represents those individuals who had not been tested in 2003 and 2004, but who were first tested positive (A) or negative (B) in 2005.

The analysis was carried out in three srages. First, the serological and parasitological prevalence among the registered population on Xiang Lu Village for the years 2003 to 2010 was investigated. As parasitological test results from individuals who didn't participate in any serological tests between 2003 and 2010 (n=136) were unavailable for analysis, these individuals were excluded. The results are based on test results of a total of 1081 people.

In the second stage, serologic changes were investigated. Here, test results of all individuals tested in two or more consecutive years were examined further. IHA titers were considered in ordered categories (1:5, 1:10, 1:20 and 1:40). As for the years 2003 and 2004, no titer values were recorded (see Table 5), only test results from 2005–2010 could be included into this part of analysis.

In this context we identified four patterns of serologic changes in patients tested in two consecutive years:

1) those with negative IHA titers in year 1 but who subsequently seroconverted (sero-conversion from negative to positive),
2) those with positive IHA titers in year 1 but whose IHA titer subsequently dropped to negative (sero-reversion from positive to negative),
3) those with persistently negative IHA titers (from negative to negative) and
4) those with persistently positive titers (from positive to positive).

The focus of this part of the analysis is on identification and examination of sero-conversions and sero-reversions. Those individuals with persistently negative IHA titers on all tests performed within the 8 year period studied were excluded from further analysis as no information could be derived from those results regarding sero-conversion or sero-reversions. Therefore, only patterns 1), 2) and 4) were investigated further. Analysis is based on IHA test results of 423 different people tested multiple times for at least two consecutive years between 2005 and 2010. Finally, we investigated individual titer course patterns over a period of several years. Included in this part of analysis were only individuals who came for IHA testing for at least 6 consecutive years within the period 2003–2010, with at least one positive IHA test result. In total, 87 individuals fit the criteria and were included in this analysis.

Age and sex differences in incidences per year and cumulative incidence proportions were examined with the x^2 test. Univarite logistic regression was performed. Ninety five per cent confidence intervals (95 % CI) for proportions were obtained from the binomial distribution.

2.5 Ethical Considerations

The study proposal was submitted and approved by the University of Heidelberg Medical Faculty Ethics Committee and the CDC Wuhan, PR China. Questionnaires on human resources in schistosomiasis were approved and distributed by CDC Wuhan. All staff members were informed about the purpose and procedure of this study. An informed consent sheet, including study information and the fact that participation was voluntary, was distributed together with the questionnaires. Consent from all participants was obtained. Official approval by CDC Wuhan to use surveillance data for analysis of diagnostic tests was obtained. For analysis, all data on human resources and surveillance was coded through allocation of an ID number to each individual person/respondent for privacy protection.

2.6 Study limitations

This work needs clarification on certain potential limitations. A study limitation regarding the investigation of Wuhan's human resources for schistosomiasis control could be that data collection relied on self-reporting by the respondents to the questionnaires based on their personal experiences with the program. This may have produced an element of bias in the findings. In investigating personal opinions on schistosomiasis control activities in Wuhan, the respondents working for the CDC Wuhan may be cautious in expressing opinions that might identify problematic issues in their work. However, all respondents were assured of anonymity and confidentiality, which was fully respected. The focus of the study was on lesson learning and this was highlighted to each interviewee with support from the CDC Wuhan. Possibly the most important limitation of the diagnostics part of the study is that we had no insight in to the data with respect to variables or data quality, since the study was conducted retrospectively. Data quality was, however, unlikely to be less than technically optimal, as the study village is a national surveillance site and high value was placed on the quality of annual data collection to meet all national standards. This was confirmed by our results on the agreement between IHA and KK and the observed PPV in our study, which were similar to respective findings by others in prospective studies performed under controlled settings. However, as in our research KK tests were performed only on subjects previously tested IHA positive, determination of specificity and sensitivity and negative predictive value (NPV) were not possible (see Discussion). Possible infections missed by the IHA test could not be determined.

Another limitation of the study is generalizability of findings. In this study, the investigation and assessment of diagnostic tests is concentrated on one focal point, Xiang Lu village. Due to personnel, budget and time limitations data on more study sites could not be investigated. Thus, it would be inappropriate to statistically generalize the situation for all of China. However, we are convinced that the patterns and mechanisms identified have some degree of general applicability elsewhere and in other situations.

3 Results

3.1 Description of schistosomiasis control system in Wuhan

The system of schistosomiasis control is barely, if at all, known in detail in Western countries, mainly because of language barriers and lack of knowledge of Chinese administrative structures. This is quite in contrast to the situation in African and American schistosomiasis control, which is easily understood due to the historical (usually colonial) history and absence of language problems. This chapter presents the results obtained from investigating local documents and from numerous informal interviews with leaders and workers in schistosomiasis control in Wuhan.

3.1.1 Historical background

Historical records related to or explicitly mentioning schistosomiasis in Wuhan date back to the late 19th century. In 1881, *Oncomelania hupensis* snails were first found and identified in Wuhan's Jiangxia district by the missionary P. Kaspar Fuchs. Hospital records from 1910 from a church hospital in Hankou district reporting on patients with symptoms typical of schistosomiasis. Schistosomiasis prevention activities in Wuhan, as in all other endemic areas in China, were conducted purely locally for a long time and remained very sporadic (Yang 2005). Only after the founding of the People's Republic of China in 1949 did schistosomiasis control appear on the health agenda and was more frequently promoted officially. In 1953, Wuhan Medical College conducted tests on 400 people and found that 248 were infected with Schistosomiasis. This was the start of population screenings in key endemic areas (Yang 2005). However, for the following fifty years, such population screenings within Wuhan were conducted irregularly and without a clear structure. On the national level, control and surveillance strategies were developed, implemented and improved over time, such as the establishment of national surveillance sites in the 1990s, or the implementation of three national large-scale sample surveys to reflect the national endemic situation. With these, the thought arose to gain reliable, complete and comprehensive data on a regular basis to reflect the actual schistosomiasis endemic situation on a local level. Under the Ministry of

Health, in 2002, the "Wuhan urban schistosomiasis monitoring program" was developed and implemented in September 2003 (Yang 2005).

3.1.2 Structure of the system

3.1.2.1 Surveillance sites

The surveillance system developed and implemented under the monitoring program continues until today. Active surveillance is performed within pre-defined surveillance sites located in endemic areas of the city. The system includes two forms of surveillance sites, permanent sites and additional non-permanent sites.

In total, thirty permanent surveillance sites were established within the twelve endemic districts of Wuhan, each comprising of between 1,000–1,500 people. In these spots, testing for schistosomiasis among permanent residents is carried out on a yearly basis. The thirty sites include one national site in Xiang Lu village, eight provincial level sites and twenty-one city-level sites. Twelve sites are located in suburban transmission-uncontrolled endemic areas, ten are located in representative villages in suburban transmission-controlled areas and eight are located in residential areas along the Jangze River in the city proper area.

In addition to these thirty permanent sites, each year the district level institutions select additional sites, where testing will also be conducted in the respective year. If the infection rate in these additional sites is between 1–5 %, the sites must be tested every two years . If the infection rate is below 1 %, the site will be checked every three years. In total, there are about 200 such additional non-permanent surveillance sites, each comprising of between 700–800 people, where tests are conducted every 2–3 years according to the infection rate. Sites are classified strictly by the amount of infected people. Unlike in Africa, classification is not upon infection intensity, i.e. how many eggs patients excrete, but simply by a yes/no record of infection.

The sizes of the different sites vary. However, in total about one quarter of Wuhan's entire endemic area (villages and land) is covered by them and under regular surveillance. Every year, between 120,000–160,000 people are screened, including preliminary serological testing, followed by parasitological testing of sero-positive residents.

3.1.2.2 Institutions and control measures

In line with the national strategy described in the introduction chapter, Wuhan follows an integrated approach in schistosomiasis control activities. Inevitably, this leads to the involvement of several different institutions, who conduct control activities within their respective area of responsibility, namely the area of water resources, forestry, agriculture and health.

Ministry of Water Resources: Water resource development projects in Wuhan are carried out by the *Changjiang Water Resources Commission* (CWRC), an authority dispatched by the Ministry of Water Resources, in charge of the Yangtze (Chinese: Changjiang) River Basin and other river basins of southwestern China. The activities carried out include repair of river dams, cleaning of cannels, concreting ditches etc. to reduce actual or potential snail breeding habitats. A few years ago, China's largest water recreation park was constructed in the embankment areas of Yangtze River that crosses the city. A shoreline area of 100,000 square-meters was turned into a green public square, not only for entertainment reasons but also as an anti-flood resource and as a mode to keep the banks of the river free from snails.

State Forestry Administration and Ministry of Agriculture: Reduction of snail susceptible land is also the motivation for all forestry and agriculture control measures, which are under the supervision of the State Forestry Administration and the Ministry of Agriculture, respectively. For example, the Bureau of Forestry under the State Forestry Administration is responsible for planting trees in outside embankment areas as a control measure. The purpose here is to create smooth surfaces and get rid of swamp areas, which are otherwise adequate snail habitats.

Agricultural activities in schistosomiasis control include sanitation measures, i.e. building sanitary lavatories (Figure 11) or methane pits, construction of fishponds, maintaining or/and digging of new channels. As bovines play a major role in the transmission of *S. japonicum* to humans in China, control activities also include the prevention of cattle herding in areas susceptible to snail infestation by cordoning off respective meadows and pastures. This is supported by the installation of fences and placement of information boards at the relevant locations (Figure 11). Numbers of performed activities are shared with Wuhan CDC Institute of schistosomiasis control.

Figure 11: Examples of control measures in Wuhan; left: information board warning of schistosomiasis endemic area; right; newly built sanitary lavatories in a village

Veterinary stations of the Veterinary Bureau under the Ministry of Agriculture are responsible for surveillance of schistosomiasis in livestock i.e. detecting infections through regular testing of livestock and treatment of the animals. All buffalos and cattle living in snail-infected areas must be checked for possible infection. Checks and tests are conducted during October and November every year. Following the new campaign "machines replacing cattle (ji dai niu)", promoted by the national control strategy over the last couple of years, the removal of bovines and their replacement by agricultural machines is also being implemented as a control measure. Cattle are sold to non-endemic areas and farmers are compensated for the cattle and also provided with one machine per buffalo as replacement. As several farmers usually share one buffalo among each other, they are now left to share the machine in the same way.

Ministry of Health: All surveillance and control activities relating to human schistosomiasis are overlooked and/or implemented by the Wuhan Center of Disease Prevention and Control (CDC) (Figure 12) which operates under the Ministry of Health. Main activities are monitoring and surveillance of human schistosomiasis in endemic areas, surveillance of snail infested areas (Figure 13), provision of health education and training for endemic population, treatment of chronic cases with praziquantel and treatment of advanced cases in hospitals. In addition, Wuhan CDC collects data from all other Ministries about their respective control and surveillance activities.

Operational structures are in place at different administrative levels as shown in Figure 12.

Figure 12: Hierarchical structure of schistosomiasis control institutions in Wuhan City

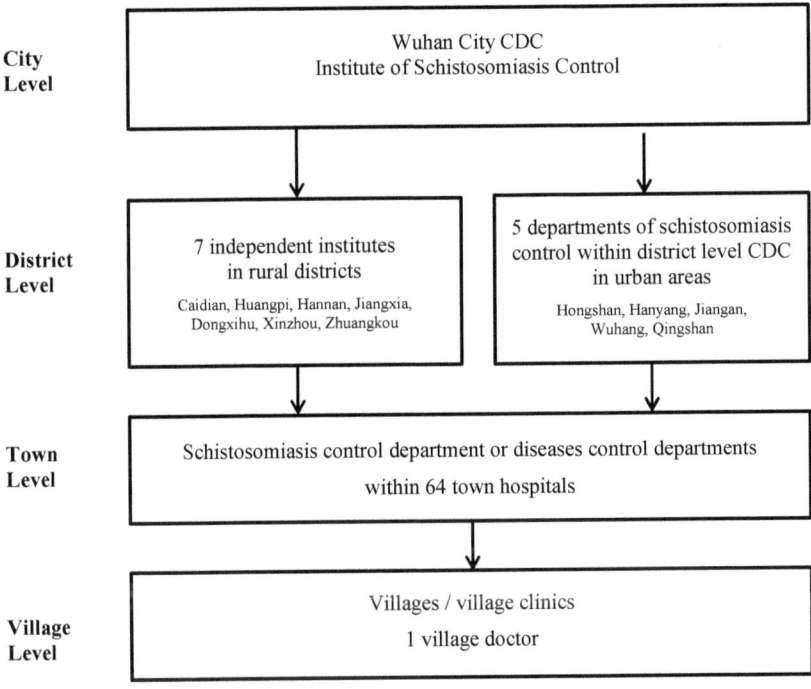

On city level there is the *Institute of Schistosomiasis Control*, an institute within the Wuhan CDC. The *Institute for Schistosomiasis Control* is one of the seven institutes integrated into the Wuhan CDC. It is further divided into the *Department for schistosomiasis control* and the *Department for the control of other endemic diseases*, i.e. malaria and filariae. The institute is responsible for providing practical professional and technical directions to the respective organizations at lower administrative levels and to supervise organization and implementation of plans issued by the health bureau.

On a district level, each of Wuhan's endemic districts has its own schistosomiasis control department. Within the Wuhan city area, the endemic situation is very light with two districts even being endemic free. The remaining five endemic districts, namely Jiangan, Wuchang, Hanyang, Qingshan and Hongshan district, are managed by the departments of schistosomiasis control, which are integrated in the district level CDC. In the suburban and rural areas of Wuhan, the seven endemic districts, namely Caidian, Huangpi, Hannan, Jiangxia, Dongxihu, Xinzhou, Zhuangkou, are managed by independent institutes that are not integrated into CDC but have an independent office and are managed and supervised directly by the Health Bureau.

On the town level, all schistosomiasis control stations are integrated in and managed by town hospitals. Some stations on district and town level also admit and treat in-patients. These hospitals are then regarded and referred to as hospitals being specialized in schistosomiasis. Within each hospital there are often designated experienced doctors who are responsible for the control and treatment of schistosomiasis and elimination of snails in the local area.

On village level, in the endemic areas, each village has a village clinic, which includes one so-called village doctor, a local health worker, who is mostly self-taught and responsible for health issues and offering very basic health services. In schistosomiasis endemic villages, the village doctor is the key person in organizing and implementing surveillance activities and works closely with control station staff.

3.1.2.3 Surveillance and control work activities

Work activities at the CDC institute of schistosomiasis control vary according to the season. In general, between May and October, activities for the prevention of acute schistosomiasis are predominantly carried out. During this period, district level stations must report to the institute on all acute schistosomiasis cases on a weekly basis. Reporting is done via phone. Surveillance sites are visited between October and November when serological and parasitological testing of population is conducted. During the winter months, the focus lies on the evaluation of all control efforts during the past year, i.e. overall management, patient testing and treatment, snail surveillance, health education etc. Stations are awarded points according to their performance.

Snail surveillance:

In Wuhan, the area surrounding Han River is snail free. The Fu River is snail-infested, as is the area along the Dongjin River. The national surveillance site, Xiang Lu village, is located along the Dongjin River. The two districts Hanyang and Wuchang no longer have snail-infested areas. Snail surveillance is carried out twice or three times a year, in Spring and Autumn.

The technique of how to measure and determine snail-infested areas in China varies according to the different endemic areas. Wuhan is categorized as a "marshland and lake area". Within this category, snail-infested areas are further differentiated between two subcategories, inside-embankment (the area protected from being flooded by dams) and outside-embankment (the area between the rivers and the dam, which is flooded, including grassy beaches and river islets). Snails are examined within square fields of 10 to 10 meters. If the distance between two examined snail-infested fields is less than 30 meters, the area between those fields is also considered as being snail-infested.

As an example, in Jiangxia district, snails are checked 3 times a year, first early in spring, then later after the application of molluscisides, and again a third time in autumn. The center sends between 7–10 people out to the field to check the snails. They spend between 5–9 hours every day, for about 15 days in a row. In Jiangxia, microscopic examinations for infection of snails are carried out solely in the district level center in Zhifang.

Figure 13: Collection of Oncomelania hupensis *snails in a schistosomiasis endemic area and microscopic examination for infections in the CDC laboratory*

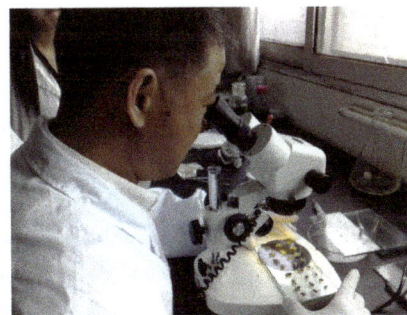

Human schistosomiasis surveillance and treatment of infections:

There are two methods used for conducting examinations at surveillance sites. The first one is to inform the target population of the surveillance site of the place and date of testing by the village head and encourage people to visit the examination place. For serological testing, the district control stations send out teams of 3–5 people, including one medical doctor, one nurse and one or more assistants, for example to help fill out forms etc. On the local side, the village head and village doctor are in charge of organizing the procedures. In addition, several local villagers are involved in the logistical assistance.

The second method is to go to peoples' homes to take the samples on the spot. This method is very time-consuming, According to the experience of control staff interviewed, it requires 4 to 5 times more investment time than the first method. As an example, Jiangxia district has three surveillance sites of roughly 1.500 people each, and all 3 sites have already implemented both methods. The testing time period for method 1 was about 10 days, while method 2 required between 30–40 days.

For the stool collection, no professional people from district level control stations are sent. Stool collections are carried out by local village people. The involvement of local people in the process ensures high population coverage and contributes to the success of activities performed. Microscopical egg examinations are also carried out locally in village or town hospitals, not in the district level laboratory as is the case with serological tests. Everybody who is tested serologically positive obtains praeziquantel treatment. In some areas, the dose for stool negative patients is lower than for the patients counted as "infected". The first get a dose of 40 mg/kg, the latter a dose of 60mg/kg, given in one dose or two doses in 2 consecutive days.

Surveillance tests are carried out in autumn, after the infection season. But some 200–300 selected people will be examined twice a year, in autumn and in spring. These are so-called 'moving people', who are not included in any surveillance sites and have plenty of water contact (boat people, moving population along small rivers within a city such as Jinkou River, the fishermen).

Wuhan CDC is responsible for disease prevention measures. There are no tests performed in the CDC directly. Those who want to get tested for infection outside of regular surveillance activities can do so at a hospital by paying a fee of 15–25 Yuan per test. CDC staff on city level is supervising activities implemented on district level and below. Staff members randomly accompany district level staff when conducting control activities and occasionally take test samples (blood for IHA test, snails) to double check at the city level laboratory as a quality measure.

All schistosomiasis patients in the city centre are treated in Wuhan Hospital. In the seven other district stations, in-patients are also treated. These stations are all integrated into hospitals, the names of which usually contain a reference to schistosomiasis. Nowadays in many areas, hospitals are competing for patients. Hospital names indicating a specialization are believed to attract patients. However, in these special schistosomiasis hospitals, other diseases are also treated.

Schistosomiasis in-patients are normally chronic cases with an average stay of between 2–3 weeks. Most patients come between April and October. On town level, not all hospitals treat in-patients. For more serious illnesses patients must go to a district level hospital.

Figure 14: Distribution of praziquantel to chronic patients (left) and treatment of a patient with advanced schistosomiasis in hospital (splenectomy for splenomegaly) (right)

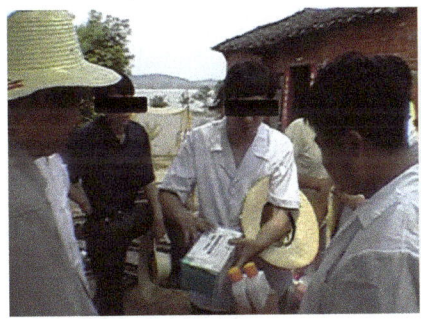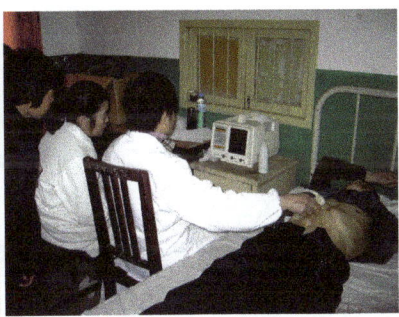

3.1.2.4 Endemic situation

Integration of health activities combined with environmental management and water resources development projects show very promising results. By the end of 2008, four districts reached the category of transmission interruption (Xinzhou, Wuchang, Qingshan and Hanyang), three districts the category of transmission control and five districts the stage of morbidity control. Details on the categories at town and village levels in Wuhan in 2008 are shown here in Table 6.

Table 6: Schistosomiasis control status of Wuhan endemic city districts, towns and villages in 2008

Control Category	City districts (%) N=12	City towns (%) N=81	City villages (%) N=604
Cat 1: uncontrolled	–	–	–
Cat 2: uncontrolled	–	–	–
Cat 3: morbidity control	5 (42 %)	9 (11 %)	103 (17 %)
Cat 4: transmission control	3 (25 %)	27 (33 %)	217 (36 %)
Cat 5: transmission interruption	4 (33 %)	45 (56 %)	284 (47 %)

For explanation of control categories, see chapter 1.2.3

Figure 15 shows a map of the endemic Jiangxia district located in the south of Wuhan (as shown in Figure 7). Endemic villages are marked with yellow and red tags, yellow representing control category 3 (morbidity control) and red representing category 4 (transmission control) villages. As can be seen, endemic villages are located alongside the Yangtze River, bordering mainly the west of the district but also the northeast part. Category 3 villages are those located at closest proximity to the river, while category 4 villages are found in the interior districts, surrounding a big lake and smaller rivers.

Figure 15: Mapping of endemic villages in Jiangxia district according to their control status

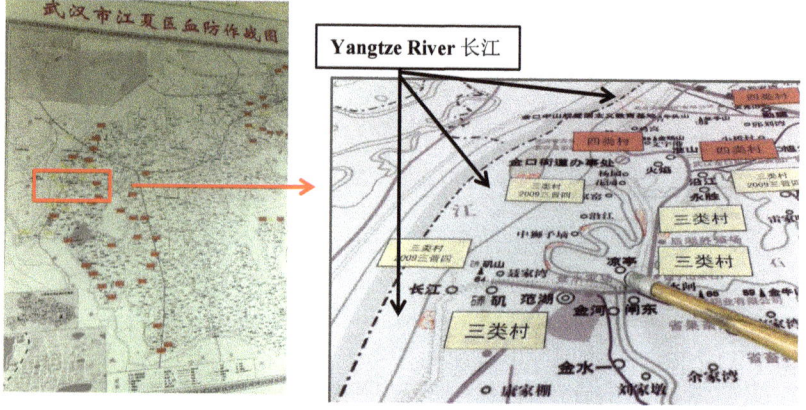

(Red boxes indicate category 4: transmission control villages, yellow boxes indicate category 3: morbidity control villages)

According to the 5-year plan for 2009–2013, an internal document compiled by the Wuhan Health Bureau, the long distance goal set by the government is to achieve the status of transmission control by 2012 and transmission interruption by 2013 for all city districts.

Each year between 120,000 and 150,000 persons are tested for infections. The average infection rate for the whole of Wuhan in 2009 was 0.41 % with considerable fluctuations between the respective endemic districts. Residents of rural areas are at risk of infection because their agricultural activities oblige them to get into contact with infested water. Transmission occurs from May to September.

Out of Wuhan's total population of 8.35 million people in 2009, only about 0.90 million people lived in a schistosomiasis-endemic area. Table 7 gives an overview of the number of endemic districts and communities in Wuhan and the respective populations affected.

Table 7: Wuhan: endemic situation overview in 2009

Endemic districts	Total population of endemic districts	Number of endemic townships	Total population of endemic townships	Number of endemic villages and communities	Total population of endemic villages and communities
Jiangan	630.000	6	208.800	23	30.000
Hanyang	456.000	5	167.500	5	10.000
Wuchang	977.000	4	271.200	6	18.600
Qingshan	434.000	4	145.000	13	29.800
EDZ*	63.800	1	63.800	13	2.100
Hongshan	590.000	4	101.000	19	25.500
Donghihu	254.100	12	167.200	64	92.600
Hannan	104.500	6	104.500	53	104.500
Caidian	462.600	10	231.100	150	184.300
Jiangxia	656.100	10	409.400	56	78.700
Huangpi	1.111.000	11	552.900	119	199.900
Xinzhou	957.600	8	618.900	83	132.100
Total	6.696.700	81	3.103.300	604	908.200

* EDZ = Economic Development Zone

In 2009, a total of 152,484 people were screened for schistosome infections, of which around 60,000 were treated. Around 200 people were late stage patients. The total snail-infested area was 13,400 ha (hectare), of which 13,250 ha were located in outside embankment and 150 ha in inside embankment areas.

3.1.3 Operation of the system

3.1.3.1 Surveillance

a) Case definition

Human schistosomiasis patients are identified according to the following decision tree.

Figure 16: Decision tree to determine human schistosome infections

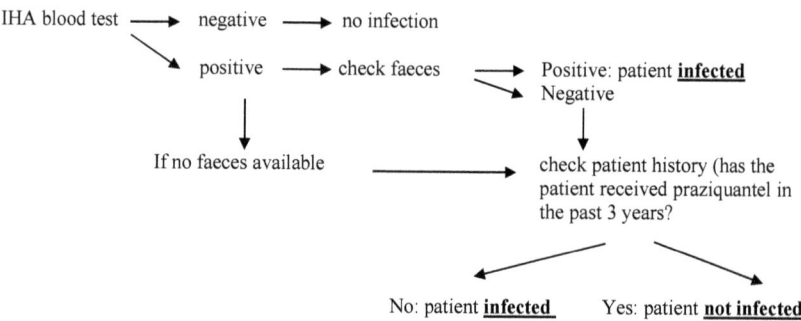

According to Figure 16 only parasitologically positive people are considered as being infected. If IHA is positive and stool examination negative or unavailable, then patients should be asked, whether or not they received PZQ in the past 3 years. If the answer is no, the patient is per definition also considered infected. However, several control personnel stated that this procedure is not always followed. Even if patients specify not having received PZQ within the previous 3 years, they are often not counted as infected (unlike the definition states in the guidelines). According to one interviewed leader of a district level control department, 3 % of all serological positive tested people would fall under this latter category. De facto, it would imply underreporting of cases by 3 %.

b) Case detection and case registration:
Standard case definitions of acute, chronic and late stage schistosomiasis are available from official guidelines published on state level. Manuals, giving detailed instructions as to how information has to be recorded (date, place, name, age and gender of the patient) and how information is to be coded, is available at all levels. Cases are detected during regular monitoring activities as described above. During transmission months, district level stations are required to report to the institute of schistosomiasis on city level on all acute schistosomiasis cases on a weekly basis per phone. Review of data from different surveillance sites made available to me for this study by CDC Wuhan showed data incompleteness in some cases. Some data was not entered in electronic form, but only available as handwritten hard copies. Some forms were filled out incorrectly by staff.

c) Case confirmation
The laboratory examination of the blood samples is done exclusively in the laboratory of respective district level control centers. On the other hand, examinations of KK tests are only carried out locally in village or town hospitals, not in district level laboratories.

The standard test performed for serological testing is IHA. Detailed instructions of how to perform the test are available (translation provided on page 43–44). According to laboratory staff interviewed, 7–8 people can examine about 200–300 blood samples a day. If the IHA test is positive, then additional parasitological test samples will be collected about ten days later. The standard test for parasitological testing of stool is KK test using 3 smear slides of the same stool sample. Detailed instructions on how to perform the test are available (translation provided on page 44–45). However, review of surveillance data made available to me for this study by CDC Wuhan showed that on some surveillance sites only two KK slides were tested. Schistosome infection is confirmed with a positive KK test result.

d) Data management (including data analysis, data interpretation)

All reporting districts share data from case reports with the Wuhan Center for Disease Control and Prevention (CDC) via excel files sent on a monthly basis. Wuhan does not have a database, which contains all combined information received by CDC from the cities endemic districts. Data analysis is done mainly on city level. Information collected each year is only available in the form of individual Excel sheets as provided by the individual districts each year. Results are shared by the city CDC with district heads.

3.1.3.2 Response

A feedback system is in place. Performance of control stations is monitored by control offices. In addition, CDC staff conducts control visits to districts on a regular basis. At the end of the year, the work of control stations is measured according to fulfilment of the target plan. Evaluations are done using detailed evaluation sheets and are based on a point system. Information on outcome of surveillance activities in endemic areas is disseminated to the respective communities. During field visits to several endemic villages, all interviewed village heads had an up-to-date knowledge of the endemic situation in their respective village, i.e. number of acute, chronic and late stage patients.

However, data regarding the endemic situation of the entire city area, especially with regard to infection numbers and stages of illness, was not made available for this study by the CDC. Even for this study, it was not possible to have insight into detailed surveillance data for the whole city.

3.1.3.3 Resources

a) Funding sources

Control measures and specific projects implemented in Wuhan are planned, decided on and financed at different administrative levels. Tables 8 and Table 9 list various state, province and city level control projects implemented in 2009 per sector and activities and the respective funding sources. Staff salaries are not included. All projects are decided upon by the Health Bureau at each respective administrative level and passed on to lower levels in the form of action plans for implementation. Table 8 gives an overview of only those projects and their respective funding, which are decided at state and province level, while Table 9 lists only the projects decided at city level. In total, 74,207,600 Yuan Renminbi (RMB) was spent on schistosomiasis prevention and control activities in Wuhan in 2009. Out of this, 53.3 % (39,556,900 RMB) was covered by city budget, 14.4 % (10,669,900 RMB) by province budget and 32.3 % (23,980,800 RMB) was paid for by state funds. The majority of the money is spent on large scale state and province level projects. Environmental modification takes up most of the budget, as there is high cost involved. Implementation costs of these projects are either financed independently through state or province funds or by contribution funds from all the three administrative levels. Other projects, such as activities for prevention measures against cattle herding at beaches, although decreed from above, must be borne entirely by the city.

Table 8: *Funding of integrated state and province level control activities in Wuhan in 2009*

Sector	Activities	Total cost in CNY* (USD*)	Proportion of overall cost in CNY* (USD*) covered by		
			State	Hubei province	Wuhan city
Water resources	Reparation of river dams, cleaning of cannels etc.	12,000,000 (1,753,200)	3,600,000 (525,960)		8,400,000 (1,227,240)
Agriculture	Sanitation measures	10,360,800 (1,513,713)	10,360,800 (1,513,713)		
	Prevention of cattle herding at river beaches; installation of fences and placement of information boards	761,000 (111,182)		761,000 (111,182)	
	Cattle surveillance and treatment	1,200,000 (175,320)			1,200,000 (175,320)

Sector	Activities	Total cost in CNY* (USD*)	Proportion of overall cost in CNY* (USD*) covered by		
			State	Hubei province	Wuhan city
Health	Human schistosomiasis; surveillance of endemic population and snail population, treatment, health training and education	9,306,300 (1,359,650)		3,228,900 (471,742)	6,077,400 (887,908)
Forestry	Planting trees in outside embankment areas	16,700,000 (2,439,870)	10,020,000 (1,463,922)	6,680,000 (975,948)	
Total		50,328,100 (7,352,935)	23,980,800 (3,503,595)	10,669,900 (1,558,872)	15,677,400 (2,290,468)

State and province level control projects

* CNY=Chinese Yuan Renminbi; USD=United States Dollar average exchange rate for 2009: 100 CNY=14.61 USD; 100CNY=10.51 Euro

State and province level projects amount to 50.3 Million RMB out of which 57.65 % was covered through state funds, 21.20 % through province funds and 31.15 % was borne by city funds.

65 % of health sector activities are funded by city funds and 35 % by provincial funds. The biggest financial item is the treatment of schistosomiasis patients. Treatment by praziquantel is generally free for patients. Drugs are provided by the province government to CDC according to the needs of the previous year, and distributed among the districts. Treatment of chronic and advanced schistosomiasis in hospitals is also free of charge for in-patients. Costs are covered by the government. The city level government pays 70 % of all treatment costs; the district covers the remaining 30 %. The average cost per hospitalized patient in 2009 was about 6,000 RMB. At the beginning of each year, districts are asked to submit a cost calculation. Based on this estimation, the office of schistosomiasis control

determines the advance payment for each district. The remaining costs are reimbursed at the end of each year.

Table 9: Funding of integrated city level control activities in Wuhan in 2009

Sector	Activities	Total cost in CNY* (USD*)	Proportion of overall cost in CNY* (USD*) covered by		
			State	Hubei province	Wuhan city
All sectors	Model district: Hannan district integrated control projects	9,643,400 (1,408,901)	–	–	9,643,400 (1,408,901)
Agriculture	"Machines replacing cattle"	9,316,800 (1,361,184)	–	–	9,316,800 (1,361,184)
	Modification inside embankment areas	2,647,800 (386,844)	–	–	2,647,800 (386,844)
Water resources	River beaches in districts Jiangxia and Jiangnan;	900,000 (131,490)	–	–	900,000 (131,490)
	Zhengguang river in Huangpi district	1,371,500 (200,376)	–	–	1,371,500 (200,376)
Total		23,879,500 (3.488.795)	–	–	23,879,500 (3.488.795)

* CNY=ChineseYuan Renminbi; USD=United States Dollars; average exchange rate for 2009: 100 CNY=14.61 USD; 100CNY=10.51 Euro

City level projects are decided by the Health Bureau of Wuhan city and funded exclusively through city funds. In 2009, the Hannan district was picked as model district among all endemic districts in Wuhan. As such, it was allocated extra funds for integrated control measures which were decided upon by all departments involved.

Between 2009 and 2010, around 1000 cattle were sold to non-endemic areas and replaced by agricultural machines. The cost here lay at approximately 9,300 RMB (equivalent to 1,359 USD) per replaced cattle.

Activities regarding modification of inside embankment areas were implemented in the four endemic districts and included the creation of fishponds, digging cannels, cleaning cannels from mud, etc. These activities apply to small rivers. Large river projects, namely cementing of cannels along Yangtse and Zhengguang rivers, were carried out in the Jiangxia, Jiangnan and Huangpi districts.

b) Equipment

As schistosomiasis control stations are integrated into institutes or hospitals, equipment and materials are available and shared. Additional equipment which is not available, such as centrifuges, is provided by the government.

Equipment and materials used for conducting serological and parasitiological tests, such as IHA kits, are provided by the province government free of charge. Surveillance teams receive 10 RMB per person tested, as well as 6 RMB per Mu (1 Mu equals to 666.67 m^2 or 0.07 ha) snail-infested area checked.

This money is not paid to the workers themselves but to the respective local authorities, the town control stations. There, the money is used to buy equipment such as glass pots for tests, pipettes, needles, syringes etc.

3.2 Health workforce for schistosomiasis control in Wuhan

3.2.1 Availability and distribution of human resources

In Wuhan city each year 80,000–90,000 people are screened for schistosomiasis (around 10 % of total population at risk). In 2008, the infection rate for endemic areas was very low at only 0.85 % with 1.216 reported cases of schistosomiasis. In the same year, 516 personnel were recorded at the Wuhan CDC as working part or full time in schistosomiasis control. Thus, with a health worker to patient ratio of 1:2.4, theoretically one health worker was available for every two to three schistosomiasis patients. Figure 17 shows their distribution among different facilities on the three administrative levels.

Figure 17: Distribution of health personnel in schistosomiasis control in Wuhan in 2008

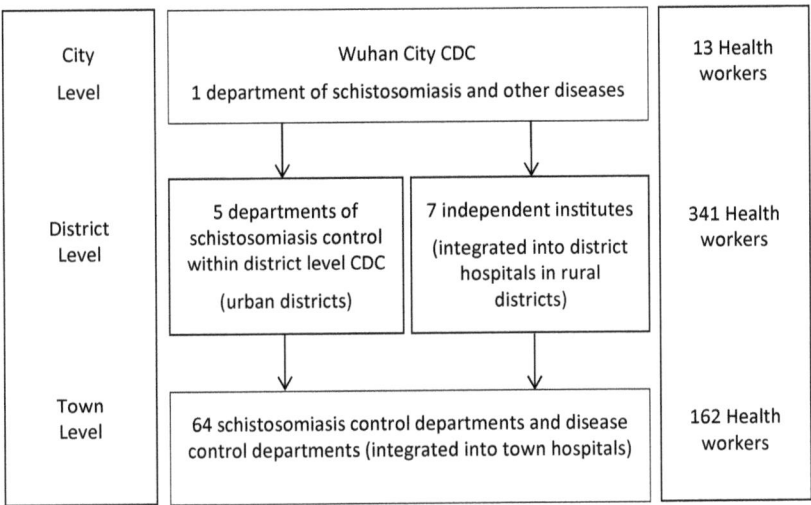

City level had the smallest number of workers with just thirteen people. At the district level, the number of health workers differs greatly between the individual control departments and institutes. Amongst the 341 staff on district level, 24 (7.04 %) were employed in the urban areas within 5 departments of schistosomiasis control of district level CDCs. In these districts the endemic situation is very small and only 2–3 people work at each institution: Jiangan and Hongshan districts each have 3 staff members, Wuchang, Hanyang and Qingshan districts 2 staff members each. In the seven suburban and rural district institutions, a total of 317 (92.96 %) staff are attached, although in varying numbers. The largest schistosomiasis control station is in Caidian district with over 100 staff members. This high number can be explained by the high number of staff in the attached hospital.

Figure 18 illustrates the number of technical and non-technical staff at each level of the system, based on results of baseline study conducted by Wuhan CDC.

Figure 18: Distribution of technical and non-technical staff at each administrative level of the schistosomiasis control system in Wuhan in 2008

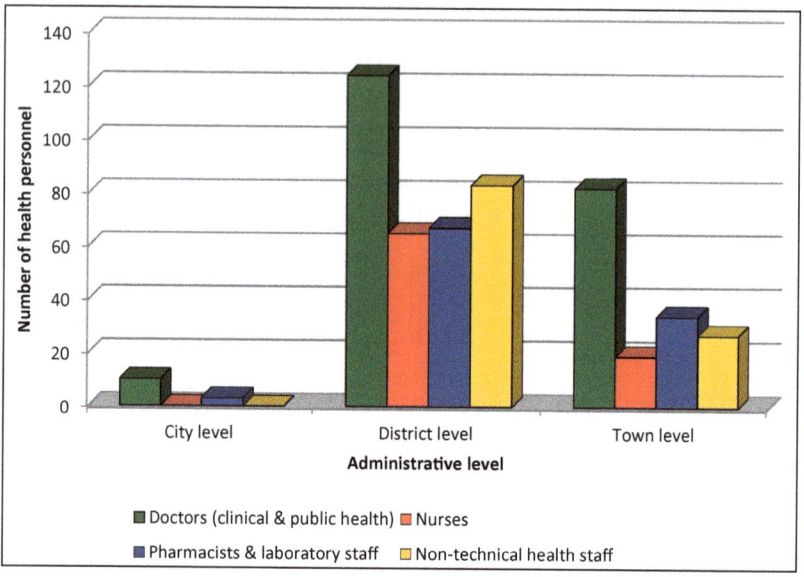

78 % of the health workers were technical staff, i.e. doctors, nurses, pharmacists and laboratory staff, and 22 % non-technical staff. With proactive case management being the priority control measure, there is a high number of doctors and nurses engaged in the screening and treatment of patients. Laboratory staff carrying out the diagnostic serological and parasitological testing is present in only district and town level institutions. In those control institutions which are integrated into hospitals, part of the clinical staff of the hospital are available for treatment of schistosomiasis patients, but not necessarily all available staff of a hospital are also involved in schistosomiasis control.

About 8 % of total staff were younger than 30 years of age, 50 % were between 30 and 40 years old and 12 % over 45 years. The proportion of younger staff was highest at the city level with almost 8 % being under 30 years and the lowest on town level with only 4 % being under 30 years old. At district and town levels, half of all staff (50 %, 53 %) were between 30 and 45 years of age. Only at city level, 53 % were older than 45 years.

Information on the distribution of the health personnel between the three administrative levels of employing facilities according to their educational background is presented here in Table 19.

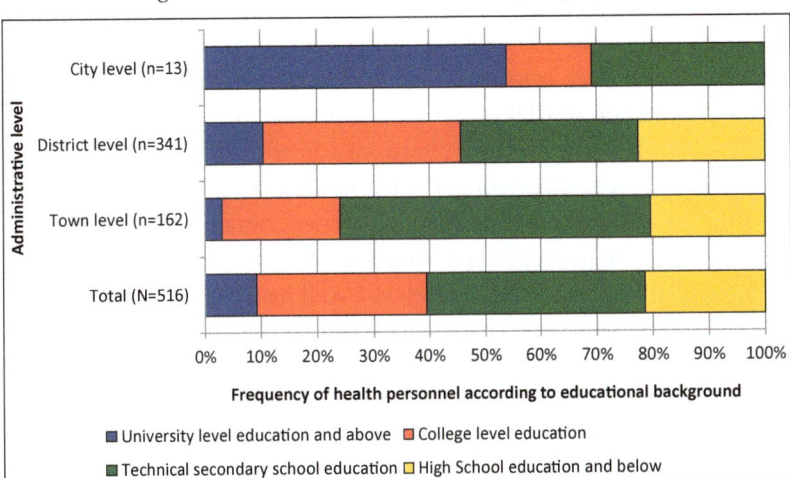

Figure 19: Distribution of health personnel according to their educational background at each administrative level of employment facility in 2008

Education level was higher at the city level, compared to district level or town levels. On city level, 54 % of staff had university level education, 15 % had college level education and 31 % technical secondary school education. There was no staff employed with a High School education or below.

On district level, only 11 % of staff had a university level education, while 27 % had a high school education or below. However, there was a difference in educational background between city proper districts and suburban and rural districts. While 45 % of staff in city proper districts had a university degree, only 8 % had a university degree in the outer city areas. Staff with high school (33 out of 317) or middle school diplomas (45 out of 317) were found only in rural districts.

Town level facilities have the lowest proportion of staff with university education (3 %) and the highest proportion of staff with technical secondary school education (56 %).

To further investigate the health worker investment for schistosomiasis control in Wuhan, questionnaires were distributed amongst all 516 health workers identified as being available to perform schistosomiasis prevention and control activities in 2008. Different questionnaires were distributed amongst the heads of schistosomiasis control stations (Annex 4), non-clinical staff (Annex 5) and clinical staff (Annex 6); clinical staff encompassed personnel employed by and working in hospitals with the main focus of work on treatment. Non-clinical staff included all workers employed by control institutes under the supervision of CDC, who are responsible for planning and carrying out prevention activities. Lastly, heads of schistosomiasis control stations are in charge of work and personnel of both hospitals and control institutes.

The information presented in this chapter was obtained by the analysis of the 216 questionnaires collected from respondents affiliated with control institutions at all administrative levels, as well as by informal interviews with leading staff members. This corresponds to a response rate of 42 %. Further analysis of the questionnaires lies in the perceptions of respondents on the availability of skilled labor forces and the workload in schistosomiasis control, as well as their opinions on the status of community health education and community participation with regard to schistosomiasis in Wuhan. Affiliations of respondents in terms of city district and work facility level are presented in Table 10.

Table 10: *Summary of respondents and their work facilities per district*

City districts	Number of respondents from work facilities at city, district and town level included in analysis (In brackets: number of different work facilities represented)						Total
	Non-clinical staff			Clinical staff		Control station leaders	
	City level	District level	Town level	District level	Town level	District and city level	
Xinzhou	–	15 (2)	–	15 (1)	–	1	31
Hannan	–	7 (1)	–	–	–	1	8
Caidian	–	6 (1)	11 (2)	2 (1)	11 (2)	1	31
Economic Development	–	–	3 (2)	–	2 (1)	–	5

City districts	Number of respondents from work facilities at city, district and town level included in analysis (In brackets: number of different work facilities represented)						Total
	Non-clinical staff			Clinical staff		Control station leaders	
	City level	District level	Town level	District level	Town level	District and city level	
Huangpi	–	9 (1)	39 (7)	34 (1)	37 (8)	1	120
Jiangxia	–	1 (1)	–	1 (1)	–	1	3
Qingshan	–	–	–	–	–	1	1
Wuchang	–	1 (1)	–	–	–	2	3
Hongshan	–	1 (1)	–	–	–	1	2
Hanyang	–	1 (1)	–	–	–	–	1
Donxihu	–	2 (1)	–	2 (1)	–	1	5
Jiangan	1 (1)	–	–	–	–	1	2
Wuhan city	3 (1)	–	–	–	–	1	4
Total	4 (2)	43 (10)	53 (11)	54 (5)	50 (11)	12 (12)	216
	100 (23)			104 (16)			
	216 (26)						

In total, 26 different work facilities from the 11 endemic districts, the economic developmental zone and the city level CDC are represented by the respondents. 56 % of respondents work in Huangpi district and 14.5 % in each Caidian and Xinzhou districts, the districts with the highest numbers of endemic villages and population at risk in Wuhan.

There is an equal distribution and number of male (n=110) and female (n=106) respondents. Their distribution according to human resource (HR) category is presented here in Table 11.

Table 11: Respondents' sex distribution per human resource (HR) category

HR category	Non-clinical staff		Clinical staff		Control station leaders		Total		
	Male	Female	Male	Female	Male	Female	Male	Female	All
Doctors	12	7	35	21	–	–	47	28	75
Nurses	0	9	2	26	–	–	2	35	37
Laboratory technicians	4	1	5	7	–	–	9	8	17
Others	34	20	2	6	–	–	36	26	72
No answer / not specified	8	4	–	–	8	4	16	8	24
Total	58	42	44	60	8	4	110	106	216

Clinical staff respondents working in hospitals are comprised of doctors (54 %), nurses (27 %) and laboratory technicians (12 %). Among non-clinical staff working in CDC institutes, the three subgroups together represent only one third (33 %) of respondents, while more than half (54 %), grouped under the subcategory "others", identified themselves as non-technical staff, such as management, financial officers, administration staff, logistic and support staff (driver etc.), data management, IT support, information officer and Communist Party representatives.

52.32 % (113) of respondents hold a university, college or technical secondary school degree. Among non-clinical staff with a higher education degree, 29 (58 %) majored in medical science and 8 (16 %) in public health; the remaining 22 % had a background in economics, natural science, computer sciences or others. Among non-clinical staff, 18 % of respondents had acquired a public health license, i.e. a special training in public health which allows successful participants to hold the title of public health doctor. 27.39 % (59) of respondents had a high school education or below.

Two thirds of respondents (143, 66.2 %) were employed full-time and 53 (24.5 %) part-time, with 8 (3.7 %) of respondents not specifying.

34 % of respondents were between 30–39 and 39 % being between 40–49 years old. 21 (9.7 %) respondents were younger than 30 years of age and 16 % between 50 and 60. Only one respondent was older than 60 years (0.9 %). There was no difference in age distribution between non-clinical and clinical staff. Out of the 12 control station leaders, half (50 %) were between 40–49 years old and the other half between 50–59 years old.

The majority of the 204 (94.4 %) respondents were born in Wuhan, another 6 (2.8 %) were from other areas still within the Hubei province and only 4 (1.9 %) were born in other provinces and had moved to Wuhan for work. Thus, geographical mobility is low and migration does not seem to be an issue.

Over 60 % of respondents had general work experience in schistosomiasis prevention and control for over 10 years, almost 9 % over 30 years. This experience did not necessarily start with a professional career. The older generations in particular had already acquired practical experience in this field during their childhood and youth, when many campaigns were set up by the government for control of schistosomiasis, which generally all of the population participated in. Among control station leaders, 10 (83 %) can build on more than 10 years' work experience, 3 (25 %) on over 30 years. Details are shown here in Table 12.

Table 12: Respondents' work experience (years) in schistosomiasis prevention and control

Work experience (years)	Non-clinical staff	Clinical staff	Control station leaders	Total
< 5	26 (26 %)	10 (9.6 %)	–	36 (16.7 %)
5–10	20 (20 %)	27 (26.0 %)	2 (16.7 %)	49 (22.7 %)
11–20	22 (22 %)	32 (30.8 %)	3 (25 %)	57 (26.4 %)
21–30	14 (14 %)	25 (24.0 %)	4 (33.3 %)	43 (19.9 %)
> 30	16 (16 %)	10 (9.6 %)	3 (25 %)	19 (8.8 %)
No answer / not specified	2 (2 %)	–	–	2 (0.9 %)
Total	100 (100 %)	104 (100 %)	12 (100 %)	216 (100 %)

There seemed to be relatively little staff turnover. Duration of job holding is quite high. 62.5 % of respondents have been in their present position for more than 10 years, of which 41 (19 %) for more than 20 years and 22 (10.2 %) even for more than 30 years.

3.2.2 Work load

To assess the self-perceived work-load of health workers in schistosomiasis control, the respondents were presented with some statements, and asked for their individual opinions. Using a Likert-type scale, respondents could express their views on the respective statements by choosing opinion boxes ranging from strongly agree to strongly disagree.

The statements referred to the development of general workload in schistosomiasis control over time (Table 13), the availability of health workers for the existing amount of work (Table 14) and the role of human resources in further reducing schistosome infection levels (Table 15).

Table 13: Respondents' view on the statement that since they started working in schistosomiasis the schistosomiasis related workload has steadily decreased

Respondents' view	Non-clinical staff	Clinical staff	Control station leaders	Total
Strongly agree	1 (1 %)	6 (5.8 %)	–	7 (3.2 %)
Agree	21 (21 %)	29 (27.9 %)	1 (8.3 %)	51 (23.6 %)
Neither agree nor disagree	17 (17 %)	36 (34.6 %)	3 (25 %)	56 (25.9 %)
Disagree	59 (59 %)	29 (27.9 %)	3 (25 %)	92 (42.6 %)
Strongly disagree	–	4 (3.9 %)	2 (16.7 %)	6 (2.8 %)
No answer / not specified	–	–	3 (25 %)	3 (1.4 %)
Total	100 (100 %)	104 (100 %)	12 (100 %)	216 (100 %)

The majority of respondents disagreed (n=88, 42.6 %), of which some even strongly disagreed (n=6, 2.8 %) with the statement that since they started working in the field of schistosomiasis, work load had steadily decreased over time (Table 13). Only 26.3 % (n=58) agree with the statement. There was a highly significant difference between non-clinical and clinical staff (p=0.001). While 60 % of clinical staff is divided in agreeing and disagreeing to this question, the majority of non-clinical staff takes a clear position against the statement. This opinion is also reflected in responses by the majority of city and district level control station leaders. In personal interviews, most of the leaders stated that the workload had increased, while the total number of health workers had steadily decreased during the past 10 years. However leaders of control stations of rural city districts did not see any change in overall staff numbers.

37 % of respondents thought that in their line of work, at this point of time, there were enough people employed for the current workload, while 31 % of all respondents thought otherwise (Table 14). One quarter of the respondents was undecided about this and neither agreed nor disagreed.

Table 14: Respondents' view on the statement that in their line of work in schistosomiasis control presently there were enough people employed for the current work load

Respondents' view	Non-clinical staff	Clinical staff	Control station leaders	Total
Strongly agree	4 (4 %)	3 (2.9 %)	1 (8.3 %)	7 (3.2 %)
Agree	40 (40 %)	33 (31.7 %)	2 (16.7 %)	73 (33.8 %)
Neither agree nor disagree	19 (19 %)	34 (32.7 %)	2 (16.7 %)	53 (24.5 %)
Disagree	22 (22 %)	32 (30.8 %)	4 (33.3 %)	54 (25.0 %)
Strongly disagree	12 (12 %)	1 (1 %)	–	13 (6.0 %)
No answer / not specified	3 (3 %)	1 (1 %)	3 (25 %)	7 (4.2 %)
Total	100 (100 %)	104 (100 %)	12 (100 %)	216 (100 %)

While the distributions of agreement and disagreement within the groups of clinical staff and control station leaders balance each other out, among non-clinical staff there is slightly less disagreement (34 %) to this statement than agreement (44 %).

A significant difference (p=0.004) was found between distributions of responses given by clinical and non-clinical staff. While one third of clinical staff neither agreed nor disagreed, 80 % of non-clinical staff took a clear stand on this question, with the majority agreeing. In addition, distribution of answers with respect to facility level of employment of respondents was also found to significantly differ (p=0.001). The highest disagreement was found among respondents working in town-level facilities, for both clinical and non-clinical staff.

District station heads were asked in their function as an employer, whether they thought it was difficult to find qualified personnel for the work required in schistosomiasis prevention and control. Opinions on this were divided. One third agreed that it was difficult, while the second third disagreed, of which half even strongly disagreed. The remaining third neither agreed nor disagreed or did not answer this question.

However, all respondents who found it difficult to find qualified personnel were leaders from those Wuhan suburban and rural area districts (Jiangxia, Xinzhou, Caidian, Dongxihu), which had the highest number of endemic villages and population at risk; disagreeing and even strongly disagreeing were city proper district heads (Jiangan, Wuchang, Hongshan). Distribution of qualified health workers was focused on city proper area, while rural districts are in need of a higher number of health workers and also of qualified health workers.

In Wuhan, a lot of emphasis was placed on the training of employees to improve their qualification in working in schistosomiasis prevention and control. All respondents reported that they had received further schistosomiasis-related education or training. The majority of the 128 respondents claimed to have received more than one training session per year (59.26 %), 70 respondents (32.41 %) received one training session per year and 2 respondents received (0.96) one training session every two years.

For the majority of respondents (87.7 %), the solution to the problem of how to achieve further decrease of schistosomiasis infections seemed to lie in the recruitment of additional personnel (Table 15).

Table 15: Respondents' view on the statement that further decrease of schistosomiasis infection rates could only be achieved by employing more people in schistosomiasis control

Respondents' view	Non-clinical staff	Clinical staff	Control station leaders	Total
Strongly agree	27 (27 %)	28 (26.9 %)	2 (16.7 %)	55 (26.4 %)
Agree	43 (43 %)	64 (61.5 %)	6 (50 %)	107 (52.3 %)
Neither agree nor disagree	3 (3 %)	4 (3.9 %)	3 (25 %)	7 (4.6 %)
Disagree	26 (26 %)	8 (7.7 %)	–	34 (15.7 %)
Strongly disagree	1 (1 %)	–	–	1 (0.5 %)
No answer / not specified	–	–	1 (8.3 %)	1 (0.5 %)
Total	100 (100 %)	104 (100 %)	12 (100 %)	216 (100 %)

Only 16 % of respondents did not share this view. However, while all control station leaders and almost 90 % of the clinical staff agreed or even strongly agreed to this, the opinion on this matter was more diverse among non-clinical staff. In this sub-group, 27 % did not agree.

3.2.3 Control activities

Leaders of schistosomiasis control stations were asked about the three, in their opinion, most labor intensive (in terms of number of people needed), time intensive and expensive control activities within the work of their respective control stations. The collective answers showed that the most labor intensive activities were 1) surveying snails, followed by 2) diagnosing patients (surveillance in endemic areas, IHA and Kato-Katz tests) and 3) spraying molluscicide. The most time-intensive activities were considered to be 1) surveying snails, followed by 2) health education activities (visiting endemic areas and educating on schistosomiasis, visiting schools, compiling information brochures and other material etc.) and 3) overall management (organizing, reports etc.). The most expensive activities according to the leaders were 1) surveying snails, followed by 2) spraying molluscacide and 3) treatment of chronic patients with praziquantel (in endemic areas).

To gain further understanding on the scope of investment in the individual control activities, clinical and non-clinical staff was asked to give an estimate of their time investment in the various control activities they were involved in. Estimates were given as days per month during the transmission period (TP: May-September) and the non-transmission period (NTP: October-April). Each self-reported time-investment includes planning, supervision and reporting/evaluation of the respective surveillance activity. Results for non-clinical staff are presented in Table 16, for clinical staff in Table 17, respectively.

Results of self-reported investment time among non-clinical staff show that involvement (by number of staff) differs greatly for various activities. Over 85–91 % of non-clinical respondents reported to be actively participating in snail surveillance during non-transmission period (NTP) and transmission period (TP), while 67 %-78% reported involvement in health education and 50 %-72% in spraying molluscacide respectively (Table 16). On the other hand, less than half of all respondents were involved in activities such as treatment of advanced cases in hospitals, improving sanitation and water supply, research and "others".

For most activities, self-reported involvement accounts for a total of one week or less (1–5 days) per month. Only for snail surveillance, management and administration were there any respondents whose self-reported time investment exceeded one or even two weeks per month.

Table 16: Non-clinical staff and self-reported estimation of work time invested in control activities

Activity*	Period**	Number of staff members active in respective activity per work investment (days per month)				Number (%) of staff involved (N=46)
		1–5 days	6–10 days	11–15 days	> 15 days	
Snail surveillance	TP	30	9	3	0	42 (91.3 %)
	NTP	31	6	2	0	39 (84.8 %)
Diagnosing patients	TP	20	4	0	0	24 (52.2 %)
	NTP	21	1	0	0	22 (47.8 %)
Treating chronic patients with PZQ	TP	30	1	0	0	31 (67.4 %)
	NTP	34	1	0	0	35 (76.1 %)

Activity*	Period**	Number of staff members active in respective activity per work investment (days per month)				Number (%) of staff involved (N=46)
		1–5 days	6–10 days	11–15 days	> 15 days	
Treatment of advanced cases in hospitals	TP	16	0	0	0	16 (34.8 %)
	NTP	17	0	0	0	17 (37.0 %)
Spraying molluscacide	TP	33	0	0	0	33 (71.7 %)
	NTP	23	0	0	0	23 (50.0 %)
Health education	TP	36	0	0	0	36 (78.3 %)
	NTP	28	3	0	0	31 (67.4 %)
Environmental Modification	TP	24	0	0	0	24 (52.2 %)
	NTP	21	0	0	0	21 (45.7 %)
Improving sanitation and water supply	TP	20	0	0	0	20 (43.5 %)
	NTP	20	0	0	0	20 (43.5 %)
Management	TP	28	1	0	0	29 (63.0 %)
	NTP	20	0	1	0	21 (45.7 %)
Administration and Support	TP	23	1	2	0	26 (56.5 %)
	NTP	19	4	0	0	23 (50.0 %)
Research	TP	11	0	0	0	11 (23.9 %)
	NTP	13	0	0	0	13 (28.3 %)
Other Activities	TP	6	0	0	0	6 (13.0 %)
	NTP	12	0	0	0	12 (26.1 %)

* all activities include planning, preparation and reporting
** TP= Transmission period; NTP= Non-transmission period

In almost all control activities, there was a higher number of staff involved during TP than NTP. The only exceptions were treatment of patients, research and "other activities".

The clinical staff reported their main work focus to lie clearly in treatment of patients in the hospitals with over 90 % of staff involved. 47 % of clinical staff respondents indicated that this work takes up at least half of their total work time, irrespective of TP or NTP (Table 17).

Table 17: Clinical staff and self-reported estimation of work time invested in control activities

Activity*	Period**	Number of staff members active in respective activity per work investment (days per month)				Number (%) of staff involved (N=42)
		1–5 days	6–10 days	11–15 days	> 15 days	
Diagnosis in hospital	TP	16	2	1	1	20 (47.6 %)
	NTP	17	2	1	0	20 (47.6 %)
Treatment in hospital	TP	13	7	7	11	38 (90.5 %)
	NTP	16	4	7	11	38 (90.5 %)
IHA testing in endemic villages	TP	18	1	3	0	22 (52.4 %)
	NTP	21	2	1	0	23 (54.8 %)
Treatment with PZQ in endemic villages	TP	22	2	0	0	24 (57.1 %)
	NTP	29	2	0	0	30 (71.4 %)
Laboratory diagnosis of IHA and KK	TP	13	1	0	0	14 (33.3 %)
	NTP	15	0	0	0	15 (35.7 %)
Health education	TP	23	0	0	0	23 (54.8 %)
	NTP	19	0	0	0	19 (45.2 %)
Research	TP	12	1	0	0	13 (31.0 %)
	NTP	10	1	0	0	11 (26.2 %)
Other Activities	TP	1	0	0	0	1 (2.4 %)
	NTP	3	0	0	0	3 (7.1 %)

* all activities include planning, preparation and reporting
** TP= Transmission period; NTP= Non-transmission period

However, the majority of clinical staff (86 %) stated that they had also been involved in schistosomiasis related work outside of their hospital. These activities included visiting endemic villages for conducting IHA test and for treatment with praziquantel. Here, between 50 % and 71 % of all respondents were involved, although their time investment was low at no more than 1–3 days per month. In other schistosomiasis related work, at least 25 % of respondents were included; however the time investment here was also rather low in days per month invested in the respective activity.

3.2.4 Community participation and community health education

a) Community participation:

The vast majority of respondents consider community participation as extremely important (63.1 %) or very important (32 %) for the success of their personal work activities in schistosomiasis control. Only 6 (2.9 %) respondents rated it as moderately important.

Cooperation with local community participants during their daily work on an occasional basis was reported by 185 respondents (90.7 %). Only 15 respondents (7.4 %) stated that they rarely had contact with community members and 4 had never had any. Of those with contact to community members, the majority of the 98 respondents (48 %) had contact on a monthly basis, 42 (20.6 %) on a weekly basis, and 57 (27.9 %) a few times per year. Weekly and monthly contact was self-reported more often among non-clinical (24 %, 53 %) compared to clinical (17.3 %, 43.3 %) staff.

Respondents, both clinical and non-clinical, were in contact with various different groups of community members as summarized in Table 16. Contact with school teachers was reported more often among non-clinical (53 %) compared to clinical (24.0 %) staff.

Table 18: Respondents' contact to different groups of community members

Respondent group	Village authorities	Village doctors	Villagers support staff	School teachers	Others	Not specified
Non-clinical (out of 100)	71 (71 %)	69 (69 %)	31 (31 %)	53 (53 %)	1 (1 %)	4 (4 %)
Clinical (out of 104)	59 (56.7 %)	54 (51.9 %)	35 (33.7 %)	25 (24.0 %)	–	–
Total (out of 204)	130 (63.7 %)	123 (60.3 %)	66 (32.4 %)	78 (38.2 %)	1 (0.5 %)	4 (2.0 %)

Based on personal experience, 79 respondents (30.8 %) regarded their cooperation relationship with local community participants in schistosomiasis control as good, 46 (26.9 %) as very good. However, 75 (40.4 %) assessed the relationship as being only moderate.

b) Community health education

All respondents viewed health education on schistosomiasis as very important (122, 60.4 %) or extremely important (80, 39.6 %) for the success of their work. Non-clinical staff in particular stressed the importance of health education in this context, with 75 % assessing it as extremely important compared to 45.2 % of clinical staff.

Among those respondents with more than five years of work experience in schistosomiasis prevention and control, the majority (134, 75.3 %) perceived that the general knowledge of the people in the communities they worked with about schistosomiasis had increased over the past 5 years. 23.6 % (42) could not see any change in knowledge over the past 5 years and 2 respondents (1.1 %) even observed an decrease in general knowledge about schistosomiasis.

In total, 187 respondents (91.7 %) believed that the majority of people (more than 50 %) in the communities they work in had sufficient knowledge about what schistosomiasis is, how it is contracted and how it can be prevented. Only 8 people (3.9 %) held the view that the majority of people in the communities did not have this knowledge.

3.3 Schistosomiasis surveillance in Xiang Lu village

This section presents results from surveillance data collected on the population of Xiang Lu village between 2003 and 2010. The original data is from the files of the CDC Wuhan, as collected officially for reporting purposes according to the duties of this office. Focus of analysis lies on serological prevalence, conversions and reversion rates as well as development of titer patterns within individuals over time.

3.3.1 Description of study population

In this study, data from all people registered as residents in Xiang Lu village was analyzed. The registration list used for surveillance purposes was compiled in 2006 and comprised of a total of 1,217 people. However, this list had not been updated between 2006 and 2010, for example by adding newborn children or emitting the deceased. Therefore, the population under surveillance is unchanged between 2006 and 2010. Not all people registered as inhabitants of Xiang Lu Village reside there at all times. Therefore, the number of tests carried out per person between 2003 and 2010 varies considerably, with some people having not being tested at all. The number of individual tests per person carried out and available for further analysis is summarized in Table 19. The maximum amount of tests per person is 8, with one test per year conducted over a total period of eight years.

Table 19: *Overview and structure of the dataset / results of IHA tests (once per year) 2003–2010*

Number of times residents were tested between 2003–2010	Number of positive IHA tests (titre ≥ 5)								
	0	1	2	3	4	5	6	7	8	Total (%)
0	136	–	–	–	–	–	–	–	–	136 (11 %)
1	149	23	–	–	–	–	–	–	–	172 (14 %)
2	113	33	6	–	–	–	–	–	–	152 (12 %)
3	84	58	15	1	–	–	–	–	–	158 (13 %)
4	61	37	25	12	5	–	–	–	–	140 (12 %)
5	52	39	30	23	8	0	–	–	–	152 (12 %)
6	72	42	26	27	14	4	2	–	–	187 (15 %)
7	43	18	18	7	12	4	0	0	–	102 (8 %)
8	7	3	2	2	2	1	1	0	0	18 (1 %)
Total	717	253	122	72	41	9	3	0	0	1,217 (100 %)

Over the period covered in this study, a total of 89 % of the village population under surveillance has been tested at least one time. However, only 18 people (1 %) were tested every year for eight consecutive years. The reason for total or partial absence here is that there exists high temporary rural-urban labour migration. For example, people may be registered in the village, but work or live somewhere else. This could be a possible explanation as to why so many participants within the time span of 8 years were tested so rarely or not at all. Another explanation is that tests are conducted on only one or 2 days per year. Although dates for testing are previously announced, villagers who are registered in the village might have been not available at these times due to other commitments.

The age distribution of the population registered as residents of Xiang Lu village in 2006 is presented in Figure 20. With no changes in the composition of population under surveillance, the age distribution for the year 2010 would still have the same shape, it would only move to the right by 4 years.

The 136 people (11 %) who were never tested were excluded from further analysis as no test result was available. For comparison, Figure 21 shows the age distribution of the village population without the 136 people who didn't come for testing. Differences in total numbers can be seen in age groups 15–20 and 20–40 years. The overall distribution shape stays the same. The population distributions are not apparently different; thus absenteeism from being tested is unlikely to induce a bias to the analysis. Table 20 and Table 21 summarize the background in occupation and education, respectively, of all individuals tested. The vast majority were farmers and had a junior high school education. There were no appreciable differences between sexes, except possibly for fishers.

Table 20: Occupation of study population in 2006

Occupation	Male	Female	No of people (%)
Farmer	459	430	889 (88.65 %)
Fishermen	21	9	30 (4.49 %)
School children	97	65	162 (6.86 %)
Primary School	29	13	42
Junior High School	38	33	71
Senior High School	30	19	49
Total	577 (53.4 %)	504 (46,6 %)	1081 (100 %)

Table 21: *Educational background of study population (including school children) in 2006*

Education level	Male	Female	No of people (%)
No school education / illiterate	3	4	7 (0.65 %)
Primary school	49	52	101 (9.34 %)
Junior High School	414	368	785 (72.62 %)
Senior High School	108	80	188 (17.39 %)
Total	242	181	1081 (100 %)

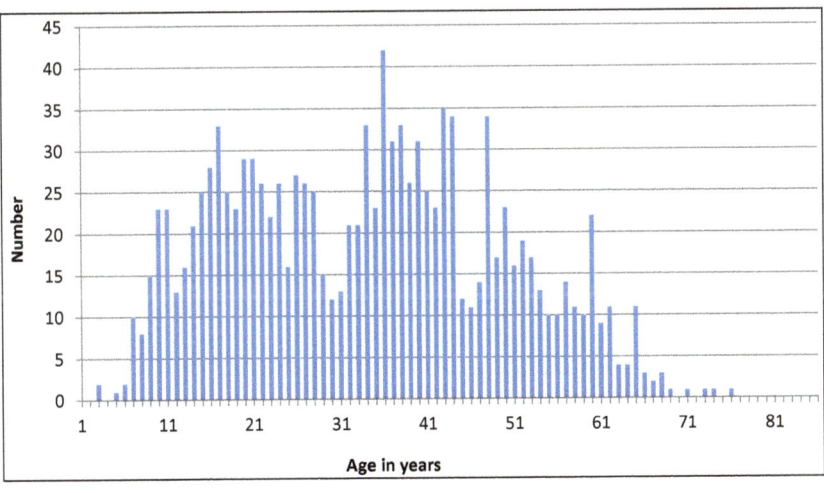

Figure 20: *Age structure of total registered population of Xiang Lu village in 2006 (N=1217)*

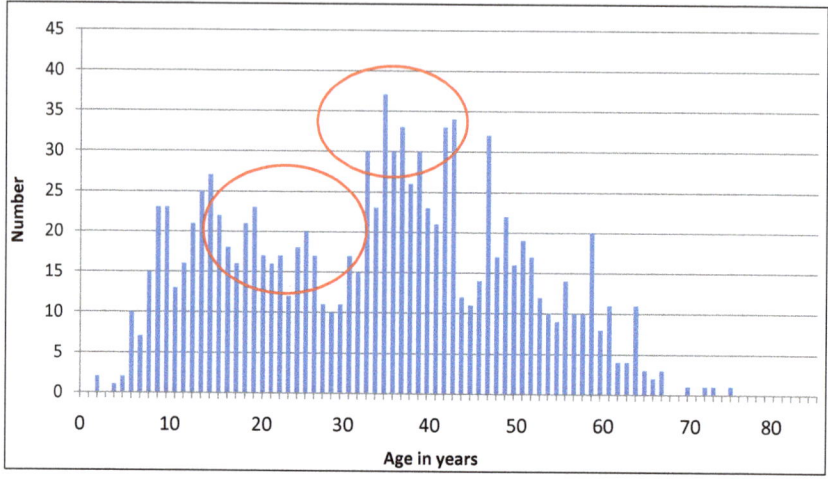

Figure 21: Age structure population of Xiang Lu village in 2006 of people tested at least one time between 2003–2010 (N=1081); the circles indicate differences compared to total registered population as presented in Figure 20

3.3.2 Serological and parasitological prevalence

Serological and parasitological prevalence rates are based on test results of N=1081 people who came at least once for testing between the years of 2003–2010. In total, 4,250 IHA tests were performed. The number of subjects detected per year is shown in Table 22. Those with a positive IHA (933 cases) were further tested for egg excretion by KK (Table 23).

Table 22: Serological prevalence of schistosomiasis japonica in Xiang Lu village (2003–2010)

Year	No of tests performed	No serologically positive	serolog. positive (%)	95 % Confidence Interval	
2003	186	22	11.83	.0800	.1797
2004	414	56	13.53	.1146	.1852
2005	603	227	37.65	.3376	.4165
2006	853	143	16.76	.1432	.1944
2007	577	164	28.42	.2494	.3247

Year	No of tests performed	No serologically positive	serolog. positive (%)	95 % Confidence Interval	
2008	486	132	27.16	.2325	.3135
2009	649	129	19.88	.1687	.2316
2010	482	60	12.45	.0964	.1573
Total	4250	933			

Table 23: Parasitological prevalence of schistosomiasis japonica in Xiang Lu village (2003–2010) as tested by KK*

Year	No of serological test	No egg positive	Infection rate (%)	95 % Confidence Interval		Infection intensity (mean EPG) AM* GM*	
2003	186	8	4.30	.0187	.0830	20	18
2004	414	4	0.97	.0026	.0247	No data available	
2005	603	31	5.14	.0352	.0721	60	35
2006	853	45	5.28	.0387	.0700	14	12
2007	577	19	3.29	.0199	.0509	25	22
2008	486	14	2.88	.0158	.0479	17	15
2009	649	14	2.16	.0118	.0359	16	14
2010	482	8	1.66	.0072	.0324	13	11
Total	4250	143					

*Abbreviations: Kato-Katz (KK), Egg per Gramm (EPG), Arithmetic Mean (AM), Geometric Mean (GM)

The infection rate or KK-positive rate ranged from 0.97 % in 2004 to 5.28 % in 2006. Infection intensity, expressed in mean EPG values for both arithmetic mean (AM) and geometric mean (GM), is very low. In 2010, in KK-positive tests, there were only 1 to 3 eggs detected, which calculates as only 8–24 EPG[2]. In 2009, in KK positive tests there were only 1 to 4 eggs counted, which calculates as only 8–32 EPG. In 2008, in KK positive tests there were only 1 to 3 eggs counted, which calculates as only 8–24 EPG.

The percentages of IHA and KK positive cases among the tested population per year are shown and compared with each other in Figure 22. Sero-prevalence of *S. japonicum* as detected by IHA was 3–14 times higher than the prevalence as determined by the KK stool examination. There are remarkable and unexpected large variations in sera-reactivity, in particular in year 2005, which need further clarification. Technical reasons could be involved, i.e. change of test kits or staff conducting, analyzing or interpreting laboratory test results. Similar variations are not apparent in the egg counts.

Figure 22: Serological and parasitological prevalence of schistosomiasis per year in Xiang Lu village (2003–2010)

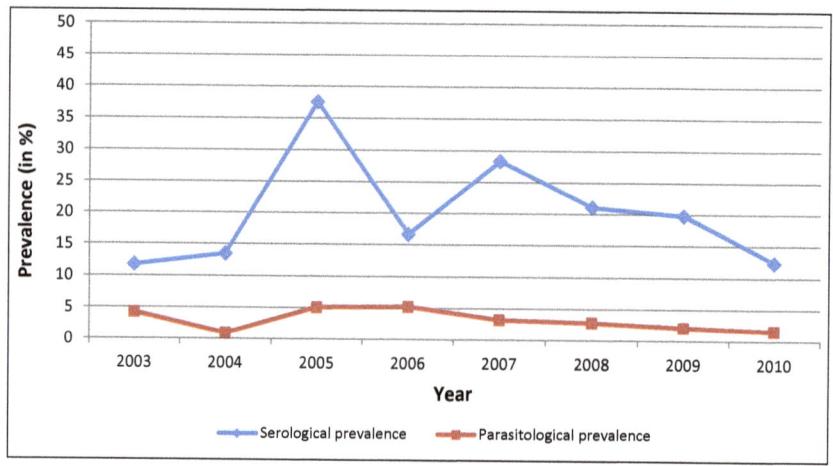

---

2   EPG values obtained from Kato-Katz thick smear readings use the multiplication factor 24 for a single, and a factor 8 for triplicate Kato-Katz thick smear readings. In this study triplicate Kato-Katz smears were collected from one stool specimen. Therefore, the multiplication factor used here is 8 for each egg identified in each of the three slides.

As expected, serologically positive cases exceeded egg positive cases by many times. However, neither curve correlates in shape, although they should. Therefore, a linear correlation between serological and parasitological test results is not apparent. However, here serological test results were only considered as a dichotomous variable (positive/negative). Thus, we further investigated whether there is a possible relationship between serological and parasitological test results when looking at IHA titer values.

3.3.2.1 IHA titer and KK test results

The results indicate that there is a statistically significant relationship between IHA titer value and result of KK test in all individual years as well as for all test results accumulated over all years 2005–2010 (Table 24).

Table 24: Association between IHA titer and KK test result per year and titer

Year	IHA titer value	No serological positive	No egg positive	Agreement between IHA and KK (%)*	95 % CI	P-value
2005	All	227	31	13.66	9.47–18.82	<0.001
	IHA ≤ 1:10	119	1	0.84	0.02–4.59	
	IHA = 1:20	41	2	4.88	5.96–16.53	
	IHA = 1:20	67	28	41.79	29.85–54.48	
2006	All	143	45	31.47	23.00–39.76	0.009
	IHA ≤ 1:10	121	32	26.45	18.84–35.24	
	IHA = 1:20	10	6	60.00	26.23–87.84	
	IHA = 1:40	12	7	58.33	27.67–84.83	
2007	All	164	19	11.59	7.12–17.50	<0.001
	IHA ≤ 1:10	70	1	1.43	0.04–7.70	
	IHA = 1:20	42	3	7.14	1.48–19.48	
	IHA = 1:40	52	15	28.85	17.13–43.08	

Year	IHA titer value	No serological positive	No egg positive	Agreement between IHA and KK (%)*	95 % CI	P-value
2008	All	132	14	10.61	5.92–17.15	0.001
	IHA ≤ 1:10	68	2	2.94	0.36–10.22	
	IHA = 1:20	24	3	12.50	0.27–32.36	
	IHA = 1:40	26	9	34.62	17.21–55.67	
2009	All	129	14	10.85	6.06–17.54	<0.001
	IHA ≤ 1:10	67	1	1.49	0.04–8.04	
	IHA = 1:20	21	3	14.29	3.05–36.34	
	IHA = 1:40	27	10	37.04	19.40–57.63	
2010	All	60	8	13.33	5.94–24.59	0.001
	IHA ≤ 1:10	47	2	4.26	0.52–14.54	
	IHA = 1:20	6	2	33.33	4.33–77.72	
	IHA = 1:40	7	4	57.14	18.41–90.10	
2005–2010	All	855	132	15.44	13.08–18.04	
	IHA ≤ 1:10	495	39	7.88	5.66–10.61	
	IHA = 1:20	150	19	12.67	7.80–19.07	
	IHA = 1:40	210	73	34.76	28.34–41.62	

* Assuming the Kato-Katz results as the gold standard reference, agreement is equivalent to the positive predictive value (PPV) for IHA test

Data shows that the frequency of agreement between a positive IHA test result and a positive KK test result rises with titer values, the lowest being from IHA titer of ≤ 1:10 and the highest IHA titer of 1:40. This trend is visible in all individual years. The positive predictive value of IHA test increases with increased titer values. However, frequency values between the individual years vary, the year 2006 showing a particularly high agreement between both tests compared to all other years. A graphical representation of the data is given in Figure 23.

Figure 23: Frequency of agreement between IHA titer and positive and KK test per year

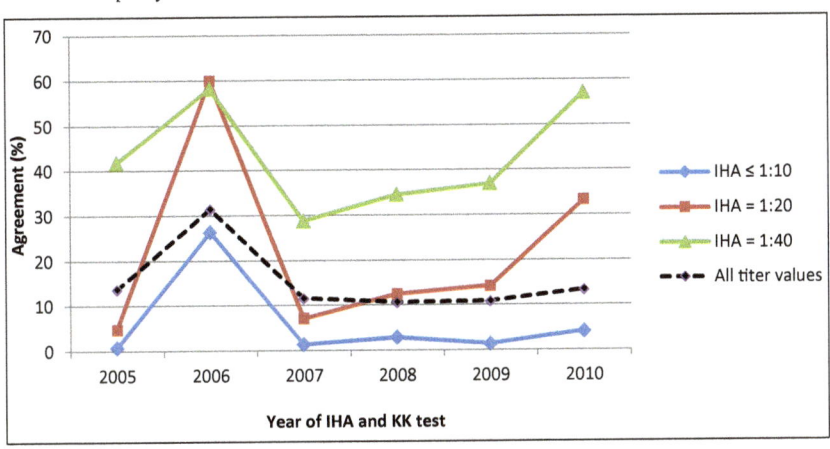

The results indicate that the IHA titer value is a statistically significant predictor of KK test result (i.e., being tested egg positive). Both, overall and separated by year, test results were found to be significantly associated with an egg positive test in univariate analysis (Table 25).

Table 25: Association of titer values and positive KK test result in univariate analysis

Titer (Year of IHA test)	Odds Ratio (OR)	Standard Error	P	95 % Confidence Interval (CI)		Pseudo R²
2005	1.149622	0.0297232	<0.001	1.092817	1.20938	0.3516
2006	1.052922	0.0217962	0.013	1.011058	1.096521	0.0365
2007	1.103651	0.0272276	<0.001	1.051555	1.158327	0.1925
2008	1.077086	0.0247968	0.001	1.029566	1.1268	0.1318
2009	1.09027	0.027175	0.001	1.038288	1.144855	0.1714
2010	1.11341	0.0354466	0.001	1.046059	1.185097	0.2786

Here, the serological prevalence will be investigated further. An in-depth analysis with respect to age and sex and other attributes of the parasitological positive cases over time would be irrelevant due to the small number of cases and very low infection intensities.

3.3.2.2 Age and sex-specific serological prevalence

Data on the yearly age-specific coverage of the population by IHA testing is available for the years 2005–2010 (Table 26), i.e. the percentage of people in each age group tested out of all people registered within the same age group. There is full coverage (100 %) of school children in age group 6–9 years. Even in the age group 10–14 years, coverage remains very high, ranging from between 89 % (2007) and 100 % (2006). However, coverage is far lower among all other age groups, i.e. among young adults of 15–19 years old, it ranged only between 12–59 %, and among adults of 20–39 years between only 15–63 %.

It can be noted that primary and Junior High School children are tested more regularly. Possible reasons for this will be discussed in the Discussion section.

The graphical illustration of the age-specific serological prevalence per year in Figure 24 shows trends of prevalence with age that are comparable for the different years. The black-dotted curve represents the accumulated values from all years. Thus, the serological prevalence is comparatively low below 20 years of age and is highest in the older age groups with a peak in age group 40–59; for individuals older than 60 years the prevalences decrease. Prevalence rates do not differ much between the sexes; with the only exception being the age group 20–39, where prevalence among men is almost double that of women (Figure 25).

Table 26: Age specific coverage of population by IHA tests and serological prevalence per year

Age group		2003	2004	2005	2006	2007	2008	2009	2010	total
6–9	Total registered N	n.a.*	n.a.*	n.a.*	34	18	12	5	3	
	Total number tested	11	34	49	34	18 (100)	12	5	3	166
	(coverage in %)**				(100 %)		(100 %)	(100 %)	(100 %)	
	IHA positive	1	0	9	5	1	0	0	0	16
10–14	Total registered N	n.a.*	n.a.*	n.a.*	96	89	81	79	58	
	Total number tested	26	68	75	96	89	75	74	55	548
	(coverage in %)**				(100 %)	(89 %)	(93 %)	(94 %)	(95 %)	
	IHA positive	3	5	9	7	2	3	0	0	29
15–19	Total registered N	n.a.*	n.a.*	n.a.*	133	132	122	102	97	
	Total number tested	12	57	16	69	16	30	38	57	295
	(coverage in %)**				(52 %)	(12 %)	(25 %)	(20 %)	(59 %)	
	IHA positive	1	1	3	10	2	0	0	1	18
20–39	Total registered N	n.a.*	n.a.*	n.a.*	496	489	484	487	473	
	Total number tested	53	126	193	311	148	105	161	69	1166
	(coverage in %)**				(63 %)	(30 %)	(22 %)	(33 %)	(15 %)	
	IHA positive	11	19	86	59	44	38	35	14	306

Age group		2003	2004	2005	2006	2007	2008	2009	2010	total
40–59	Total registered N	n.a.*	n.a.*	n.a.*	379	396	417	434	466	
	Total number tested	83	120	240	302	260	216	315	240	1776
	(coverage in %)**				(80 %)	(99 %)	(52 %)	(73 %)	(52 %)	
	IHA positive	7	34	112	60	99	82	78	38	510
≥ 60	Total registered N	n.a.*	n.a.*	n.a.*	74	85	96	109	119	
	Total number tested	1	9	30	41	56	48	56	58	299
	(coverage in %)**				(55 %)	(66 %)	(50 %)	(51 %)	(49 %)	
	IHA positive	0	2	8	2	17	9	16	7	61
Total		23	61	227	143	(577)	(486)	129	60	849
		(186)	(414)	(603)	(853)			(649)	(482)	(4250)

* Not applicable: registry of 2006 was used as basis for this analysis. Composition of total population under surveillance varied 2003–2005. Therefore, total registered numbers for 2003–2005 are not considered.
** Coverage refers to the percentage of persons tested out of the total population registered in each year within each individual age group.

Figure 24: Age specific serological prevalence (IHA positive test) per year and accumulated for all years 2003–2010

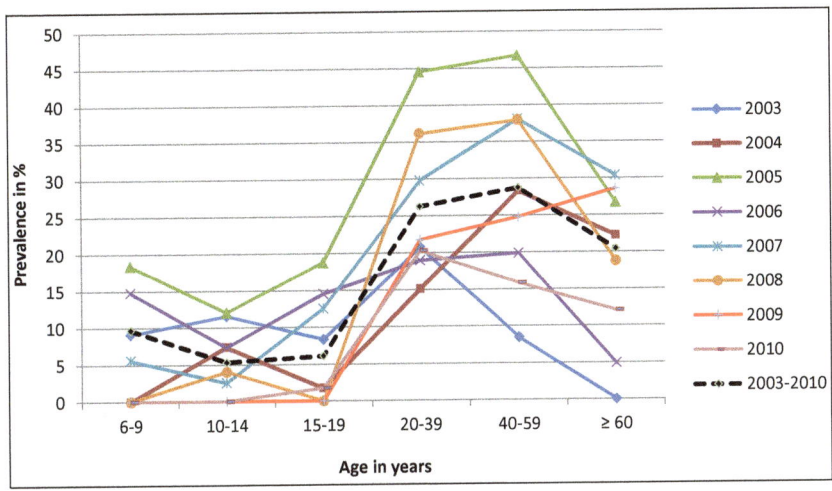

Figure 25: Age and sex specific serological prevalence (IHA positive test) accumulated for all years 2003–2010

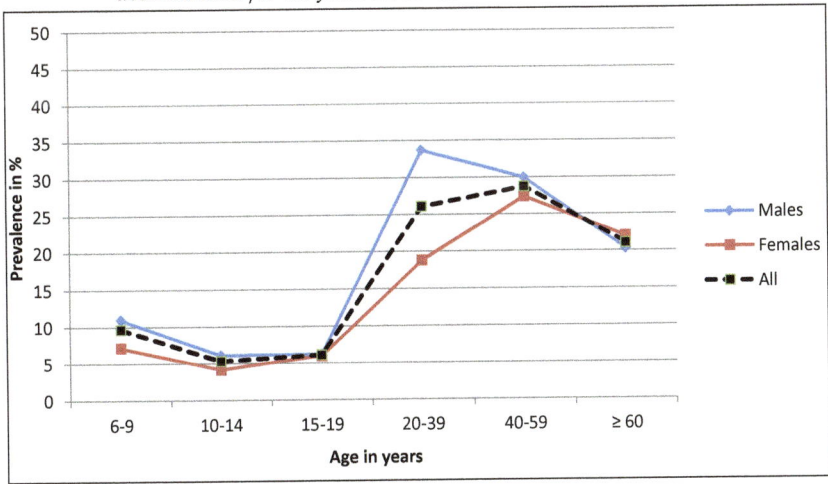

3.3.2.3 Titer value-specific serological prevalence

Here, serological prevalence according to titer values is analyzed and a potential correlation between titer values and sex or age is investigated (Table 27).

Table 27: Serological prevalence according to titer values (2005–2010)

Year	No of serological positive test	Titer value ≤10	Titer value =20	Titer value =40
2005	227 (100 %)	119 (52.42 %)	41 (18.06 %)	67 (29.52 %)
male	124 (100 %)	71 (57.26 %)	18 (14.52 %)	35 (28.23 %)
female	103 (100 %)	48 (46.60 %)	23 (22.33 %)	32 (31.07 %)
2006	143 (100 %)	121 (84.62 %)	10 (6.99 %)	12 (8.39 %)
male	86 (100 %)	73 (84.88 %)	7 (8.14 %)	6 (6.98 %)
female	57 (100 %)	48 (84.21 %)	3 (5.26 %)	6 (10.53 %)
2007	165 (100 %)	71 (43.03 %)	42 (25.45 %)	52 (31.52 %)
male	95 (100 %)	41 (43.16 %)	20 (21.05 %)	34 (35.79 %)
female	70 (100 %)	30 (42.86 %)	22 (31.43 %)	18 (25.71 %)
2008	132 (100 %)	70 (53.03 %)	27 (20.45 %)	35 (26.52 %)
male	77 (100 %)	39 (50.65 %)	17 (22.08 %)	21 (27.27 %)
female	55 (100 %)	31 (56.36 %)	10 (18.18 %)	14 (25.45 %)
2009	129 (100 %)	68 (52.71 %)	24 (18.60 %)	37 (28.68 %)
male	77 (100 %)	43 (55.84 %)	15 (19.48 %)	19 (24.68 %)
female	52 (100 %)	25 (48.08 %)	9 (17.31 %)	18 (34.62 %)
2010	60 (100 %)	47 (78.33 %)	6 (10.0 %)	7 (11.67 %)
male	33 (100 %)	25 (75.76 %)	3 (9.09 %)	5 (15.15 %)
female	27 (100 %)	22 (81.48 %)	3 (11.11 %)	2 (7.41 %)
Total (2005–2010)	856 (100 %)	496 (57.94 %)	150 (17.52 %)	210 (24.53 %)
male	492 (100 %)	292 (59.35 %)	80 (16.29 %)	120 (24.39 %)
female	364 (100 %)	204 56.04 %)	70 (19.23 %)	90 (24.73 %)

The graphical illustration of the titer-specific serological prevalence per year in Figure 26 shows that the serological prevalence is highest for titer levels of at least 1:10. Titre-related prevalence rates do not differ at all between the sexes. As seen in Table 27, prevalence rates among men and women in all three titre value groups accumulated for all years (2005–2010) are almost the same. Values between different individual years show insignificant minor variations.

Figure 26: IHA Titer level-specific serological prevalence per year (2005–2010)

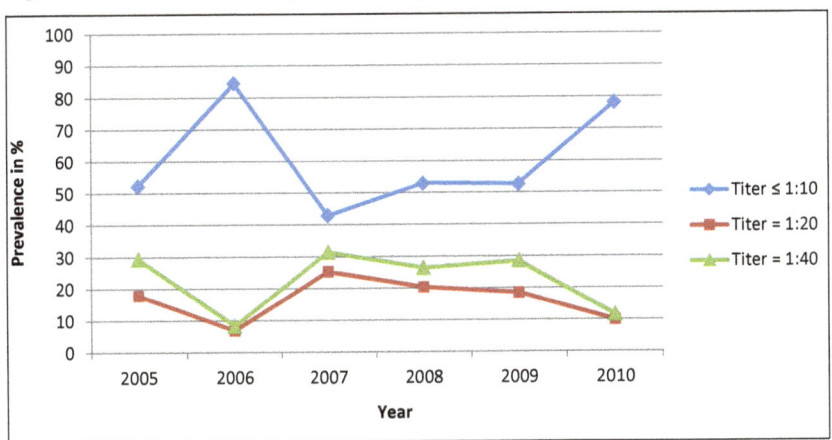

The results indicate that titers were relatively low in the younger age groups. 87 % of all children in the age group 6–9 years with positive IHA titers showed a level of ≤ 1:10, and less than 7 % showed titers of 1:20 or 1:40 (Figure 27). However, titer levels rose gradually with increasing age. In particular, the curve for titer level ≤ 1:10 shows almost a linear decrease with increasing age and with it the curves for titer values of 1:20 and 1:40, rise respectively, with titer values of 40 being more often tested after reaching adulthood at the age of over 20 years.

Figure 27: Age-specific serologic prevalence per titer-level; age calculated according to year of test

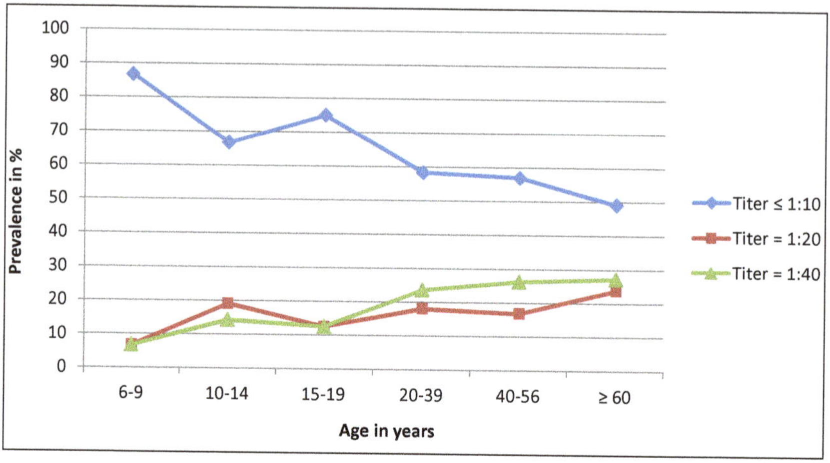

3.3.3 Sero-conversion and sero-reversion

In this section we determined sero-reversion (SR) and sero-conversion (SC) rates for IHA tests done within the time period 2003–2010. Seroconversion is defined as the conversion from a seronegative to a seropositive state. Sero-converters are assumed to have acquired an infection. Accordingly, sero-reversion is defined as the reversion from a seropositive to a seronegative IHA result. Sero-reverters are assumed to have been successfully cured by therapy.

Included in this part of the analysis were only individuals who came for IHA testing for at least <u>2 consecutive years</u> within the period 2003–2010. For all positive IHA tests within the 2 consecutive years, <u>IHA titers must have been recorded</u>.

Determination of SC is based on matching tests from only those individuals who have been tested IHA-negative in the first and IHA-positive in the second of any two consecutive years. The number of individuals fitting in this scheme is 227. Correspondingly, determination of SR is based on matching test results from only those individuals who have been tested IHA-positive in the first year. The number of individuals with these conditions is 377. There is an overlap between the individuals included for analysis of SC and SR, as in the course of the six years between 2005–2010, 181 individuals experienced episodes of both sero-conversion and sero-reversion. Thus, the total number of different individuals analysed in this section is 423.

Table 28: Occupation of study population

Occupation	Male	Female	Total (%)
Farmer	208	167	375 (88.65 %)
Fishermen	16	3	19 (4.49 %)
School children	18	11	29 (6.86 %)
Primary School	5	2	7
Junior High School	10	7	17
Senior High School	3	2	5
Total	242 (57.3 %)	181 (42.8 %)	423 (100 %)

The subgroup of 423 people studied here can be considered as representative of the entire village study population, the proportions of farmers, fishermen and students being even fully equivalent in both groups (compare Table 28 with Table 18), and proportions of different age groups being very similar (see Table 20).

Table 29 gives an overview of the age and sex distribution of the study population used for the analysis of SR and SC rates. The age of the 423 people was calculated at the time point when the respective individual came for IHA testing for the first time.

Table 29: Number of available IHA test results according to age (at time of first IHA test) and sex

Age group	Sex	Number of available IHA tests per person							Total
		2	3	4	5	6	7	8	
6–9	Male	–	–	–	–	7	2	2	11	15
	Female	–	–	–	–	2	1	1	4	
10–14	Male	–	2	3	–	4	2	–	11	18
	Female	–	2	2	–	3	–	–	7	
15–19	Male	1	5	1	–	1	–	–	8	10
	Female	1	–	1	–	–	–	–	2	

Age group	Sex	Number of available IHA tests per person								
		2	3	4	5	6	7	8	Total	
20–39	Male	7	16	16	20	22	7	1	89	156
	Female	8	5	12	15	17	9	1	67	
40–59	Male	2	14	21	30	24	19	4	114	205
	Female	4	6	14	27	24	14	2	91	
≥ 60	Male	–	–	2	2	3	2	–	9	19
	Female	–	3	1	2	3	1	–	10	
Total	Male	10	37	43	52	61	32	7	242	423
	Female	13	16	30	44	49	25	4	181	
Total		23	53	73	96	110	57	11	423	

Furthermore, Table 29 shows the number of available IHA tests per persons according to age group and sex. For all children within the age group 6–9, results are available for 6–8 years, most of which are consecutive. This corresponds to the earlier observation that the coverage of IHA testing is highest among primary and secondary school children. The highest absolute number of tests available is from the age group 40–59, the lowest in the age group 15–19.

Since the calculation of SC and SR is based on the multiple IHA results from the same individuals, it could be argued that this inevitably creates dependencies between results over the years, which might lead to the distortion of analysis. This issue is addressed in the discussion section.

In this population-based retrospective cohort study comprising 423 people, a low incidence of SC and a high incidence of SR were found (Figure 28). The SC curve indicates a trend with variations being relatively small. As for the SR curve, there is no clear trend visible and there are high variations between the years.

Assuming that these events reflect acquisition and loss of schistosome infections, respectively, the overall prevalence of the infection appears to decline over the following years.

Figure 28: Sero-conversion and sero-reversion rates

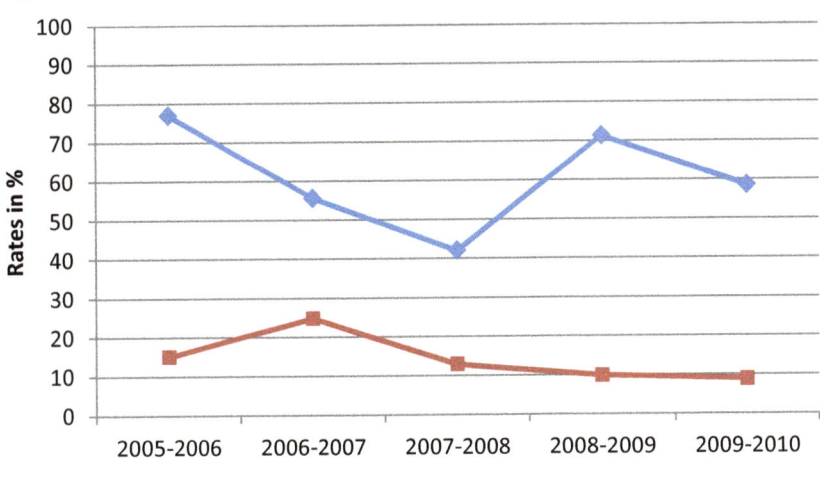

3.3.3.1 Sero-conversion and titer values

In the years 2005–2010, SC occurred with an average of 15.1 %, ranging between 9.8 % and 24.8 %. The clear majority of cases in all years (67.9 %) converted to a titer value of 1:10 or below (Table 30). There is no significant difference between SC to titer values of 1:20 and 1:40. Average frequency of conversions to these titer values accumulated for all years was 16.9 % and 15.2 %, respectively.

Table 30: Sero-conversion (IHA test negative in t_0, but positive in t_1) with respect to titer values

Period t_0	Total sero negative cases in t_0	Remaining sero negative in t_1	Sero positive in t_1	Conversion in t_1 to		
				titre value ≤ 1:10	titre value = 1:20	titre value = 1:40
2005	333	283	50 (15 %)	45 (90 %)	3 (6 %)	2 (4 %)
2006	400	301	99 (24.8 %)	50 (50.6 %)	24 (24.2 %)	25 (25.3 %)
2007	280	244	36 (12.9 %)	27 (75 %)	6 (16.7 %)	3 (8.3 %)

Period t_0	Total sero negative cases in t_0	Remaining sero negative in t_1	Sero positive in t_1	Conversion in t_1 to		
				titre value ≤ 1:10	titre value = 1:20	titre value = 1:40
2008	337	304	33 (9.8 %)	22 (66.7 %)	5 (15.2 %)	6 (18.2 %)
2009	352	321	31 (8.9 %)	25 (80.7 %)	4 (12.9 %)	2 (6.5 %)
2005–2009	1702	1343	249 (14.6 %)	169 (67.9 %)	42 (16.9 %)	38 (15.2 %)

3.3.3.2 Age and sex-specific sero-conversion rates

In this section of analysis we investigated the occurrence of SC within different sex and age groups. Table 31 presents a breakdown of all SC cases into males and females. Graphic illustration of data as presented in Figure 29 shows almost no difference between sexes in children and teen-agers. However, in the age group 20–39, considerably more men than women experienced a sero-conversion.

Table 31: Age and sex-specific sero-conversion (2005–2010)

Age group in t_0	Total sero negative cases in t_0		Sero positive in t_1	
	Male	Female	Male	Female
6–9	69	32	4 (5.8 %)	2 (6.3 %)
10–14	209	150	5 (2.4 %)	4 (2.7 %)
15–19	62	33	3 (4.8 %)	1 (3.0 %)
20–39	146	214	39 (26.7 %)	33 (15.4 %)
40–59	331	329	75 (22.6 %)	62 (18.8 %)
60+	62	65	12 (19.35 %)	10 (15.4 %)
Total	879	823	138 (15.7 %)	112 (13.6 %)

Previous results on age-specific serologic prevalence showed that titer levels were lowest in the younger age groups and gradually increased with age. In accordance with this finding, age-specific sero-conversion data confirmed that seroconversion to lower titer levels is at its highest in younger age groups, i.e. 100 % of all children in the age group 6–9 sero-converted to a titer of ≤1:10 (Table 32).

Table 32: Age and titer value-specific sero-conversion (2005–2010)

Age group in t_0	Total sero negative cases in t_0	Sero positive in t_1	Conversion in t_1 to		
			titre value ≤ 1:10	titre value = 1:20	titre value = 1:40
6–9	101	5 (5 %)	5 (100 %)	0	0
10–14	359	9 (2.5 %)	8 (88.9 %)	0	1 (11.1 %)
15–19	95	4 (4.2 %)	3 (75 %)	1 (25 %)	0
20–39	360	72 (20 %)	50 (69.4 %)	12 (16.7 %)	10 (13.9 %)
40–59	660	137 (20.8 %)	90 (65.7 %)	23 (16.8 %)	24 (17.5 %)
60+	127	22 (17.3 %)	13 (59.1 %)	6 (27.3 %)	3 (13.6 %)
Total	1702	249 (14.6 %)	169 (67.9 %)	42 (16.9 %)	38 (15.2 %)

Graphic illustration of data in Figure 30 demonstrates the trend that the percentage of cases converting to a titer value of ≤1:10 within age groups falls steadily with increasing age. The trends titer curves 1:20 and 1:40 are not as clear and obvious as for titer 1:10. However, due to the very small number of cases with these titer levels, particularly for the age group 15–19, the actual values can fluctuate considerably.

Figure 29: Sex-specific sero-conversion accumulated for all years (2005–2010)

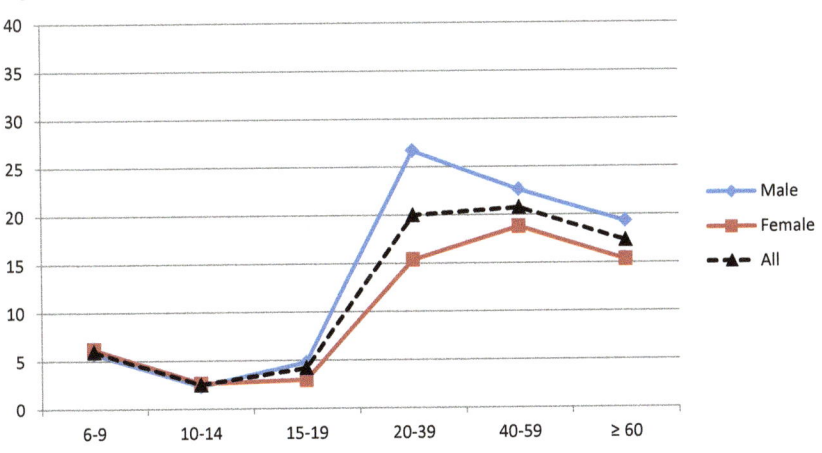

Figure 30: Age-specific sero-conversion to different titer levels (2005–2010)

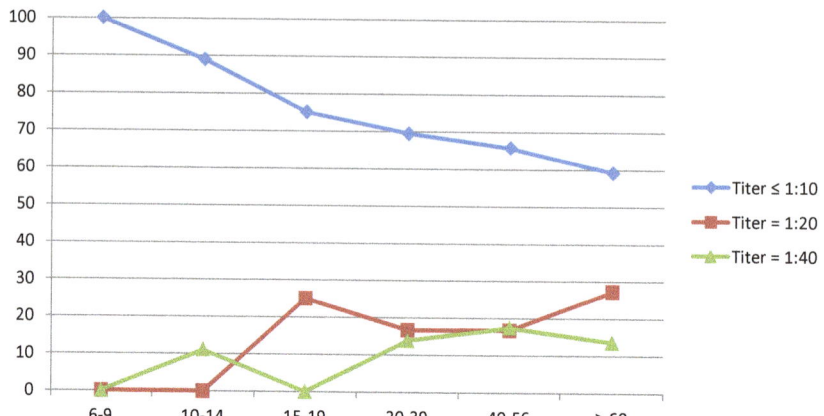

3.3.3.3 Sero-reversion and post-treatment titer values

Each seropositive case is treated with praziquantel according to the rules of CDC. Table 33 shows the results of renewed IHA tests one year after therapy (in period t_1) and whether SR occurred. In case of no SR in t_1, we also examined the development of titer values between the two years. According to the rules, repeated treatment with praziquantel was carried out at t_1 and test results in the following period t_2 examined (Table 33).

Over five pairs of consecutive years, SR one year after treatment with praziquantel occurred in an average of 66.8 % of cases, ranging from 42.1 % in 2007 to 78.6 % in 2009. In case of absence of SR one year after treatment, and re-treatment with praziquantel, after two years of treatment SR with an average rate of 81 % was observed, ranging from 63.3 % for reversion between 2006 and 2008 to 88.4 % for reversion between 2008 and 2010.

Table 33: Sero-reversion rates one or two years after IHA positive testing

Period t_0	Total sero-positive cases at t_0*	Sero reversion after one year at t_1 (%)	Remaining positive in t_1* and sero-reverting in t_2	Total sero-reversion after two years (%)
2005	205	158 (76.96 %)	16	174 (84.87 %)
2006	90	50 (55.56 %)	7	57 (63.33 %)
2007	107	45 (42.06 %)	39	84 (78.50 %)
2008	129	92 (71.32 %)	22	114 (88.37 %)
2009	84	66 (78.57 %)	No data for 2011 available	No data for 2011 available
2005–2009	615	411 (66.83 %)		

* All sero-positive individuals received therapy at this time

Considering all cases accumulated over the years, almost half of all cases (48.5 %) showed no change in titer levels, 30 % showed a falling titer level and in only one-fifth of all cases (20.5 %) was a rise in the titer values observed. However, the variations between the individual pairs of years are considerable. In the year 2006–2007, the situation was completely reversed. Here, 57.5 % of cases showed a rise of titer values, while no one showed a drop in titer values (Table 34).

Table 34: Development of titers one year after treatment

Period t_0	Total sero positive cases at t_0	Remaining positive at t_1 (% of t_0)	Remaining positive at t_1 (% of t_1) with titer values in		
			$t_0 > t_1$	$t_0 = t_1$	$t_0 < t_1$
2005	205	47	26 (55.32 %)	18 (38.30 %)	3 (6.38 %)
2006	90	40	0 (0 %)	17 (42.50 %)	23 (57.50 %)
2007	107	62	20 (32.26 %)	34 (54.84 %)	8 (12.90 %)
2008	129	37	7 (18.92 %)	22 (59.46 %)	8 (21.62 %)
2009	84	18	10 (55.56 %)	8 (44.44 %)	0 (0 %)
2005-2009	615	204 (33.17 %)	63 (30.88 %)	99 (48.53 %)	42 (20.52 %)

3.3.3.4 Sero-reversion and pre-treatment titer values

Results in the previous section showed that sero-reversion one year after treatment with praziquantel was observed in an average of 66.8 % of cases. In this section of analysis we investigated, whether or not sero-reversion one year after treatment is related to the level of the initial titer in the first period at t_0.

Table 35 shows the frequency of sero-reversion one year after treatment according to pre-treatment titers. When considering sero-reverters after one year, it appears that patients with lower titer before treatment were more likely to become sero-negative after one year than patients with a higher pre-treatment titer. Througout all the years, sero-reversion is highest if pre-treatment titer is 1:10, with frequency values ranging from 54.8 % to 88.1 %. Sero-reversion with initial titers of 1:20 was 66 % and for 1:40 52 %.

Table 35: Frequency of sero-reversion one year after treatment (%) per pre-treatment titer value

Pre-treatment titer value	Frequency of sero-reversion after treatment (%)				
	2005–2006	2006–2007	2007–2008	2008–2009	2009–2010
10	88.1	59.5	54.8	74.6	82.5
20	82.5	16.7	41.4	70.4	78.9
40	50.9	40.0	27.8	65.7	72.0

Table 36 gives an overview of titer value developments one year after treatment (t_1) in relation to titer values in period t_0. An IHA titer of Zero in t_1 indicates sero-reversion.

Table 36: Overview of IHA titer values for 2 consecutive years

(Red: number of people with <u>dropping titers</u> in the year after treatment; grey: number of people with <u>remaining titers</u> in year after treatment; green: number of people with <u>rising titers</u> in year after treatment.)

IHA titer 2005	IHA titer 2006				
	0	10	20	40	Total
10	96	12	0	1	109
20	33	5	0	2	40
40	28	19	2	6	55
Total	157				204

IHA titer 2006	IHA titer 2007				
	0	10	20	40	Total
10	47	14	6	12	79
20	1	0	0	5	6
40	2	0	0	3	5
Total	50				90

IHA titer 2007	IHA titer 2008				
	0	10	20	40	Total
10	23	13	5	1	42
20	12	11	4	2	29
40	10	5	4	17	36
Total	45				107

IHA titer 2008	IHA titer 2009				
	0	10	20	40	Total
10	50	12	3	2	67
20	19	3	2	3	27
40	23	1	3	8	35
Total	92				129

IHA titer 2009	IHA titer 2010				
	0	10	20	40	Total
10	33	7	0	0	40
20	15	4	0	0	19
40	18	4	2	1	25
Total	66				84

3.3.3.5 Age and sex-specific sero-reversion rates

An overview of age and sex-specific SR cases and rates one year after treatment is presented in Table 37. Within the 66.8 % SR after one year, reversion is at its highest in the younger age groups, with an average of 92.9 % reversion in the age group 6–9, average of 87.5 % in the age group 10–14 and 100 % in the age group 15–19. However, the number of cases available within these age groups is relatively low, with almost no cases at all available for the years 2008–2010. The reason for this is that the number of children as well as the serological prevalence in these age groups, as previously shown, has significantly dropped in particular in the years after 2008. The lowest rates of sero-reversions are found within age groups 20–39 with an average of 68.2 % of cases sero-reverting one year after treatment and age group 40–59 with 61.5 % of cases sero-reverting one year after treatment. A graphical representation of the results is given in Figure 31.

There are no significant differences in accumulated sero-reversion rates among men and women (Figure 32).

Table 37: Age and sex specific sero-reversion rates one year after treatment

Age group		2005–2006	2006–2007	2007–2008	2008–2009	2009–2010	total
6–9	Total cases	9 (100 %)	4 (100 %)	1 (100 %)	0	0	14 (100 %)
	Male	8 (100 %)	2 (100 %)	1 (100 %)	n.a.*	n.a.*	11 (100 %)
	Female	1 (100 %)	2 (100 %)	0	n.a.*	n.a.*	3 (100 %)
	Sero-reverted cases	8 (88.9 %)	4 (100 %)	1 (100 %)	n.a.*	n.a.*	13 (92.9 %)
	Male	8 (100 %)	2 (100 %)	1 (100 %)	n.a.*	n.a.*	11 (100 %)
	Female	0 (0 %)	2 (100 %)	n.a.*	n.a.*	n.a.*	2 (66.7 %)
10–14	Total cases	9 (100 %)	2 (100 %)	2 (100 %)	3 (100 %)	0	16 (100 %)
	Male	5 (100 %)	0	2 (100 %)	2 (100 %)	n.a.*	9 (100 %)
	Female	4 (100 %)	2 (100 %)	0	1 (100 %)	n.a.*	7 (100 %)
	Sero-reverted cases	9 (100 %)	2 (100 %)	0 (0 %)	3 (100 %)	n.a.*	14 (87.5 %)
	Male	5 (100 %)	n.a.*	0 (0 %)	2 (100 %)	n.a.*	7 (77.8 %)
	Female	4 (100 %)	2 (100 %)	n.a.*	1 (100 %)	n.a.*	7 (100 %)
15–19	Total cases	3 (100 %)	1 (100 %)	2 (100 %)	0	0	6 (100 %)
	Male	2 (100 %)	0	2 (100 %)	n.a.*	n.a.*	4 (100 %)
	Female	1 (100 %)	1 (100 %)	0	n.a.	n.a.*	2 (100 %)

Age group		2005–2006	2006–2007	2007–2008	2008–2009	2009–2010	total
	Sero-reverted cases	3 (100 %)	1 (100 %)	2 (100 %)	n.a.*	n.a.*	6 (100 %)
	Male	2 (100 %)	n.a.*	2 (100 %)	n.a.*.	n.a.*.	4 (100 %)
	Female	1 (100 %)	1 (100 %)	n.a.*	n.a.*	n.a.*	2 (100 %)
20–39	Total cases	77 (100 %)	33 (100 %)	28 (100 %)	38 (100 %)	16 (100 %)	192 (100 %)
	Male	38 (100 %)	21 (100 %)	16 (100 %)	29 (100 %)	9 (100 %)	113 (100 %)
	Female	39 (100 %)	12 (100 %)	12 (100 %)	9 (100 %)	7 (100 %)	79 (100 %)
	Sero-reverted cases	59 (76.6 %)	19 (57.6 %)	10 (35.7 %)	29 (76.3 %)	14 (87.5 %)	131 (68.2 %)
	Male	28 (73.7 %)	12 (57.1 %)	5 (31.3 %)	22 (75.9 %)	8 (88.9 %)	75 (66.4 %)
	Female	31 (79.5 %)	7 (58.3 %)	5 (41.7 %)	7 (77.8 %)	6 (85.7 %)	56 (70.9 %)
40–59	Total cases	102 (100 %)	49 (100 %)	61 (100 %)	82 (100 %)	54 (100 %)	348 (100 %)
	Male	58 (100 %)	29 (100 %)	33 (100 %)	43 (100 %)	32 (100 %)	195 (100 %)
	Female	44 (100 %)	20 (100 %)	28 (100 %)	39 (100 %)	22 (100 %)	153 (100 %)
	Sero-reverted cases	75 (73.5 %)	23 (46.9 %)	23 (37.7 %)	55 (67.1 %)	38 (70.4 %)	214 (61.5 %)
	Male	40 (69 %)	12 (41.4 %)	15 (45.5 %)	30 (69.8 %)	25 (78.1 %)	122 (62.6 %)
	Female	35 (79.5 %)	11 (55 %)	8 (28.6 %)	25 (64.1 %)	13 (59.1 %)	92 (60.1 %)

Age group		2005–2006	2006–2007	2007–2008	2008–2009	2009–2010	total
≥ 60	Total cases	5 (100 %)	1 (100 %)	13 (100 %)	6 (100 %)	14 (100 %)	39 (100 %)
	Male	3 (100 %)	1 (100 %)	7 (100 %)	3 (100 %)	8 (100 %)	22 (100 %)
	Female	2 (100 %)	0	6 (100 %)	3 (100 %)	6 (100 %)	17 (100 %)
	Sero-reverted cases	4 (80 %)	1 (100 %)	9 (69.2 %)	5 (83.3 %)	14 (100 %)	33 (84.6 %)
	Male	3 (100 %)	1 (100 %)	5 (71.4 %)	2 (66.7 %)	8 (100 %)	19 (86.4 %)
	Female	1 (50 %)	0	4 (66.7 %)	3 (100 %)	6 (100 %)	14 (82.4 %)
Total	Total cases	205 (100 %)	90 (100 %)	107 (100 %)	129 (100 %)	84 (100 %)	615 (100 %)
	Male	114 (100 %)	53 (100 %)	61 (100 %)	77 (100 %)	49 (100 %)	354 (100 %)
	Female	91 (100 %)	37 (100 %)	46 (100 %)	52 (100 %)	35 (100 %)	261 (100 %)
	Sero-reverted cases	158 (77.1 %)	50 (55.6 %)	45 (42.1 %)	92 (71.3 %)	66 (78.6 %)	411 (66.8 %)
	Male	86 (75.4 %)	27 (50.9 %)	28 (45.9 %)	56 (72.7 %)	41 (83.7 %)	238 (67.2 %)
	Female	72 (79.1 %)	23 (62.2 %)	17 (37 %)	36 (69.2 %)	25 (71.4 %)	173 (66.3 %)

* not applicable

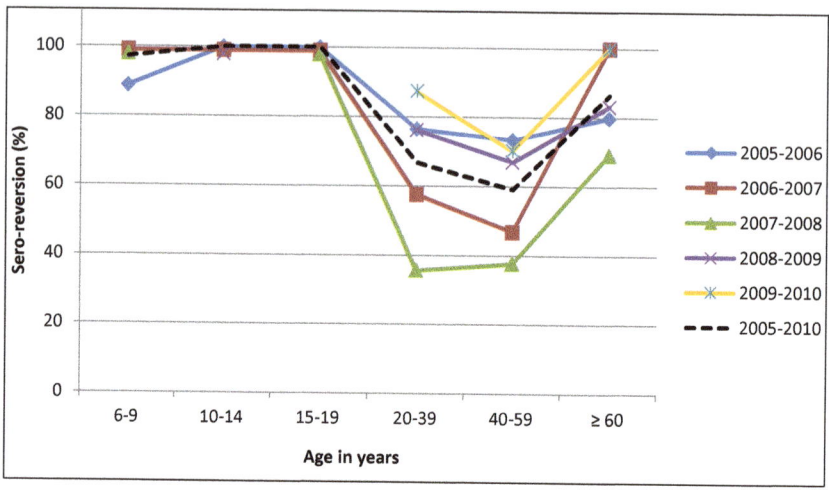

Figure 31: Age specific sero-reversion rates one year after treatment per year and accumulated for all years 2005–2010

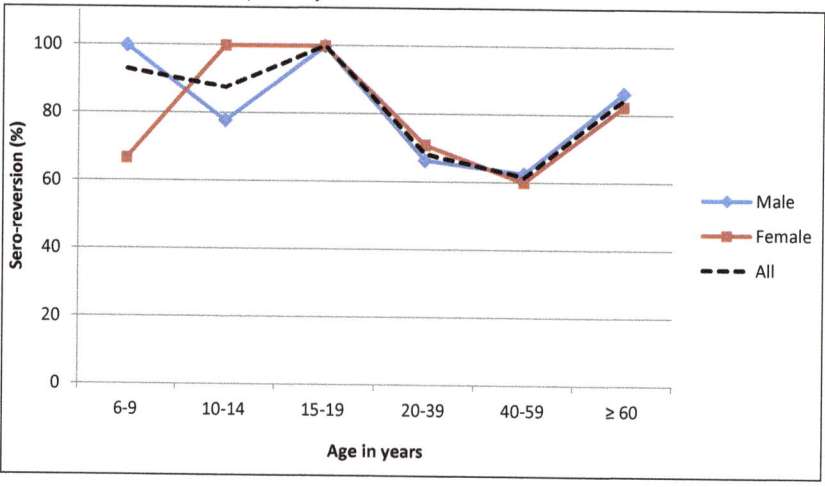

Figure 32: Age and sex-specific sero-reversion rates one year after treatment accumulated for all years 2005–2010

3.3.4 Individual titer courses over 6–8 consecutive periods

We investigated the individual time course of IHA titers of people who had been IHA-tested in six or more consecutive years. In particular, special interest lies in the development of titers after treatment.

Included in this part of analysis were individuals who came for IHA testing for at least <u>6 or more consecutive years</u> within the time period 2003–2010. Test results for each of these individuals can be read in Annex 1, 2 or 3. People who were tested in 6 consecutive years are marked in green color, those who came for 7 consecutive years are marked in blue color and those who came for 8 consecutive years are marked in yellow color.

Furthermore, people must have been tested <u>at least one time IHA positive</u>. Excluded were cases whose only one positive test within the whole period was at the first or last year of testing, as this does not allow any conclusions about the prior or later course of titers.

In total, 87 people were included into this part of analysis, out of which 51 were males and 36 females. Among the cases 13 were children aged 6–12 years, 22 were adults between 20–39 years of age, 45 were between 40–59 years of age and 7 people were over 60 years. Table 38 gives an overview of the number of tests and the number of positive test results.

Table 38: Test results of people with 6 or more consecutive tests

Number of consecutive tests (2003–2010)	Number of positive IHA tests (titre ≥ 5)								
	1	2	3	4	5	6	7	8	Total
6	9	7	14	9	2	1	–	–	42
7	11	11	3	7	3	0	0	–	35
8	2	2	2	2	1	1	0	0	10
Total	22	20	19	18	6	2	0	0	87

Longitudinal analysis of patients who have been followed up for six or more consecutive years, led to the identification of four different patterns of serologic change. Figure 33 illustrates for each of the four patterns A-D one example of a possible titer curve.

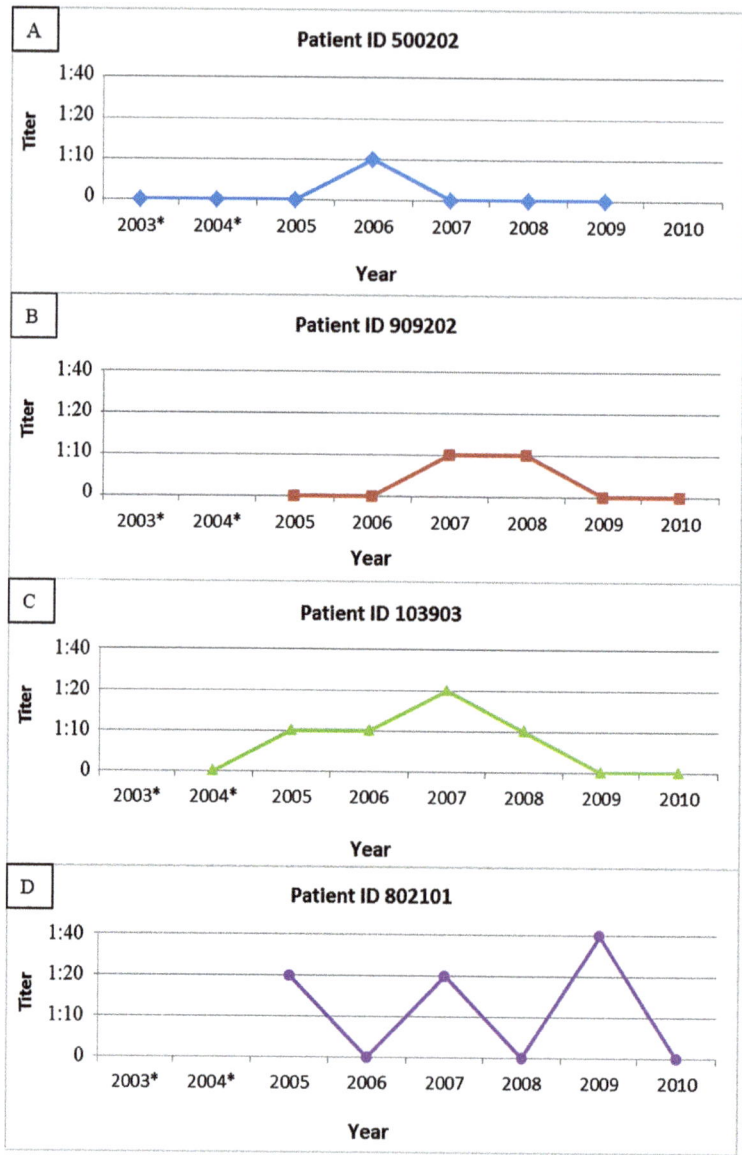

Figure 33: Individual patient patterns of changes in IHA titers over ≥ 6 consecutive years. Each pattern is exemplified by one patient.

* no titer values available for years 2003 and 2004

Pattern A:

This category comprises all cases with an initially negative IHA titer which sero-converted (irrespective of the titer value) and who subsequently sero-reverted one year after treatment. Should one person have experienced more than one episode of sero-conversion within the 6–8 consecutive years, the case was only included into this category if after the first sero-reversion the person stayed sero-negative for at least one additional period.

After sero-conversion the patient received treatment that resulted in immediate sero-reversion, whereby the disappearance of antibodies is taken as a cure of infection. Therefore, under the assumption, that the test is correct, such a case would be interpreted as a new infection that has been cleared one year after treatment

Pattern B:

This category comprises all cases with an initially negative IHA titer that stayed positive (irrespective of titer-value) in the subsequent two years and then eventually sero-reverted. Should one person have experienced more than one episode of sero-conversion within the 6–8 consecutive years, the case was only included into this category, if after first sero-reversion the person remained sero-negative for at least one additional period. The interpretation is analogous to pattern A. However, here the infection is only assumed to have been cleared after two years of treatment.

Pattern C:

This category comprises all cases where titers (irrespective of specific titer-values) remained positive for at least three consecutive periods. One interpretation of this could be a persistence of infection due to an incomplete cure, or – alternatively and considered unlikely – a persistence of antibodies despite a complete cure. Also, there could have been a complete cure and a sero-reversion, but at the same time a reinfection occurring in the months between testing.

Pattern D:

This category comprises all cases where subsequent titers changed from positive to negative to positive etc. over at least four consecutive periods. Assuming that the tests are serologically correct, the conclusion from the course of this curve would be that the infection cleared after treatment with a subsequent new infection. However, this pattern may also reflect technical mistakes.

Over the course of 6–8 consecutive years, the titer course of some individuals was such that it fulfilled the criteria for more than one of the categories above, showing a mix of different patterns. Here, the respective cases were counted in more than one category. Equally, titer courses of 14 individuals (16 %) did not fit into any of the four groups described above.

In this study, the most common pattern of serologic change was with 33 cases (38 %) a sero-reversion one year after treatment (Pattern A). 76.7 % (n=25) of all cases in this category involved a titer value of 1:10, only 6.7 % (n=4) to a value of 1:20 and another 16.6 % (n=6) to a value of 1:40. In total, ten cases (11.5 %) experienced sero-reversion after two periods as described in pattern B. Among these, after sero-conversion six cases (60 %) showed no change in titer value and two cases showed a rise or fall of titer values, respectively (20 %).

The second most common category, however, was pattern C with 25 people (29 %) showing positive titer values for three or more consecutive periods. Unlike the cases of pattern B, here the majority of cases (11; 44 %) showed a rise in titer values after sero-conversion, in 9 cases (36 %) the titer value remained equally high in all three consecutive periods and only 5 cases (20 %) showed a declining titer after sero-conversion.

A titer course with subsequently changes from negative to positive to negative etc. over at least four periods as described in pattern D was found for 8 individuals (9.2 %). However, 7 more people experienced at least 4 sero-changes within the 6–8 years period, although not all of them occurred in consecutive years.

4 Discussion

After the considerable progress made in the control of schistosomiasis japonica in China over the past fifty years, some areas are now aiming for interruption of transmission or complete elimination of the disease. In diseases targeted for elimination, the closer one gets to the goal the greater emphasis must be laid on the completeness and accuracy of reporting disease occurrence. This often requires substantially intensive monitoring and control methods (King 2009). Moving from low transmission to elimination of schistosomiasis in China holds many challenges in terms of effective surveillance (Spear *et al.* 2011). In view of this ambitious goal, this study examined the practical implementation of the national control strategy at grass root level in the city of Wuhan in the province Hubei, central China, with a focus on availability and composition of human resources for control efforts and on the performance of diagnostic tests for case-detection for effective surveillance. This section provides a thorough discussion of the results on human resources in schistosomiasis control, and on the analysis of diagnostic tools used in the field as based on research performed in cooperation with our partners in Wuhan.

4.1 Human resources in schistosomiasis control in Wuhan

4.1.1 Availability and distribution of human resources

There is clear evidence that suggests that human resources for health affect health outcomes and that an increase of health worker density will lead to a significant reduction of disease burden, especially the burden associated to communicable diseases (Castillo-Laborde 2011). In this study, we found a very high health worker to patient ratio in Wuhan, with theoretically one health worker being available for every two to three confirmed schistosomiasis patients. At first glance, this seems very high, but this impression may, however, be misleading when drawing conclusions on whether or not a sufficient number of health workers is available in schistosomiasis control.

Most literature and studies on health workforce look into how many clinical workers, i.e. doctors and nurses, are available for treatment of patients within a given population. In this context, lack or inequalities of human resources is often discussed using health worker to patients density measurements as references (Dal Poz *et al.* 2009). This study, however, deals with workforce available for the control of a specific disease and looks not only at workers available for treatment but also for activities aiming at the prevention of this disease. Up to now, only few, mainly Chinese, studies have been published on China's human resources for disease control in general or for the control of schistosomiasis in particular (Jiang *et al.* 2011; Xie *et al.* 2005). However, these studies only looked at the overall supply of health workers for disease control and did not consider the demand side; also, they did not distinguish health worker availability for different work activities.

Education levels of staff were highest at city level facilities and city proper district levels, while rural districts also had a considerable number of staff with a junior high school education and below. Control station leaders in rural districts found it difficult to find qualified staff required for the work in schistosomiasis control. This supports other studies that showed that poorer provinces are also likely to be disadvantaged in terms of less educated workforces and that there is a mal-distribution of health professionals, who tend to serve in provincial urban centers rather than in rural areas (Anand 2010; Anand *et al.* 2008).

Large disparities in distribution of workers available for the control of schistosomiasis were, however, not observed in our study. While Anand *et al.* (2008) reported a high inter-county inequality in the distribution of both doctors and nurses in China, which in large part was due to urban-rural disparities in health worker density (Anand *et al.* 2008), in our study the local distribution of health personnel was found to correspond to the respective population at risk and infection cases, with almost two thirds of all personnel being employed in district level facilities. Over the past ten years, Wuhan experienced some changes in its schistosomiasis control staff structure. At city level and in city proper district level facilities, the total number of staff was steadily reduced. These observations have also been reported in a study by Jiang *et al.* (2011) who compared changes in the number of health workers in county anti-schistosomaisis institions between 2007 and 2010. In our study, suburban and rural district facilities seemed to have been unaffected by staff reduction. Nevertheless, in these districts, the number of staff available in schistosomiasis control was perceived – according to self-administered questionnaires – as still being too few for the existing workload.

4.1.2 Workload and activities

Differences were observed between the self-perceived work situations of clinical and non-clinical staff. Workload of clinical staff seems to have been reduced by more than that of non-clinical staff over the past ten plus years. One explanation might be the small overall number of patients treated in the hospitals, as infection levels are steadily declining. It is thus not surprising that most clinical staff in Wuhan agreed that for treatment of schistosomiasis patients, there were enough personnel available.

On the other hand, for non-clinical staff involved in prevention activities, the workload seemed to have increased in the past years. In 2004, after increasing re-emergence of schistosomiasis in formerly controlled areas was observed, the Chinese government renewed its dedication to the fight of schistosomiasis by classifying the disease, together with HIV / AIDS, tuberculosis and hepatitis B, as the top priority in the control of communicable diseases (Wang *et al.* 2008). The goal set by the government, namely reduction of infection prevalence among humans in all endemic counties, led to the formulation of detailed surveillance guidelines and the requirement of more rigorous reporting and, thus, leading and adding to a higher workload.

Most labour-intensive activities were prevention activities, i.e. snail surveillance, spraying molluscicide, followed by the treatment of patients in endemic areas. Additionally, activities identified as the most time-intensive included surveilling snails, followed by health education and overall management. Therefore, it can be argued that in the control of schistosomiasis in Wuhan, the majority of the work lies in prevention rather than treatment activities. Thus, the number of available clinical staff, i.e. doctors and nurses, may no longer be crucial for the success of schistosomiasis control, but rather the number of non-clinical staff. China has previously proven that it has the capability to respond to a public health crisis, for example in the successful dealing of SARS and other crises. However, there are still gaps in prevention. Public health still remains an underfunded area (Freeman III & Lu 2009). In view of the structural changes within China's health care system over the past decades, which have led to decentralization and underfinancing of public health services, public health organizations have frequently turned to revenue-generating services as their main source of income (Blumenthal & Hsiao 2005; Yip & Hsiao 2008). The provision of schistosomiasis control has adapted to the increased exposure to market forces in the same way (Bian *et al.* 2004; Xiang *et al.* 1998), often resulting in the neglect of non-profitable public health activities.

In summary, a considerable human resource investment in schistosomiasis control is being made in Wuhan, and the health worker to patient ratio is very high. The number of patients does not necessarily positively correlate with the number of health workers needed, and a reduction in the total number of patients does not necessarily lead to, require, or justify a reduction in the number of health workers. Considering the low endemicity in Wuhan, the focus of all activities lays in prevention of disease by interrupting the transmission cycle. Thus, detection of intermediate host snails as well as detection of these very few human cases, which still keep the transmission cycle active and therefore need to be detected and treated as early as possible, requires the same amount of work or maybe even more, as one has to be more accurate and complete.

However, when talking about interruption of the transmission cycle, other activities should be mentioned, such as environmental modification to reduce snail susceptible areas, or the dealing of the zoonotic transmission, in particular by buffaloes, which is probably similarly relevant to the interruption of the transmission cycle. This need was stated in the national control policy and was recently reinforced (Hong *et al.* 2013). From available information on the costs of control activities, both approaches represented an appreciable portion (see Table 8 and 9). However, the actions to reduce snail susceptible areas and water buffaloes as a source of transmission are not the responsibility of the Ministry of Health, but the Ministries of Water Resources and Agriculture and were not a topic for detailed analysis in this case.

4.2 Diagnostics

In low-transmission areas, with the steady decrease of transmission and reduction of parasite burden through transmission and morbidity control, both monitoring and diagnosis of infection become more difficult (WHO 2009). Monitoring of transmission requires the most accurate measures of who is infected. Thus the most sensitive monitoring tools are needed in areas of very low endemicity (WHO 2009). This study is – to our knowledge – the first follow-up study to investigate the quality of IHA tests used in field settings in China and examines titer-sequences of individual patients over the course of several years.

4.2.1 Study population

Among the village population, primary and junior high school children were tested the most often on a regular basis. The likely reasons for this is that because of China's one-child policy, single children are particularly well cared for. In addition, with tests being conducted in schools, children within these two age groups are very easily accessible. In China, school education comprises six years of primary, three years of junior secondary and then three years of senior secondary schooling. At the end of their junior secondary education at the age of 15 years, pupils take a decision whether or not to continue with school education. The educational background of the population in the village revealed that formerly most village people had stopped education after junior high school, and pursued farming as their main occupation. However, nowadays, many young people who decide to stop school education at the age of 15 as well as the young workforce in their 20 and 30s, often leave the village to find work in the Wuhan city proper area. Therefore, many members of these age groups, although registered in the village, are not actually living there anymore and, consequently, had not been tested on a regular basis if even at all. Older generations of famers and fisherman appeared somewhat unaffected by migration.

It is noteworthy, that the total number of children below ten years of age in this study was very low. In view of the fact that the registry list used for surveillance had not been updated since 2006, there were no new additions to the population under surveillance. Thus, the total number of cases within the lowest age-group dropped continuously to less than ten cases after 2008.

In general, after 2007 sero-prevalence rates in age-groups below twenty years were close to zero and analysis of IHA positive test results was based on a very small numbers of cases. Thus, variations of numbers in the respective age-groups were high, which needs to be considered when interpreting findings.

In official reports, low or zero prevalence, especially among younger children, are often highlighted as a success of control measures. This may of course well be the reason. In the case of Xiang Lu village, however, it may equally be due to the fact that there simply were very few children of less than ten years included in surveillance, thus probably leading to inaccurate calculations, especially in later years of this survey.

4.2.2 Serological and parasitological prevalence

In this study, remarkable and unexpected large variations in sera-reactivity were observed. Particularly, the year 2005 with a sero-prevalence of almost 38 % had been an exceptional year. The peculiarity of the year 2005 is visible at all stages of analysis of serology in this study. In analysis of accumulated values for all years, however, these variations are leveled out.

There are various reasons that may have led to such a large increase in prevalence in only one year. On the technical side, change of test kits or staff conducting, analyzing or interpreting laboratory tests might contribute to the variability of the results. Although technical reasons cannot be excluded in this case, the increase in sero-positivity may have been due to heavy floods which occurred earlier in the same year, with water levels of the Han River reaching 35 meters. Due to its geographical location, Wuhan is prone to flooding, which generally favors the spread of schistosomiasis. Therefore, it is conceivable that a high incidence of new infections or re-infections occurred in 2005 as a result of the flood.

Whichever of the above explanations would apply, the serologic results of 2005 illustrate an inherent problem for evaluating or measuring prevalence of schistosomiasis. Serological determination of antibodies is known to result in higher values of prevalence as compared to microscopic egg detection, including IHA testing (Mott & Dixon 1982; Sorgho *et al.* 2005). Microscopic egg detection is known to result in lower values of prevalence as compared to serological antibody determination (Mott & Dixon 1982) including IHA test (Gui et al. 1991; Idris et al. 2003; Sorgho et al. 2005; Yu et al. 2007; Zhou et al. 2008; Zhou et al. 2007b). Conversely, KK is known to result in under-estimation of egg counts due to limited sensitivity (Lin et al. 2008a; Ruppel et al. 1990; Yu et al. 2007; Zhang et al. 2009), yet KK is widely held as the "gold standard" for serology. As a consequence serology results in "false positive" cases and egg-detection in "false negatives". This issue was reviewed and discussed amply by Hamilton et al. (1998) and Doenhoff et al. (2004), including consequences for situations of low infection prevalence and intensity, as is the case for the population of the current study.

4.2.2.1 Agreement between IHA und KK

In our study, we found the agreement between IHA and KK to range between 10.6 %-31.5 % and is thus within the range of agreements found in similar studies conducted in China (Zhou et al. 2011) Assuming the KK test as the conventional golden standard, agreement would be expressed by the positive predictive value (PPV) of IHA. In our study, variations of PPV determined between different years were considerable and reached almost 20 %, even though the tests had been conducted at the same site and in the same way. These results show that the PPV may only give information on agreement of tests at one specific point in time. Similarly, in their longitudinal study of comparison of the KK technique and IHA for the detection of schistosomiasis japonica in China, Zhou et al. (2008) found variations of PPV values ranging from 19–30 % in different years. In this context, reference is again made to the reviews mentioned in the previous paragraph.

Unlike other studies, which investigated the agreement between IHA and KK based only on a positive or negative test result, the current study further investigated a possible agreement between KK and IHA with respect to IHA titer values. In this approach, agreement was found to positively correlate with IHA titer values, the lowest being with an IHA titer of ≤ 1:10 (ranging from 1 %-26%) and highest with IHA titer of 1:40 (ranging between 29 %-58%).

Titer values in serological tests reflect the amount of antibodies in the blood. However, a conclusion from titer values regarding infection intensities is not straightforward. Several earlier studies (Deelder et al. 1989;

Gui *et al.* 1991; Mott & Dixon 1982; Sorgho *et al.* 2005) investigated a possible correlation between antibody titers in IHA and quantitative egg measurements for patients infected with *S. mansoni* or *S. haematobium*. Significant correlations could only be confirmed at the population level, but not for single individuals. Our results agree with these observations in that no conclusions can be drawn from titer values about infection intensities as measured by quantitative egg excretion. However, an apparently better agreement between both tests was observed with higher IHA titers.

4.2.2.2 Age and sex specific serological prevalence

In this study, serological evidence found *S. japonicum* prevalence to be related to age. Serological prevalence below 20 years was comparatively low and was highest in older people, with a peak in the age group 40–59. This pattern of serologic prevalence was also found in a previous study conducted by Zhou et al (2008) and seems to be specific to *S. japonicum*. Studies on *S. mansoni* or *S. haematobium* observed different age-specific prevalence patterns. In African schistosomiasis, typical age-prevalence curves in an endemic setting show that the prevalence of infection normally peaks in school-aged children, adolescents or young adults. In older age groups, the prevalence decreases, although it does not reach zero (Massara *et al.* 2004; Raso *et al.* 2007).

The shift in age-related prevalence of *S. japonicum* curves to the right when compared to patterns found for African schistosomiasis could be explained by the different statuses of infection intensity in the respective endemic areas. Immune responses in populations subject to different transmission rates, even within the same parasite species, show differences in age-distribution (Mutapi *et al.* 1997). With infections being most severe in high transmission areas, endemic populations are prone to accumulate infections more rapidly and at a younger age than their counterparts in low transmission areas. This pattern of lower levels of infection occurring in older age groups is referred to as a 'peak shift' (Fulford *et al.* 1992; Woolhouse 1998). Data from our study is consistent with the concept of age-related peaks resulting from different infection intensities and prevalence rates. Another explanation for the sharp increase in *S. japonicum* infections, which we observed from an age of twentyyears onwards, could be due to professional activities. School-age children and adolescents may not spend much time in swampy or wet-transmission areas, as school workload limits leisure time and spending the latter in semi-flooded grassland may not seem an attractive idea. However, adults often work as fishermen of farmers in this community, and it is easily conceivable that they acquire their infections whilst assuming professional activities.

We did not observe any association between serologic evidence of *S. japonicum* and sex in this study.

4.2.2.3 Age specific serological prevalence and titer values

In almost all cases, the lowest schistosome antibody levels were observed within the youngest age-groups. Low antibody levels became rarer with increasing age. Serologic observations in this study indicate that the antibody response, i.e. the development of antibodies, is age-related. Antibody levels in adults could be the result of continued exposure to cumulative multiple infections. Similar observations of a tendency towards a greater incidence of high titers in age were made by Zhou *et al.* (2008) in their longitudinal study of comparison of the KK technique and IHA for the detection of schistosomiasis japonica in China. The presence of antibodies can only indicate that the examined population is, or has been, infected with schistosomiasis. In particular, the possible persistence of antibodies following chemotherapy has not been clarified as of yet and, therefore, sound conclusions on the transmission status have not yet been possible. More meaningful information on schistosomiasis transmission may be obtained from longitudinal serologic profiles on population and individual levels. Therefore, this study investigated individual post-therapeutic serologic profiles over the course of time.

4.2.3 Sero-conversions and sero-reversions

In this study, the calculation of sero-conversion (SC) and sero-reversion (SR) is based on the multiple IHA results from the same individuals. From a statistical point of view, it could be argued that this inevitably creates dependencies between results over the years, which might lead to the distortion of analysis. This issue is briefly addressed in the following section.

4.2.3.1 Dependencies in data

Analysis of SC and SR was carried out with the two following assumptions in mind:

1) The IHA test result is not dependent on time, i.e. it is technically reproducible and the test was performed and interpreted each year in the same way. Therefore, time periods can be categorized for analysis.
2) The results are not influenced if people were assigned to the study cohort at different time categories (the same people but in different years).

A <u>time category</u> is defined for the purpose of this analysis as a pair of two consecutive years, for both of which IHA test results are available for the same individual. Thereby, for calculation of SR, in the first of the two years the IHA test has to be positive, whereas the result of the IHA test in the second year can be either negative or once again positive. In total there are 5 different time categories, for which the number of eligible tests is listed in Table 39.

Table 39: Number of tests included into analysis of SR per time category

Time category	No of tests included in analysis
2005–2006	205
2006–2007	90
2007–2008	107
2008–2009	129
2009–2010	84
Total	615

Table 40: Number of time categories covered by test results from individual persons

No of time categories	No of people
1 category	228
2 categories	82
3 categories	47
4 categories	18
5 categories	2
Total	377

As shown in Table 40, from 228 people, data are available for only one time category, i.e. for each of the 228 people's data is only available for one pair of 2 consecutive years. However, others have been tested more frequently and data are then available for 2 or more time categories (Table 40). Inevitably this leads to dependencies between the individual time categories. For example, constant non-clearers, i.e. individual persons who always or often tested sero-positive and, therefore, did not sero-revert, contribute to a low reversion rate.

From a statistical point of view, the only way to avoid such dependencies would be to restrict the inclusion of test results to only one time category per person. However, the question then arises, which result should be counted if multiple different results for one person are available, as this reflection would directly influence SR rates. In order to evaluate the relevance of this theoretical consideration, Table 41 gives an overview of all possible combinations and how they influence the SR rate. In this context, we use non-reverter categories. A non-reverter category is defined as being a pair of two consecutive years for which both IHA test results are available for the same individual (one time-category), and are both positive, i.e. the respective individual did not sero-revert. In total there are five different non-reverter categories (Table 41).

As shown in Table 41, 245 people out of 377 (65.0 %) sero-reverted any time between 2005 and 2010, although the number of time categories that remained positive (i.e. did not sero-revert) varied between persons. At the same time there are 35 persons, highlighted in grey, who did not sero-revert (9.3 %), irrespective of how many categories they belonged to. Weighted with the number of non-reverter categories, those 35 people contributed to the overall result with 66 non-reverting cases.

Table 41: *Number of non-reverters with respect to their belonging to different categories*

Number of time categories	Number of non-reverter categories per person						Total
	0	1	2	3	4	5	
1	212	16	n.a.*	n.a.*	n.a.*	n.a.*	228 (53.9 %)
2	31	39	12	n.a.*	n.a.*	n.a.*	82 (19.4 %)
3	2	26	16	3	n.a.*	n.a.*	47 (11.11 %)
4	0	0	8	7	3	n.a.*	18 (4.3 %)
5	0	0	0	0	1	1	2 (0.5 %)
Total	245	81	36	10	4	1	377 (100 %)

* not applicable

The SR rate therefore lies between 65.0 % and 90.7 %, depending on the selection procedure for the allowed onetime categories for all 377 people.

To circumvent the problem of selection, which may lead to a difference in SR rate of almost 25 %, in this study we assume that there were no co-dependencies within the same people tested in different years, and that all tests were considered in the analysis.

The application of this approach allows for consideration of all test results recorded, irrespective of the number of tests available for individual patients. At the same time, this approach provides results which fall into the lower range among all possible SR outcomes and, thus, avoids possible over-reporting of sero-reversion.

4.2.3.2 Sero-conversion and -reversion and titer-values

Total cases of sero-conversion within the study population were found steadily decreasing over the years. Under the assumption that sero-conversion reflects acquisition of a new schistosome infection, the overall incidence of infections has apparently declined over the observed time span.

Most cases in this study sero-converted to a low titer value, with the probability of converting to a higher titer value rising according to age. The majority of all cases (67 %, see Table 33) were observed to then have sero-reverted one year after chemotherapy. Two years after acquisition of infection, reversion was observed in a total of almost 80 % of all cases. Thus, two thirds of all cases can be considered as cured of infection one year after treatment and 80 % after two annual treatments. However, "cure" must be considered under two aspects: absence of antibodies (serological cure) and absence of living worms (parasitological cure). Whereas the first includes the second, parasitological cures may have been achieved in spite of persisting antibodies. This phenomenon is called "serological scar". It will be discussed in the last chapter in the light of our findings.

Sero-reversion was found to be associated with pre-treatment titers. It seems that patients with lower titers before treatment became sero-negative after one year more likely than patients with higher pre-treatment titers. Sero-reversion was also found to be associated with age, with cases in younger age-groups more likely having sero-revered already one year after chemotherapy than cases in older age groups. Both associations are interrelated in view of our above mentioned findings that almost all children showed very low titer values, and higher titers were found only in the older age groups.

Our findings in the longitudinal analysis of patients over the course of six or more consecutive years confirm immediate sero-reversion one year after treatment as the most prevalent pattern. This evidence can be taken to illustrate a high cure rate through chemotherapy within the population. However, an additional technical explanation cannot be excluded for individual cases: The reading of IHA titer values is done by optical grading of individual wells between "negative, plus/minus, one plus, two plus, three plus". This procedure implicitly depends on high inter-personal consistency and reproducibility over long time intervals. Both factors become increasingly critical with low or borderline agglutination dots on the bottom of the wells, i.e. judgment of the shape, spreading or sharpness of the agglutination dot. Even though in the Wuhan schistosomiasis control program only well-trained staff with long term experience performs and reads the screening tests, it would be unrealistic, and even unfair, to assume that complete reproducibility between negative and borderline positive or low positive titers could be achieved over the years. Changes in test charges, manufacturing and in staff over the years are known to present serious challenges and necessarily lead to less than 100 % reproducibility. On the other side, for the screening purposes of the control activities the disadvantage of a few individual misclassifications has to be balanced against, and is accepted for the benefit of rapid, economic and meaningful screening by deciding on one titer value for IHA. Consequently, some sero-converters to a low value might present apparently wrong positives and the mistake may be corrected in the following screening period. Thus, single "one time low IHA positive" individuals cannot all be taken to represent true sero-converters and subsequent reverters. Our data does not allow measuring the extent of such potential complications. However, there is no reason to assume that these would be more than a few percent, i.e. a well acceptable variability for any dichotomous diagnostic decision (negative/positive) with borderline measurements.

4.2.4 Serological non-reverters

Our study identified several individuals, whose titer levels after acquisition of infection remained positive despite repeated chemotherapy. Longitudinal analysis even identified a sub-population of around 1 % of the total population, where individuals showed persisting titers for up to more than four consecutive years. In almost all of these cases, infection was confirmed by KK stool examination at least in one year.

Among all those cases, no clear trend of dropping titer-levels after treatment could be observed. On the contrary, almost half of all cases, which did not sero-revert after one period, showed no change in titer-levels, while in others even a rising titer value was observed after chemotherapy. In this context, two aspects deserve discussion, which had been forwarded as potential confounders, delivering "false positive" serological results:

First, antibody titers in schistosomiasis serology have been repeatedly discussed in terms of potential cross-reactivity, in particular with other parasitic infections (Alarcon de Noya *et al.* 1996). However, cross-reactivity between schistosome antigens and other, non-schistosome parasites were neither detectable in studies from endemic areas in Sudan (Idris & Ruppel 1988; Ruppel *et al.* 1990) or Oman (Idris *et al.* 2003) nor from China (Li *et al.* 1994; Ruppel *et al.* 1987). Thus, it is safe to assume that positive IHA-values in our study were not the result of potential other parasitic infections. In addition, praziquantel which is used for therapy of schistosomes, is also active against the flukes *Paragonimus* and *Taenia solium*, which may occasionally occur in China, but had been shown not to cross-react with schistosome antigens (Li *et al.* 1994). Thus, persistently positive IHA titers in the few individuals of our study, are the result of schistosome infections and quite unlikely of other helminths.

Second, as described in detail by Hamilton *et al.* (1998) and Doenhoff *et al.* (2003) the concept of serological positivity or negativity, i.e. titers or readings of optical densities, cannot be discussed without being clear about the reference standards (see also 4.2.2). Conventionally, serologic specificity and sensitivity are based on parasitological evidence, i.e. detection of parasite eggs (in the stool for *S. japonicum*). Detection is normally based on microscopic egg detection through KK, which is also the technique used in the present study. This is, however, prowen since long to underestimate true infection rates (Idris *et al.* 2003; Mott & Dixon 1982; Ruppel *et al.* 1990; Sorgho *et al.* 2005), particularly if only one or few stool slides are read (as in the present study). Recently, Zhang *et al.* (2009) claims that up to 80 % of *S. japonicum* cases were not detected by single slides of KK in a low endemic area. Thus, to use KK as a "gold standard" for formally calculating sensitivity or specificity of serologic tests is highly questionable and misclassifications because of "false positive" and "false negative" serology results may introduce significant bias for "specificity" or "sensitivity" (Doenhoff *et al.* 2003). As already Hamilton *et al.* (1998) put it: "The problem will thus be exacerbated particularly when the prevalence and intensity of schistosomiasis is being reduced through the introduction of effective control measures". The occurrence of sero-conversion and sero-reversion as observed in our study will have to be interpreted in light of the low specificity of the serological results. These are most likely due to a high number of "false positive" results.

The above discussion will aid to interpret the actually detected individual antibody patterns, which are based on consistently using the same antibody test (IHA) and reflect variations of individual antibody levels over the years. These patterns will be discussed in the next and last chapter.

4.2.5 Determination of the "serological scar"

In order to evaluate the time span of individual IHA titres, a discussion is first necessary on previous observations that chemotherapy, even if successful as judged by absence detectable eggs, is not necessarily followed by a rapid drop of antibodies. The influence of chemotherapy on antibody levels has been a matter of discussion for a long time. In the first international collaborative study on immune-diagnosis of schistosomiasis (Mott & Dixon 1982), "adult worm antigen in most test systems detected persistent antibodies in the sera of individuals who had (…) no eggs in their faeces after specific chemotherapy". In a control programme in Iraq based on chemotherapy, "a significant proportion of positive reactions (in ELISA) could be attributed to the persistence of antibodies after successful cure" (Yacoub *et al.* 1987).

In cases of persisting antibody levels observed within a population living in an endemic area (Gazzinelli *et al.* 1985), treatment failure, due to potential development of resistance to praziquantel has been discussed as one possible explanation, although – fortunately – not a probable one (Doenhoff *et al.* 2008). However, re-infections after chemotherapy are likely to occur in highly endemic areas and would re-stimulate antibody production. Thus persistence of specific antibodies after cure ("immunological scar") needs to be differentiated from persistent antibodies due to re-infections.

Re-infections can be ruled out in travellers with imported cases of schistosomiasis. However, also in these cases, elevated levels of schistosomiasis antibodies after treatment have been observed, sometimes even for several years after treatment (De Jonge *et al.* 1990b; Duus *et al.* 2009; Helleberg & Thybo 2010). In the study by Helleberg & Thybo (2010) a decrease in titer was not found to be a reliable marker for the success of treatment, as viable ova were found in biopsies of the rectal mucosa of a patient, in whom the titer had decreased. In addition, these cases of imported schistosomiasis where re-infection can be ruled out, it might be argued that the long-term persistence of antibodies found in patients could be an indication of a less than complete success of treatment. Praziquantel is known to kill only adult worms, but to be relatively ineffective against juvenile schistosomes (Sabah *et al.* 1986). Treatment of travellers upon their return home might have been given before all worms had matured.

Further complications with interpretations may arise from worms persisting after therapy as shown in experimental infections of mice (Ruppel *et al.* 1991): even one single, although stunted worm surviving at least one year after treatment with praziquantel, was sufficient to stimulate continued antibody production. Of course, single worms (or single-sex infections) would not be discoverable in humans.

In the context of our study, antibody levels after chemotherapy would appear to result from possible re-infections only in a minority of cases, since prevalence and intensities of schistosome infections in this population are low and are consistent with a low incidence rate. Incomplete cure due to the presence of juvenile worms also appears as an infrequent possibility, since infections accumulate over a year's time span, thus making the presence of juvenile worms unlikely. Consequently, it can be reasonably assumed that changes in IHA titers would reflect – in most cases – the effect of an optimally possible chemotherapy. Consequently, antibodies persisting after chemotherapy can likely instruct on the "immunological scar"

The majority of sero-reversions (67 %) occurred one year after therapy (see 4.3.2.3), which implies that in one third of patients they did not. Independently of whether the reversions might have been in part due to technical issues discussed above (4.2.3.2), sero-reversion is possible within the first year. However, an "immunological scar" appears to persist in a third of people beyond this time, but in the large majority of people (80 %) no longer than two years (which also implies two cycles of treatment).

This is the first study, to our knowledge, from an endemic schistosomiasis area to elucidate not only the existence of the "immunological scar". Also its duration could be narrowed down to last normally no longer than two years. This claim is substantiated on individual antibody patterns of a large population and over a long time period.

Our study also detected rare individual cases, where antibody titres persisted over several years. We would not suggest that "immunological scars" are a likely explanation for those situations. Rather, these individuals may differ from the rest of the population in aspects unknown to us. We would like to refer to a recent study investigating the existence of high-risk sub-populations for helminthic infections in China and which found clustering of infections which were not fully explained by host exposure (Carlton *et al.* 2013). These individuals who were considered either very susceptible to schistosomiasis or did not clear from infection, were suspected to be potentially future reservoirs of *S. japonicum*. However, we suggest that this claim should be balanced against the fact that schistosomiaisis japonica is nowadays still predominantly a zoonosis, as is also documented in the national control strategy (Wang *et al.* 2009a).

4.3 Conclusion

In summary, Wuhan makes an enormous effort in its fight against schistosomiasis. The investment in human resources was found to be extensive, but also necessary to achieve the objectives of control. Local control mechanisms and infrastructure are well-developed and in place. Infection rates remain at a low level and also sero-prevalence apparently declined over the years with the number of IHA positive cases and sero-conversions going down. Equally, infection intensities and schistosome antibody levels in the population remain low.

This study demonstrates the benefit to not only interpret surveillance data within the context of the respective years, but to merge the individual results as a follow-up of serological titer courses over longer periods of time. With such analysis, the surveillance activities as currently performed, may lead to identification of potential non-clearers, the potential relevance of which has recently been revealed (Carlton *et al.* 2013). The extension of analysis of regular surveillance by including longitudinal serological profiling on population and individual levels may, therefore, proof helpful. In this context, we anticipate that further investigation of those few individuals identified in this study with persisting IHA titers over the course of many years, even though infections have not yet been confirmed by KK stool examination could help to identify possible persisting sources for transmission of infections.

The distribution of schistosomiasis is very focal. Control activities, although planned on national and provincial level, are tackled locally in villages and towns. Aggregated data is undoubtedly useful for the bigger picture, but to achieve elimination, even in a comparatively small area like Wuhan City, may require a closer look at the available data to fully understand the situation at each single local point.

From a public health perspective, IHA appears as a useful tool to determine need for treatment. Since at an individual level, the reliability of IHA results is limited, when aiming at elimination, treatment should not solely depend on IHA test results. However, in the absence of more sensitive and specific tests, it is essential to make best use possible of the tools available today. IHA testing at this point is reasonable and worthwhile. Meaningful information on schistosomiasis transmission can be obtained from longitudinal serologic profiles, not only on population but also on individual level. Control activities should include longitudinal serologic survey of individual endemic villages to gain a deeper understanding of the level of schistosomiasis transmission.

In conclusion, this study highlights the need and benefit to invest considerable financial resources and manpower to achieve the goal of schistosomiasis elimination. Contrary to high prevalence situations, which occurred historically in China and persist in large parts of Africa today, the success of control in a low endemicity setting – as for the one in this study – has led to a change in paradigms: interventions based on mass drug administration as a tool with relatively low costs per schistosomiasis patient are now substituted by complex and relatively expensive surveillance activities. These, however, offer the chance to proceed from control to elimination of schistosomiasis in Wuhan.

5 References

Al-Sherbiny MM, Osman AM, Hancock K, Deelder AM, Tsang VC. 1999. Application of immunodiagnostic assays: detection of antibodies and circulating antigens in human schistosomiasis and correlation with clinical findings. *Am J Trop Med Hyg*, **60**: 960–6.

Alarcon de Noya B, Colmenares C, Losada S, Fermin Z, Masroua G, Ruiz L, Soto L, Noya O. 1996. Do intestinal parasites interfere with the seroepidemiologic surveillance of *Schistosoma mansoni* infection? *Epidemiol Infect*, **116**: 323–9.

Alonso D, Munoz J, Gascon J, Valls ME, Corachan M. 2006. Failure of standard treatment with praziquantel in two returned travelers with *Schistosoma haematobium* infection. *Am J Trop Med Hyg*, **74**: 342–4.

Anand S. 2010. Measuring health workforce inequalities: methods and application to China and India. in: *Human Resources for Health Observer*, Vol. 5, World Health Organization. Geneva.

Anand S, Fan VY, Zhang J, Zhang L, Ke Y, Dong Z, Chen LC. 2008. China's human resources for health: quantity, quality, and distribution. *Lancet*, **372**: 1774–81.

Appleton CC, Mbaye A. 2001. Praziquantel – quality, dosages and markers of resistance. *Trends in Parasitology*, **17**: 356–357.

Aragon AD, Imani RA, Blackburn VR, Cupit PM, Melman SD, Goronga T, Webb T, Loker ES, Cunningham C. 2009. Towards an understanding of the mechanism of action of praziquantel. *Mol Biochem Parasitol*, **164**: 57–65.

Balen J, Zhao ZY, Williams GM, McManus DP, Raso G, Utzinger J, Zhou J, Li YS. 2007. Prevalence, intensity and associated morbidity of *Schistosoma japonicum* infection in the Dongting Lake region, China. *Bull World Health Organ*, **85**: 519–26.

Bergquist NR, Colley DG. 1998. Schistosomiasis vaccine: research to development. *Parasitol Today*, **14**: 99–104.

Bergquist R, Johansen MV, Utzinger J. 2009. Diagnostic dilemmas in helminthology: what tools to use and when? *Trends in Parasitology*, **25**: 151–156.

Bergquist R, Utzinger J, McManus DP. 2008. Trick or treat: The role of vaccines in integrated schistosomiasis control. *PLoS Negl Trop Dis*, 2: e244.

Bethony JM, Diemert DJ, Oliveira SC, Loukas A. 2008. Can schistosomiasis really be consigned to history without a vaccine? *Vaccine*, 26: 3373–6.

Bian Y, Sun Q, Zhao Z, Blas E. 2004. Market reform: a challenge to public health--the case of schistosomiasis control in China. *Int J Health Plann Manage*, **19 Suppl 1**: S79-94.

Blumenthal D, Hsiao W. 2005. Privatization and its discontents--the evolving Chinese health care system. *N Engl J Med*, 353: 1165–70.

Booth M, Vounatsou P, N'Goran E K, Tanner M, Utzinger J. 2003. The influence of sampling effort and the performance of the Kato-Katz technique in diagnosing *Schistosoma mansoni* and hookworm co-infections in rural Cote d'Ivoire. *Parasitology*, 127: 525–31.

Botros S, Sayed H, Amer N, El-Ghannam M, Bennett JL, Day TA. 2005. Current status of sensitivity to praziquantel in a focus of potential drug resistance in Egypt. *Int J Parasitol*, 35: 787–91.

Caffrey CR, Secor WE. 2011. Schistosomiasis: from drug deployment to drug development. *Curr Opin Infect Dis*, 24: 410–7.

Capron A, Riveau GJ, Bartley PB, McManus DP. 2002. Prospects for a schistosome vaccine. *Curr Drug Targets Immune Endocr Metabol Disord*, 2: 281–90.

Carlton EJ, Hsiang M, Zhang Y, Johnson S, Hubbard A, Spear RC. 2010. The impact of *Schistosoma japonicum* infection and treatment on ultrasound-detectable morbidity: a five-year cohort study in Southwest China. *PLoS Negl Trop Dis*, 4: e685.

Carlton EJ, Hubbard A, Wang S, Spear RC. 2013. Repeated *Schistosoma japonicum* infection following treatment in two cohorts: evidence for host susceptibility to helminthiasis? *PLoS Negl Trop Dis*, 7: e2098.

Castillo-Laborde C. 2011. Human resources for health and burden of disease: an econometric approach. *Hum Resour Health*, 9: 4.

CDC. 2009. Image Library Schistosomiasis.

Chen MG. 2005. Use of praziquantel for clinical treatment and morbidity control of schistosomiasis japonica in China: a review of 30 years' experience. *Acta Trop*, 96: 168–76.

Chitsulo L, Engels D, Montresor A, Savioli L. 2000. The global status of schistosomiasis and its control. *Acta Trop*, **77**: 41–51.

Collins C, Xu J, Tang S. 2012. Schistosomiasis control and the health system in P.R. China. *Inf Dis Pov*, **1**:8.

Corachan M. 2002. Schistosomiasis and international travel. *Clin Infect Dis*, **35**: 446–50.

Dal Poz MR, Gupta N, Quain E, Soucat AL. 2009. Handbook on Monitoring and Evaluation of Human Resources for Health, World Health Organization. Geneva.

De Jonge N, Gryseels B, Hilberath GW, Polderman AM, Deelder AM. 1988. Detection of circulating anodic antigen by ELISA for seroepidemiology of schistosomiasis mansoni. *Trans R Soc Trop Med Hyg*, **82**: 591–4.

De Jonge N, Kremsner PG, Krijger FW, Schommer G, Fillie YE, Kornelis D, van Zeyl RJ, van Dam GJ, Feldmeier H, Deelder AM. 1990a. Detection of the schistosome circulating cathodic antigen by enzyme immunoassay using biotinylated monoclonal antibodies. *Trans R Soc Trop Med Hyg*, **84**: 815–8.

De Jonge N, Polderman AM, Hilberath GW, Krijger FW, Deelder AM. 1990b. Immunodiagnosis of schistosomiasis patients in The Netherlands: comparison of antibody and antigen detection before and after chemotherapy. *Trop Med Parasitol*, **41**: 257–61.

De Jonge N, Schommer G, Feldmeier H, Krijger FW, Dafalla AA, Bienzle U, Deelder AM. 1990c. Mixed *Schistosoma haematobium* and *S. mansoni* infection: effect of different treatments on the serum level of circulating anodic antigen (CAA). *Acta Trop*, **48**: 25–35.

Deelder AM, De Jonge N, Fillie YE, Kornelis D, Helaha D, Qian ZL, De Caluwe P, Polderman AM. 1989. Quantitative determination of circulating antigens in human schistosomiasis mansoni using an indirect hemagglutination assay. *Am J Trop Med Hyg*, **40**: 50–4.

Deelder AM, Klappe HT, van den Aardweg GJ, van Meerbeke EH. 1976. *Schistosoma mansoni*: demonstration of two circulating antigens in infected hamsters. *Exp Parasitol*, **40**: 189–97.

Deelder AM, Miller RL, de Jonge N, Krijger FW. 1990. Detection of schistosome antigen in mummies. *Lancet*, **335**: 724–5.

Doenhoff MJ. 1998. A Vaccine for Schistosomiasis: alternative approaches. *Parasitol Today*, **14**: 105–9.

Doenhoff MJ, Chiodini PL, Hamilton JV. 2004. Specific and sensitive diagnosis of schistosome infection: can it be done with antibodies? *Trends in Parasitology*, **20**: 35–39.

Doenhoff MJ, Cioli D, Utzinger J. 2008. Praziquantel: mechanisms of action, resistance and new derivatives for schistosomiasis. *Curr Opin Infect Dis*, **21**: 659–67.

Doenhoff MJ, Wheeler JG, Tricker K, Hamilton JV, Sturrock RF, Butterworth AE, Ouma JH, Mbugua GG, Kariuki C, Koech D. 2003. The detection of antibodies against *Schistosoma mansoni* soluble egg antigens (SEA) and CEF6 in ELISA, before and after chemotherapy. *Ann Trop Med Parasitol*, **97**: 697–709.

Duus LM, Christensen AV, Navntoft D, Tarp B, Nielsen HV, Petersen E. 2009. The *Schistosoma*-specific antibody response after treatment in non-immune travellers. *Scand J Infect Dis*, **41**: 285–90.

Engels D, Chitsulo L, Montresor A, Savioli L. 2002. The global epidemiological situation of schistosomiasis and new approaches to control and research. *Acta Trop*, **82**: 139–46.

Engels D, Sinzinkayo E, Gryseels B. 1996. Day-to-day egg count fluctuation in *Schistosoma mansoni* infection and its operational implications. *Am J Trop Med Hyg*, **54**: 319–24.

Engels D, Wang LY, Palmer KL. 2005. Control of schistosomiasis in China. *Acta Trop*, **96**: 67–8.

Fallon PG. 1998. Schistosome resistance to praziquantel. *Drug Resist Updat*, **1**: 236–41.

Feldmeier H, Poggensee G. 1993. Diagnostic techniques in schistosomiasis control. A review. *Acta Trop*, **52**: 205–20.

Finkelstein JL, Schleinitz MD, Carabin H, McGarvey ST. 2008. Decision-model estimation of the age-specific disability weight for schistosomiasis japonica: a systematic review of the literature. *PLoS Negl Trop Dis*, **2**: e158.

Freeman III CW, Lu X. 2009. China's Capacity to Manage Infectious Diseases. A Report of the CSIS Freemen Chai in China Studies. Center for Strategic & International Studies.

Fulford AJ, Butterworth AE, Sturrock RF, Ouma JH. 1992. On the use of age-intensity data to detect immunity to parasitic infections, with special reference to Schistosoma mansoni in Kenya. *Parasitology*, **105** : 219–27.

Gazzinelli G, Lambertucci JR, Katz N, Rocha RS, Lima MS, Colley DG. 1985. Immune responses during human schistosomiasis mansoni. XI. Immunologic status of patients with acute infections and after treatment. *J Immunol*, **135**: 2121–7.

Gold R, Rosen FS, Weller TH. 1969. A specific circulating antigen in hamsters infected with *Schistosoma mansoni*. Detection of antigen in serum and urine, and correlation between antigenic concentration and worm burden. *Am J Trop Med Hyg*, **18**: 545–52.

Gray DJ, Williams GM, Li Y, Chen H, Forsyth SJ, Li RS, Barnett AG, Guo J, Ross AG, Feng Z, McManus DP. 2009. A cluster-randomised intervention trial against *Schistosoma japonicum* in the Peoples' Republic of China: bovine and human transmission. *PLoS One*, **4**: e5900.

Gross MD. 2010. Chasing snails: Anti-schistosomiasis campaigns in the People's Republic of China, Ph.D., University of California, San Diego. United States -- California, pp. 749.

Guangjin S, Mingdao J, Qiyang L, Hui X, Jiangming H, Xiaomei Y. 2002. Study on histopathology, ultrasonography and some special serum enzymes and collagens for 38 advanced patients of schistosomiasis japonica. *Acta Trop*, **82**: 235–46.

Gui M, Idris MA, Shi YE, Muhling A, Ruppel A. 1991. Reactivity of *Schistosoma japonicum* and *S. mansoni* antigen preparations in indirect haemagglutination (IHA) with sera of patients with homologous and heterologous schistosomiasis. *Ann Trop Med Parasitol*, **85**: 599–604.

Guo J, Li Y, Gray D, Ning A, Hu G, Chen H, Davis GM, Sleigh AC, Feng Z, McManus DP, Williams GM. 2006. A drug-based intervention study on the importance of buffaloes for human *Schistosoma japonicum* infection around Poyang Lake, People's Republic of China. *Am J Trop Med Hyg*, **74**: 335–41.

Guo JG, Ross AG, Lin DD, Williams GM, Chen HG, Li Y, Davis GM, Feng Z, McManus DP, Sleigh AC. 2001. A baseline study on the importance of bovines for human *Schistosoma japonicum* infection around Poyang Lake, China. *Am J Trop Med Hyg*, **65**: 272–8.

Guo JG, X.N. Z, M.G. C. 2005. Epidemiology and control of schistosomiasis in China. in: *Asian Parasitology Series monograph vol. 6: Schistosomiasis in Asia*, (Eds.) Chen MG, Zhou XN, Hirayama K, Vol. 5. Chiba, Japan, pp. 8–28.

Hamilton JV, Klinkert M, Doenhoff MJ. 1998. Diagnosis of schistosomiasis: antibody detection, with notes on parasitological and antigen detection methods. *Parasitology*, **117**: S41-57.

Hatz C, Jenkins JM, Tanner M, UNDP/World Bank/WHO Special Programme for Research and Training in Tropical Diseases. 1992. *Ultrasound in schistosomiasis*. Elsevier Science Publishers, Amsterdam.

Helleberg M, Thybo S. 2010. High rate of failure in treatment of imported schistosomiasis. *J Travel Med*, **17**: 94–9.

Hong XC, Xu XJ, Chen X, Li YS, Yu CH, Yuan Y, Chen YY, Li RD, Qiu J, Liu ZC, Yi P, Ren GH, He HB. 2013. Assessing the effect of an integrated control strategy for schistosomiasis japonica emphasizing bovines in a marshland area of Hubei Province, China: a cluster randomized trial. *PLoS Negl Trop Dis*, 7: e2122.

Hsiang MS, Carlton EJ, Zhang Y, Zhong B, Dongchuan Q, Cohen PA, Stewart CC, Spear RC. 2010. Use of ultrasonography to evaluate *Schistosoma japonicum*-related morbidity in children, Sichuan Province, China, 2000–2007. *Am J Trop Med Hyg*, **82**: 103–11.

Huang YX, Manderson L. 2005. The social and economic context and determinants of schistosomiasis japonica. *Acta Trop*, **96**: 223–31.

Idris MA, Ruppel A. 1988. Diagnostic Mr31/32,000 *Schistosoma mansoni* proteins (Sm31/32): reaction with sera from Sudanese patients infected with *S. mansoni* or *S. haematobium*. *J Helminthol*, **62**: 95–101.

Idris MA, Shaban M, Richter J, Mone H, Mouahid G, Ruppel A. 2003. Emergence of infections with *Schistosoma mansoni* in the Dhofar Governorate, Oman. *Acta Trop*, **88**: 137–44.

James K, Rino R, Merry B. 2005. Vaccine Development: Current status and future needs. A report by the American Academy of Microbiology.

Jaureguiberry S, Paris L, Caumes E. 2010. Acute schistosomiasis, a diagnostic and therapeutic challenge. *Clin Microbiol Infect*, **16**: 225–31.

Jia TW, Utzinger J, Deng Y, Yang K, Li YY, Zhu JH, King CH, Zhou XN. 2011. Quantifying quality of life and disability of patients with advanced schistosomiasis japonica. *PLoS Negl Trop Dis*, 5: e966.

Jia TW, Zhou XN, Wang XH, Utzinger J, Steinmann P, Wu XH. 2007. Assessment of the age-specific disability weight of chronic schistosomiasis japonica. *Bull World Health Organ*, **85**: 458–65.

Jiang QW, Wang LY, Guo JG, Chen MG, Zhou XN, Engels D. 2002. Morbidity control of schistosomiasis in China. *Acta Tropica*, **82**: 115–125.

Jiang XR, Yuan ZK, Fang X, Huang RH, Wan YP, Duan CH. 2011. [Investigation on health workforce in county anti-schistosomiasis institutions of Jiangxi Province, 2010]. *Zhongguo Xue Xi Chong Bing Fang Zhi Za Zhi*, **23**: 714–8.

Katz N, Chaves A, Pellegrino J. 1972. A simple device for quantitative stool thick-smear technique in schistosomiasis mansoni. *Rev Inst Med Trop Sao Paulo*, **14**: 397–400.

Kikuchi S, Ohgihara A, Hasegawa A, Miki K, Kaneko E, Mizukoshi H. 2004. Seroconversion and seroreversion of *Helicobacter pylori* antibodies over a 9-year period and related factors in Japanese adults. *Helicobacter*, **9**: 335–41.

King CH. 2008. Schistosomiasis japonica: The DALYs Recaptured. *PLoS Negl Trop Dis*, **2**: e203.

King CH. 2009. Toward the elimination of schistosomiasis. *N Engl J Med*, **360**: 106–9.

King CH. 2010. Parasites and poverty: the case of schistosomiasis. *Acta Trop*, **113**: 95–104.

King CH, Bertino AM. 2008. Asymmetries of poverty: why global burden of disease valuations underestimate the burden of neglected tropical diseases. *PLoS Negl Trop Dis*, **2**: e209.

King CH, Dangerfield-Cha M. 2008. The unacknowledged impact of chronic schistosomiasis. *Chronic Illn*, **4**: 65–79.

King CH, Dickman K, Tisch DJ. 2005. Reassessment of the cost of chronic helmintic infection: a meta-analysis of disability-related outcomes in endemic schistosomiasis. *The Lancet*, **365**: 1561–1569.

King CH, Muchiri EM, Ouma JH. 2000. Evidence against rapid emergence of praziquantel resistance in *Schistosoma haematobium*, Kenya. *Emerg Infect Dis*, **6**: 585–94.

Klumpp RK, Chu KY. 1977. Ecological studies of *Bulinus rohlfsi*, the intermediate host of *Schistosoma haematobium* in the Volta Lake. *Bull World Health Organ*, **55**: 715–30.

Knopp S, Mgeni AF, Khamis IS, Steinmann P, Stothard JR, Rollinson D, Marti H, Utzinger J. 2008. Diagnosis of soil-transmitted helminths in the era of preventive chemotherapy: effect of multiple stool sampling and use of different diagnostic techniques. *PLoS Negl Trop Dis*, 2: e331.

Kumar V. 1999. *Trematode infections and diseases of man and animals.* Kluwer; Institute of Tropical Medicine, Dordrecht; Boston; Antwerp.

Kusel J, Hagan P. 1999. Praziquantel--its use, cost and possible development of resistance. *Parasitol Today*, 15: 352–4.

Lengeler C, Utzinger J, Tanner M. 2002. Questionnaires for rapid screening of schistosomiasis in sub-Saharan Africa. *Bull World Health Organ*, 80: 235–42.

Li YL, Liu W, Ruppel A. 2003. Hybridoma cell agglutination as a novel test to detect circulating antigen of *Schistosoma japonicum*. *Trop Med Int Health*, 8: 73–7.

Li YL, Song WJ, Han JJ, Ruppel A. 1994. Detection of *Schistosoma japonicum* antigen (Sj31/32) in sera of Chinese patients using a sandwich ELISA based on monoclonal antibody. *Trop Med Parasitol*, 45: 115–8.

Li YS, Raso G, Zhao ZY, He YK, Ellis MK, McManus DP. 2007. Large water management projects and schistosomiasis control, Dongting Lake region, China. *Emerg Infect Dis*, 13: 973–9.

Liang S, Seto EY, Remais JV, Zhong B, Yang C, Hubbard A, Davis GM, Gu X, Qiu D, Spear RC. 2007. Environmental effects on parasitic disease transmission exemplified by schistosomiasis in western China. *Proc Natl Acad Sci U S A*, 104: 7110–5.

Liang S, Yang C, Zhong B, Qiu D. 2006. *Re-emerging schistosomiasis in hilly and mountainous areas of Sichuan, China.*

Lin DD, Liu JX, Liu YM, Hu F, Zhang YY, Xu JM, Li JY, Ji MJ, Bergquist R, Wu GL, Wu HW. 2008a. Routine Kato-Katz technique underestimates the prevalence of *Schistosoma japonicum*: a case study in an endemic area of the People's Republic of China. *Parasitol Int*, 57: 281–6.

Lin DD, Xu JM, Zhang YY, Liu YM, Hu F, Xu XL, Li JY, Gao ZL, Wu HW, Kurtis J, Wu GL. 2008b. Evaluation of IgG-ELISA for the diagnosis of *Schistosoma japonicum* in a high prevalence, low intensity endemic area of China. *Acta Trop*, 107: 128–33.

Liu R, Dong HF, Guo Y, Zhao QP, Jiang MS. 2011. Efficacy of praziquantel and artemisinin derivatives for the treatment and prevention of human schistosomiasis: a systematic review and meta-analysis. *Parasit Vectors*, 4: 201.

Logan OT. 1905. A case of dysentery in Hunan province, caused by the trematode *Schistosoma japonicum*. *Chin Med J (Engl)*, 19: 243–245.

Mao CP. 1948. A review of the epidemiology of schistosomiasis japonica in China. *Am J Trop Med Hyg*, 28: 659–72.

Mao SP, Shao BR. 1982. Schistosomiasis control in the people's Republic of China. *Am J Trop Med Hyg*, 31: 92–9.

Massara CL, Peixoto SV, Barros Hda S, Enk MJ, Carvalho Odos S, Schall V. 2004. Factors associated with schistosomiasis mansoni in a population from the municipality of Jaboticatubas, State of Minas Gerais, Brazil. *Mem Inst Oswaldo Cruz*, 99: 127–34.

Mathers CD, Ezzati M, Lopez AD. 2007. Measuring the burden of neglected tropical diseases: the global burden of disease framework. *PLoS Negl Trop Dis*, 1: e114.

McCarthy JS, Lustigman S, Yang GJ, et al. 2012. A research agenda for helminth diseases of humans: diagnostics for control and elimination programmes. PLoS Negl Trop Dis, 6: e1601.

McManus DP, Loukas A. 2008. Current status of vaccines for schistosomiasis. *Clin Microbiol Rev*, 21: 225–42.

Melman SD, Steinauer ML, Cunningham C, Kubatko LS, Mwangi IN, Wynn NB, Mutuku MW, Karanja DM, Colley DG, Black CL, Secor WE, Mkoji GM, Loker ES. 2009. Reduced susceptibility to praziquantel among naturally occurring Kenyan isolates of *Schistosoma mansoni*. *PLoS Negl Trop Dis*, 3: e504.

Michelson MK, Azziz FA, Gamil FM, Wahid AA, Richards FO, Juranek DD, Habib MA, Spencer HC. 1993. Recent trends in the prevalence and distribution of schistosomiasis in the Nile delta region. *Am J Trop Med Hyg*, 49: 76–87.

Ministry of Health. 2006a. Criteria for control and elimination of Schistosomiasis. in: *GB 15976–2006*, Standards Press of China. (Chinese). Beijing.

Ministry of Health. 2006b. Diagnostic Criteria for Schistosomiasis. in: *WS 261–2006*, Standards Press of China. (Chinese). Beijing.

Moestue H, Mahumane B, Zacher A, Issae W, Kihamia CM, Wen ST, Adjei S, Bundy DA, Hall A. 2003. Ill-health reported by schoolchildren during questionnaire surveys in Ghana, Mozambique and Tanzania. *Trop Med Int Health*, **8**: 967–74.

Molyneux DH, Hotez PJ, Fenwick A. 2005. "Rapid-impact interventions": how a policy of integrated control for Africa's neglected tropical diseases could benefit the poor. *PLoS Med*, **2**: e336.

Montresor A, Crompton DWT, Hall A, Bundy DAP, Savioli L, World Health Organization. Division of Control of Tropical Diseases. Schistosomiasis and Intestinal Parasites Unit. 1998. *Guidelines for the evaluation of soil-transmitted helminthiasis and schistosomiasis at community level : a guide for managers of control programmes*. World Health Organization, Geneva.

Mott KE, Dixon H. 1982. Collaborative study on antigens for immunodiagnosis of schistosomiasis. *Bull World Health Organ*, **60**: 729–53.

Mott KE, Dixon H, Carter CE, Garcia E, Ishii A, Matsuda H, Mitchell G, Owhashi M, Tanaka H, Tsang VC. 1987. Collaborative study on antigens for immunodiagnosis of *Schistosoma japonicum* infection. *Bull World Health Organ*, **65**: 233–44.

Mutapi F, Ndhlovu PD, Hagan P, Woolhouse ME. 1997. A comparison of humoral responses to *Schistosoma haematobium* in areas with low and high levels of infection. *Parasite Immunol*, **19**: 255–63.

Noya O, Alarcon de Noya B, Losada S, Colmenares C, Guzman C, Lorenzo MA, Bermudez H. 2002. Laboratory diagnosis of schistosomiasis in areas of low transmission: a review of a line of research. *Mem Inst Oswaldo Cruz*, **97 Suppl 1**: 167–9.

Ofoezie IE, Asaolu SO. 1997. Water level regulation and control of schistosomiasis transmission : a case study in Oyan Reservoir, Ogun State, Nigeria. *Bull World Health Organ*, **75** 435–441.

Ofoezie IE, Imevbore AM, Balogun MO, Ogunkoya OO, Asaolu SO. 1991. A study of an outbreak of schistosomiasis in two resettlement villages near Abeokuta, Ogun State, Nigeria. *J Helminthol*, **65**: 95–102.

Paperna I. 1970. Study of an outbreak of schistosomiasis in the newly formed Volta lake in Ghana. *Z Tropenmed Parasitol*, **21**: 411–25.

Partnership for Child Development. 1999. *Self-diagnosis as a possible basis for treating urinary schistosomiasis : a study of schoolchildren in a rural area of the Unted Republic of Tanzania.*

Pica-Mattoccia L, Ruppel A, Xia CM, Cioli D. 2008. Praziquantel and the benzodiazepine Ro 11–3128 do not compete for the same binding sites in schistosomes. *Parasitology*, **135**: 47–54.

Pontes LA, Dias-Neto E, Rabello A. 2002. Detection by polymerase chain reaction of *Schistosoma mansoni* DNA in human serum and feces. *Am J Trop Med Hyg*, **66**: 157–62.

Qian ZL, Deelder AM. 1983. *Schistosoma japonicum*: immunological response to circulating polysaccharide antigens in rabbits with a light infection. *Exp Parasitol*, **55**: 394–403.

Raso G, Vounatsou P, McManus DP, N'Goran EK, Utzinger J. 2007. A Bayesian approach to estimate the age-specific prevalence of *Schistosoma mansoni* and implications for schistosomiasis control. *Int J Parasitol*, **37**: 1491–500.

Richter J, Hatz C, Campagne G, Bergquist NR, Jenkins JM, UNDP/World Bank/WHO Special Programme for Research and Training in Tropical Diseases. 2000. *Ultrasound in schistosomiasis : a practical guide to the standard use of ultrasonography for assessment of schistosomiasis-related morbidity : Second international workshop, October 22–26 1996, Niamey, Niger. Revised and updated. ed.* World Health Organization, Geneva.

Richter J, Ruppel A. 2010. Schistosomiasis oder Bilharziose. In: Loescher T, Burchard G-D (eds.). *Tropenmedizin in Klinik und Praxis*. 4 edn. Stuttgart, New York: Georg Thieme Verlag, 676 ff.

Ross AG, Sleigh AC, Li Y, Davis GM, Williams GM, Jiang Z, Feng Z, McManus DP. 2001. Schistosomiasis in the People's Republic of China: prospects and challenges for the 21st century. *Clin Microbiol Rev*, **14**: 270–95.

Ruppel A, Diesfeld HJ, Rother U. 1985. Immunoblot analysis of *Schistosoma mansoni* antigens with sera of schistosomiasis patients: diagnostic potential of an adult schistosome polypeptide. *Clin Exp Immunol*, **62**: 499–506.

Ruppel A, Idris MA, Sulaiman SM, Hilali AM. 1990. *Schistosoma mansoni* diagnostic antigens (Sm 31/12): a sero-epidemiological study in the Sudan. *Trop Med Parasitol*, **41**: 127–30.

Ruppel A, Shi YE, Wei DX, Diesfeld HJ. 1987. Sera of *Schistosoma japonicum*-infected patients cross-react with diagnostic 31/32 kD proteins of *S. mansoni*. *Clin Exp Immunol*, **69**: 291–8.

Ruppel A, Xing Y, Dell R, Numrich P, Shi YE. 1991. *Schistosoma mansoni* and *S. japonicum*: decline of antibodies against diagnostic adult worm antigens (Sm31/32) following praziquantel treatment of mice. *Trop Med Parasitol*, **42**: 325–31.

Sabah AA, Fletcher C, Webbe G, Doenhoff MJ. 1986. *Schistosoma mansoni*: chemotherapy of infections of different ages. *Exp Parasitol*, **61**: 294–303.

Seto EY, Remais JV, Carlton EJ, Wang S, Liang S, Brindley PJ, Qiu D, Spear RC, Wang LD, Wang TP, Chen HG, Dong XQ, Wang LY, Hao Y, Bergquist R, Zhou XN. 2011a. Toward sustainable and comprehensive control of schistosomiasis in China: lessons from Sichuan. *PLoS Negl Trop Dis*, **5**: e1372.

Seto EY, Wong BK, Lu D, Zhong B. 2011b. Human schistosomiasis resistance to praziquantel in China: should we be worried? *Am J Trop Med Hyg*, **85**: 74–82.

Shi YE, Jiang CF, Han JJ, Li YL, Ruppel A. 1990. *Schistosoma japonicum*: an ultraviolet-attenuated cercarial vaccine applicable in the field for water buffaloes. *Exp Parasitol*, **71**: 100–6.

Sorgho H, Bahgat M, Poda JN, Song W, Kirsten C, Doenhoff MJ, Zongo I, Ouedraogo JB, Ruppel A. 2005. Serodiagnosis of Schistosoma mansoni infections in an endemic area of Burkina Faso: performance of several immunological tests with different parasite antigens. *Acta Trop*, **93**: 169–80.

Spear RC, Seto EY, Carlton EJ, Liang S, Remais JV, Zhong B, Qiu D. 2011. The challenge of effective surveillance in moving from low transmission to elimination of schistosomiasis in China. *Int J Parasitol*, **41**: 1243–7.

Steinmann P. 2008. Epidemiology and diagnosis of *Schistosoma japonicum*, other helminth infections and multiparasitism in Yunnan province, People's Republic of China. in: *Philosophisch-Naturwissenschaftliche Fakultät*, Vol. Doktor der Philosophie, Universität Basel. Basel.

Steinmann P, Keiser J, Bos R, Tanner M, Utzinger J. 2006. Schistosomiasis and water resources development: systematic review, meta-analysis, and estimates of people at risk. *Lancet Infect Dis*, **6**: 411–25.

Su J. 2010. Wuhan Statistical Yearbook 2010, Vol. 22, China Statistics Press. Beijing.

Tan H, Yang M, Wu Z, Zhou J, Liu A, Li S, Yang T, Zhou Y, Sun Z. 2004. Rapid screening method for *Schistosoma japonicum* infection using questionnaires in flood area of the People's Republic of China. *Acta Trop*, 90: 1–9.

UNDP/World Bank/WHO. 1995. *Identification of high-risk communities for schistosomiasis in Africa : a multicountry study*. World Health Organization, Geneva.

United Nations. Department of Economic and Social Affairs. 2013. Population estimates and projections section; Country profile: China.

Utzinger J, Bergquist R, Shu-Hua X, Singer BH, Tanner M. 2003. Sustainable schistosomiasis control--the way forward. *Lancet*, 362: 1932–4.

Utzinger J, Xiao S, N'Goran EK, Bergquist R, Tanner M. 2001. The potential of artemether for the control of schistosomiasis. *Int J Parasitol*, 31: 1549–62.

Utzinger J, Xiao SH, Tanner M, Keiser J. 2007. Artemisinins for schistosomiasis and beyond. *Curr Opin Investig Drugs*, 8: 105–16.

Utzinger J, Zhou XN, Chen MG, Bergquist R. 2005. Conquering schistosomiasis in China: the long march. *Acta Trop*, 96: 69–96.

van der Werf MJ, de Vlas SJ, Brooker S, Looman CW, Nagelkerke NJ, Habbema JD, Engels D. 2003. Quantification of clinical morbidity associated with schistosome infection in sub-Saharan Africa. *Acta Trop*, 86: 125–39.

Vennervald BJ, Dunne DW. 2004. Morbidity in schistosomiasis: an update. *Curr Opin Infect Dis*, 17: 439–47.

Wang L, Utzinger J, Zhou XN. 2008. Schistosomiasis control: experiences and lessons from China. *Lancet*, 372: 1793–5.

Wang LD, Chen HG, Guo JG, Zeng XJ, Hong XL, Xiong JJ, Wu XH, Wang XH, Wang LY, Xia G, Hao Y, Chin DP, Zhou XN. 2009a. A strategy to control transmission of *Schistosoma japonicum* in China. *N Engl J Med*, 360: 121–8.

Wang LD, Guo JG, Wu XH, Chen HG, Wang TP, Zhu SP, Zhang ZH, Steinmann P, Yang GJ, Wang SP, Wu ZD, Wang LY, Hao Y, Bergquist R, Utzinger J, Zhou XN. 2009b. China's new strategy to block *Schistosoma japonicum* transmission: experiences and impact beyond schistosomiasis. *Trop Med Int Health*, **14**: 1475–83.

Watts S, El Katsha S. 1997. Irrigation, farming and schistosomiasis: a case study in the Nile delta. *International Journal of Environmental Health Research*, 7: 101.

Wei DX, Yang WY, Huang SQ, Lu YF, Su TC, Ma JH, Hu WX, Xie NF. 1980. Parasitological investigation on the ancient corpse of the Western Han Dynasty unearthed from tomb No. 168 on Phoenix Hill in Jiangling county. *Acta Acad Med Wuhan*, 3: 1–6.

WHO. 1953. The control of schistosomiasis: second report of the WHO Expert Committee. World Health Organization.

WHO. 1983. The Role of Chemotherapy in Schistosomiasis Control. in: *Unpublished Document (WHO/SCHISTO/83.70 Rev. 1)*, WHO. Geneva.

WHO. 1990. *Health education in the control of schistosomiasis*. World Health Organization, Geneva.

WHO. 1993. The control of schistosomiasis: second report of the WHO Expert Committee. World Health Organization.

WHO. 2001. *Report of the WHO Informal Consultation on Schistosomiasis in Low Transmission Areas: Control Strategies and Criteria for Elimination*. World Health Organization, Geneva.

WHO. 2002. Prevention and control of schistosomiasis and soil-transmitted helminthiasis: report of a WHO expert committee. World Health Organization.

WHO. 2006. *Neglected tropical diseases: preventive chemotherapy and transmission control: soil-transmitted helminthiasis, onchocerciasis, lymphatic filariasis, schistosomiasis, Guinea-worm disease*. WHO, Geneva.

WHO. 2009. *Elimination of schistosomiasis from low-transmission areas : report of a WHO informal consultation, Salvador, Bahia, Brazil, 18–19 August 2008*. World Health Organization, Geneva.

WHO. 2010. Schistosomiasis. *WHO Weekly epidemiological record No.18*, **85**: 157–164.

WHO. 2013. Factsheet No 115: Schistosomiasis.

WHO. 2014. Status of schistosomiasis endemic countries [Online]. Available: http://apps.who.int/neglected_diseases/ntddata/sch/sch.html [Accessed 15.04.2016].

WHO. 2016. Schistosomiasis: number of people treated worldwide in 2014. *WHO Weekly epidemiological record No.5*, **91**: 53–60.

Woolhouse ME. 1998. Patterns in parasite epidemiology: the peak shift. *Parasitol Today*, **14**: 428–34.

Wu G. 2002. A historical perspective on the immunodiagnosis of schistosomiasis in China. *Acta Trop*, **82**: 193–8.

Wu XH, Zhang SQ, Xu XJ, Huang YX, Steinmann P, Utzinger J, Wang TP, Xu J, Zheng J, Zhou XN. 2008. Effect of floods on the transmission of schistosomiasis in the Yangtze River valley, People's Republic of China. *Parasitol Int*, **57**: 271–6.

Wu ZD, Lu ZY, Yu XB. 2005. Development of a vaccine against Schistosoma japonicum in China: a review. *Acta Trop*, **96**: 106–16.

Xiang H, Yu S, Yi S, Dai Y. 1998. Financing changes of schistosomiasis control programmes in China 1980–1995: a case study in Songzi county. *Trop Med Int Health*, **3**: 454–61.

Xianyi C, Liying W, Jiming C, Xiaonong Z, Jiang Z, Jiagang G, Xiaohua W, Engels D, Minggang C. 2005. Schistosomiasis control in China: the impact of a 10-year World Bank Loan Project (1992–2001). *Bull World Health Organ*, **83**: 43–8.

Xie HB, Luo L, Su ZX, Wang WC, Wang Y, Sun M, Ma N, Yu J, Yu M, Duan Y, Gong X, Chen Z, Wang H, Shi P, Liang Z, Yang F, Wang D, Yue J, Luo S, Hao M. 2005. [Human resources allocation in centers of disease prevention and control in China]. *Wei Sheng Yan Jiu*, **34**: 390–2.

Yacoub A, Southgate BA, Lillywhite JE. 1987. The epidemiology of schistosomiasis in the later stages of a control programme based on chemotherapy: the Basrah study. 2. The serological profile and the validity of the ELISA in seroepidemiological studies. *Trans R Soc Trop Med Hyg*, **81**: 460–7.

Yang G. 2006. Potential impact of climate change and water resources development on the epidemiology of schistosomiasis in China, Universität Basel, Basel. Basel, Switzerland, pp. 171 p.

Yang Y. 2005. Study on surveillance and status of infection of schistosomiasis in Wuhan. in: *Department of Epidemiology*, Vol. Thesis (Master), School of Public Health, Huazhong University of Science and Technology. Wuhan.

Ye XP, Fu YL, Wu ZX, Anderson RM, Agnew A. 1997. The effects of temperature, light and water upon the hatching of the ova of *Schistosoma japonicum*. *Southeast Asian J Trop Med Public Health*, **28**: 575–80.

Yip W, Hsiao WC. 2008. The Chinese health system at a crossroads. *Health Aff (Millwood)*, **27**: 460–8.

Yu JM, de Vlas SJ, Jiang QW, Gryseels B. 2007. Comparison of the Kato-Katz technique, hatching test and indirect hemagglutination assay (IHA) for the diagnosis of *Schistosoma japonicum* infection in China. *Parasitol Int*, **56**: 45–9.

Zhang YY, Luo JP, Liu YM, Wang QZ, Chen JH, Xu MX, Xu JM, Wu J, Tu XM, Wu GL, Zhang ZS, Wu HW. 2009. Evaluation of Kato-Katz examination method in three areas with low-level endemicity of schistosomiasis japonica in China: A Bayesian modeling approach. *Acta Trop*, **112**: 16–22.

Zhang Z, Zhu R, Ward MP, Xu W, Zhang L, Guo J, Zhao F, Jiang Q. 2012. Long-term impact of the World Bank Loan Project for schistosomiasis control: a comparison of the spatial distribution of schistosomiasis risk in China. *PLoS Negl Trop Dis*, **6**: e1620.

Zhao GM, Zhao Q, Jiang QW, Chen XY, Wang LY, Yuan HC. 2005. Surveillance for schistosomiasis japonica in China from 2000 to 2003. *Acta Trop*, **96**: 288–95.

Zhou H, Ross AG, Hartel GF, Sleigh AC, Williams GM, McManus DP, Luo XS, He Y, Li YS. 1998. Diagnosis of schistosomiasis japonica in Chinese schoolchildren by administration of a questionnaire. *Trans R Soc Trop Med Hyg*, **92**: 245–50.

Zhou XN, Chen JX, Chen MG, Bergquist R. 2005a. The National Institute of Parasitic Diseases, Chinese Center for Disease Control and Prevention: a new administrative structure for schistosomiasis control. *Acta Trop*, **96**: 296–302.

Zhou XN, Guo JG, Wu XH, Jiang QW, Zheng J, Dang H, Wang XH, Xu J, Zhu HQ, Wu GL, Li YS, Xu XJ, Chen HG, Wang TP, Zhu YC, Qiu DC, Dong XQ, Zhao GM, Zhang SJ, Zhao NQ, Xia G, Wang LY, Zhang

SQ, Lin DD, Chen MG, Hao Y. 2007a. Epidemiology of schistosomiasis in the People's Republic of China, 2004. *Emerg Infect Dis*, **13**: 1470–6.

Zhou XN, Wang LY, Chen MG, Wu XH, Jiang QW, Chen XY, Zheng J, Utzinger J. 2005b. The public health significance and control of schistosomiasis in China--then and now. *Acta Trop*, **96**: 97–105.

Zhou YB, Liang S, Jiang QW. 2012. Factors impacting on progress towards elimination of transmission of schistosomiasis japonica in China. *Parasit Vectors*, **5**: 275.

Zhou YB, Yang MX, Tao P, Jiang QL, Zhao GM, Wei JG, Jiang QW. 2008. A longitudinal study of comparison of the Kato-Katz technique and indirect hemagglutination assay (IHA) for the detection of schistosomiasis japonica in China, 2001–2006. *Acta Trop*, **107**: 251–4.

Zhou YB, Yang MX, Wang QZ, Zhao GM, Wei JG, Peng WX, Jiang QW. 2007b. Field comparison of immunodiagnostic and parasitological techniques for the detection of Schistosomiasis japonica in the People's Republic of China. *Am J Trop Med Hyg*, **76**: 1138–43.

Zhou YB, Zheng HM, Jiang QW. 2011. A diagnostic challenge for schistosomiasis japonica in China: consequences on praziquantel-based morbidity control. *Parasit Vectors*, **4**: 194.

Zhu HM, Xiang S, Yang K, Wu XH, Zhou XN. 2008. Three Gorges Dam and its impact on the potential transmission of schistosomiasis in regions along the Yangtze River. *Ecohealth*, **5**: 137–48.

6 Annexes

Annex 1A: IHA test results of 163 individual persons who were tested IHA negative in 2003 and followed for up to 8 consecutive years until 2010

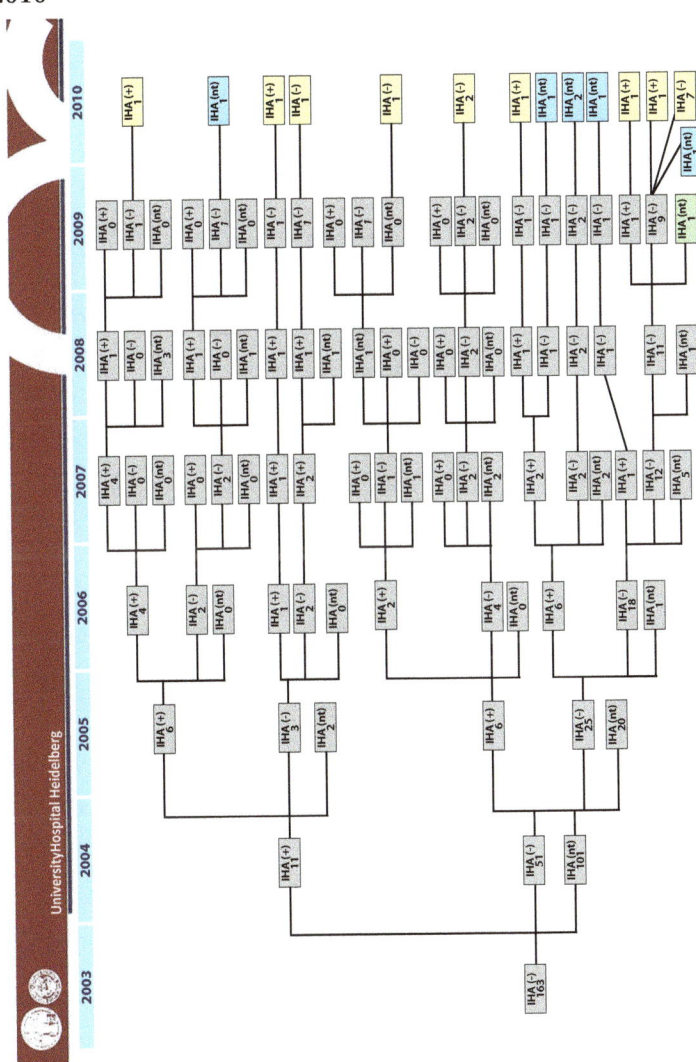

IHA (-): negative IHA test; IHA (+): positive IHA test; IHA (nt): person was not tested (nt) in the respective year. Green: persons tested for 6 consecutive years (2003–2008); blue: people tested for 7 consecutive years starting (2003–2009); yellow: people tested for a total of 8 consecutive years (2003–2010).

Annex 1B: IHA test results of 23 individual persons who were tested IHA positive in 2003 and followed for up to 8 consecutive years until 2010

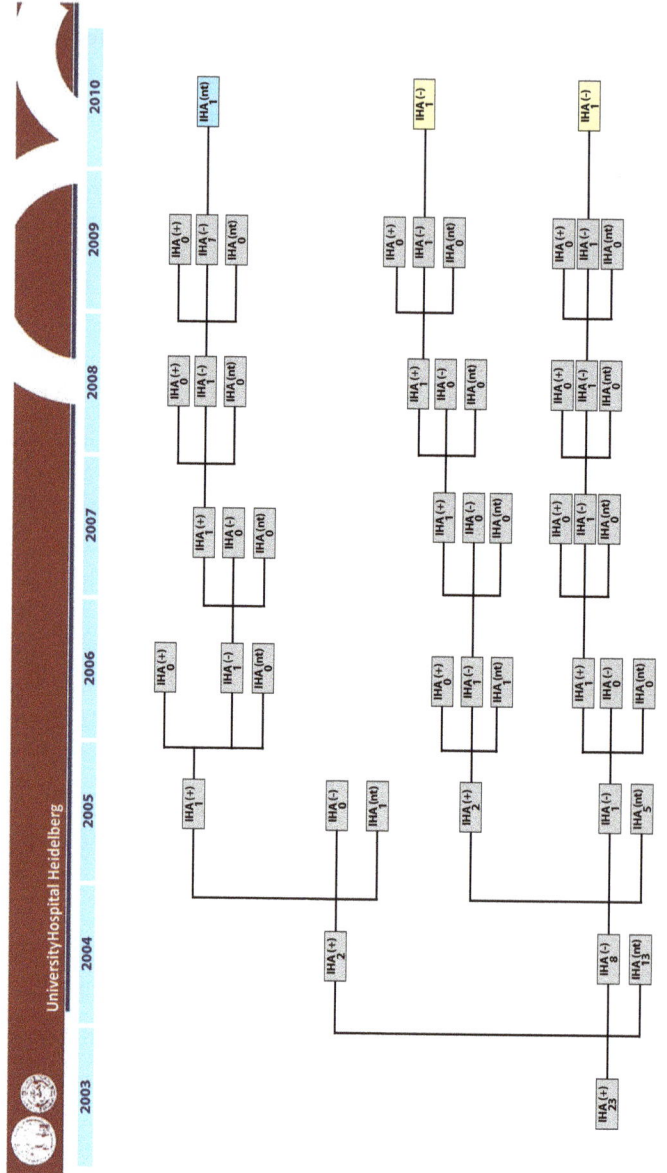

IHA (-): negative IHA test; IHA (+): positive IHA test; IHA (nt): person was not tested (nt) in the respective year. Green: persons tested for 6 consecutive years (2004–2008); blue: people tested for 7 consecutive years starting (2004–2009);

Annex 2A: **IHA test results of 293 individual persons who were not tested in 2003, but tested IHA negative in 2004 and followed for up to 7 consecutive years until 2010**

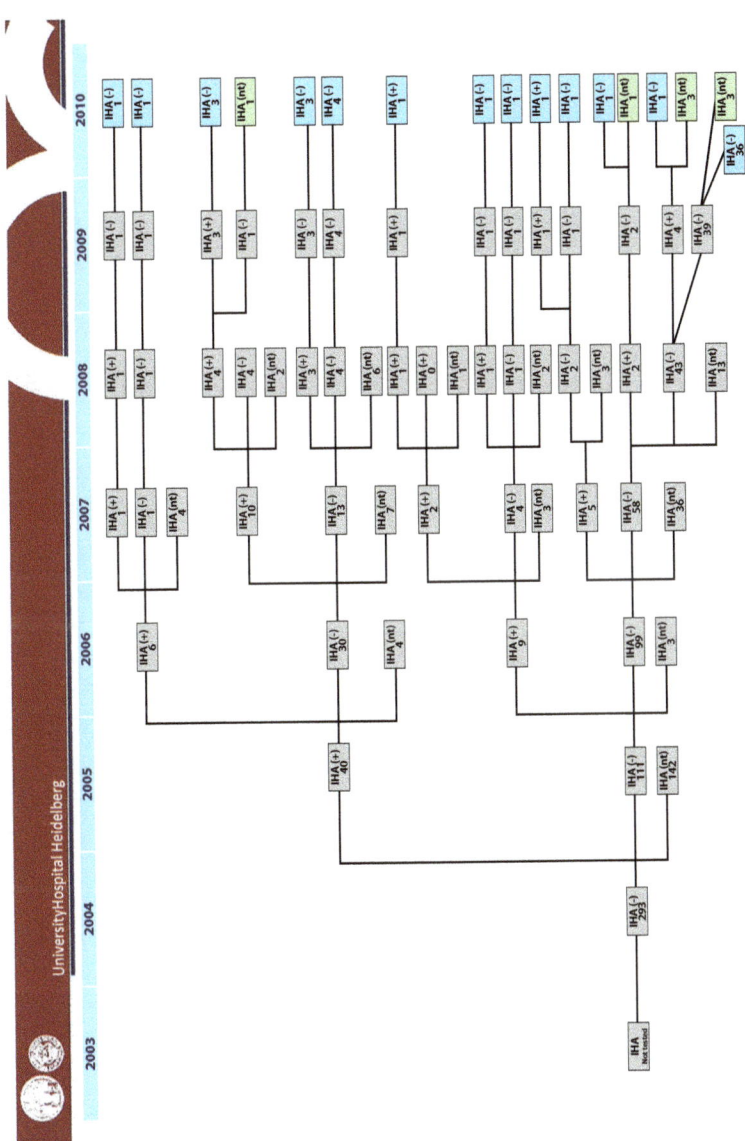

IHA (-): negative IHA test; IHA (+): positive IHA test; IHA (nt): person was not tested (nt) in the respective year. Green: persons tested for 6 consecutive years (2004–2008); blue: people tested for 7 consecutive years starting (2004–2009);

Annex 2B: IHA test results of 48 individual persons who were not tested in 2003, but tested IHA positive in 2004 and followed for up to 7 consecutive years until 2010

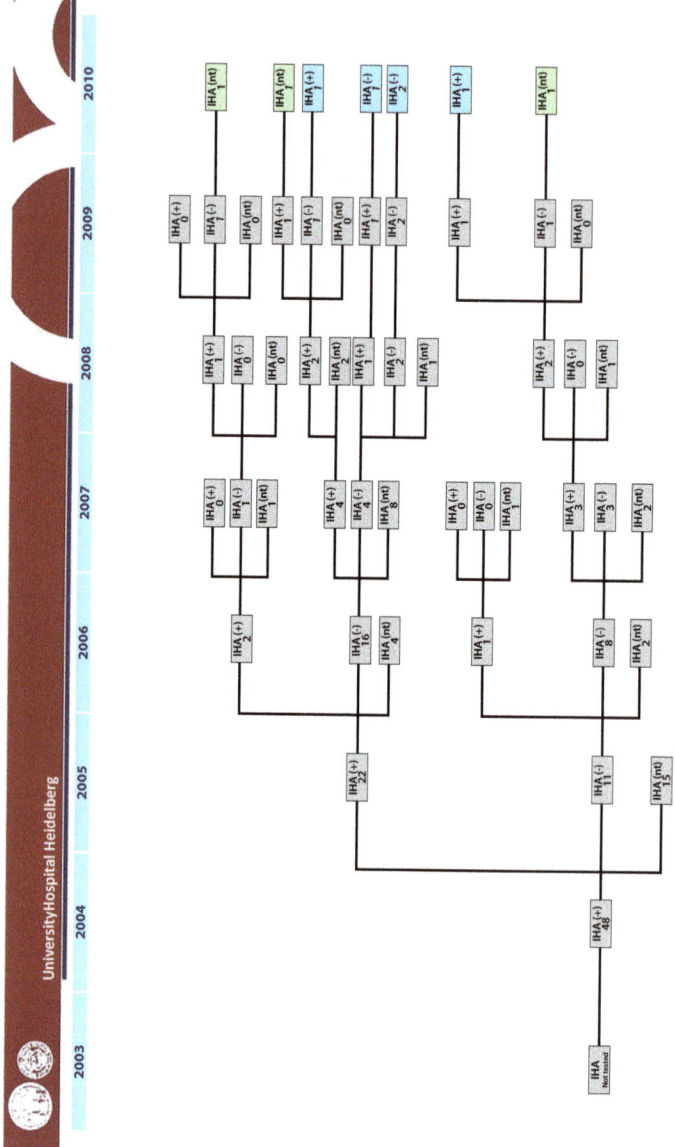

IHA (-): negative IHA test; IHA (+): positive IHA test; IHA (nt): person was not tested (nt) in the respective year. Green: persons tested for 6 consecutive years (2004–2008); blue: people tested for 7 consecutive years starting (2004–2009);

Annex 3A: IHA test results of 185 individual persons who were not tested in 2003 and 2004, but tested IHA negative in 2005 and followed for up to 6 consecutive years until 2010

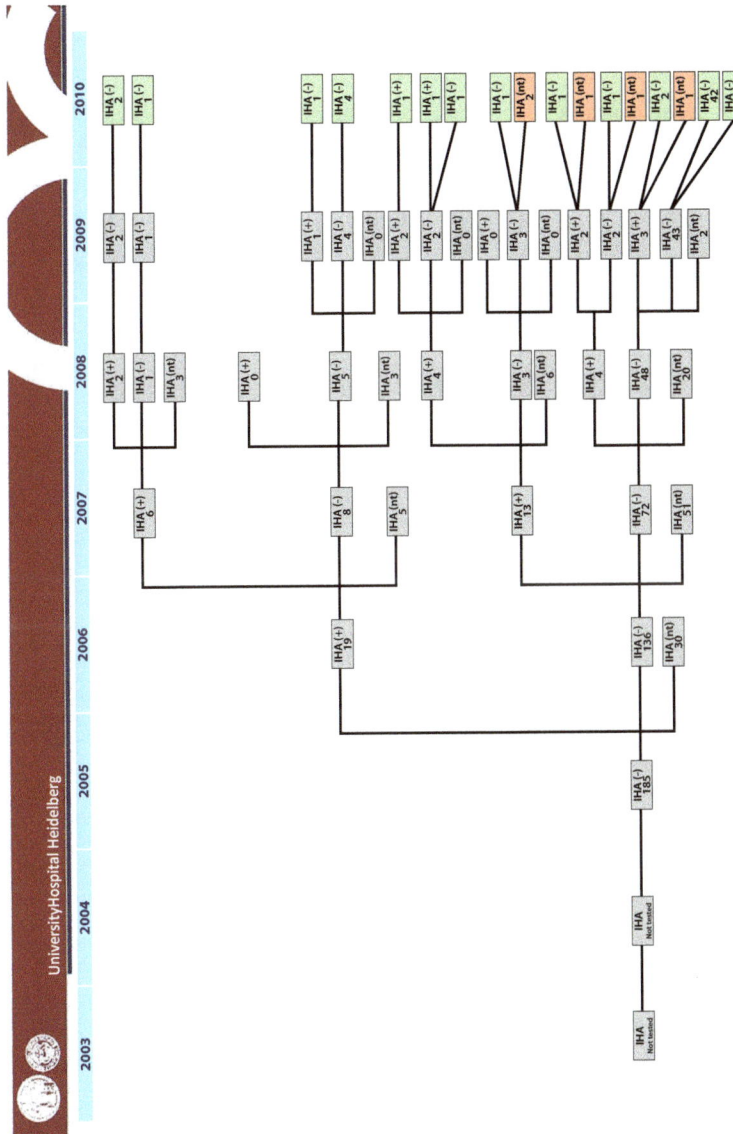

IHA (-): negative IHA test; IHA (+): positive IHA test; IHA (nt): person was not tested (nt) in the respective year. Green: persons tested for 6 consecutive years (2005–2010); red: people tested for 5 consecutive years starting (2005–2009);

Annex 3B: IHA test results of 155 individual persons who were not tested in 2003 and 2004, but tested IHA positive in 2005 and followed for up to 6 consecutive years until 2010

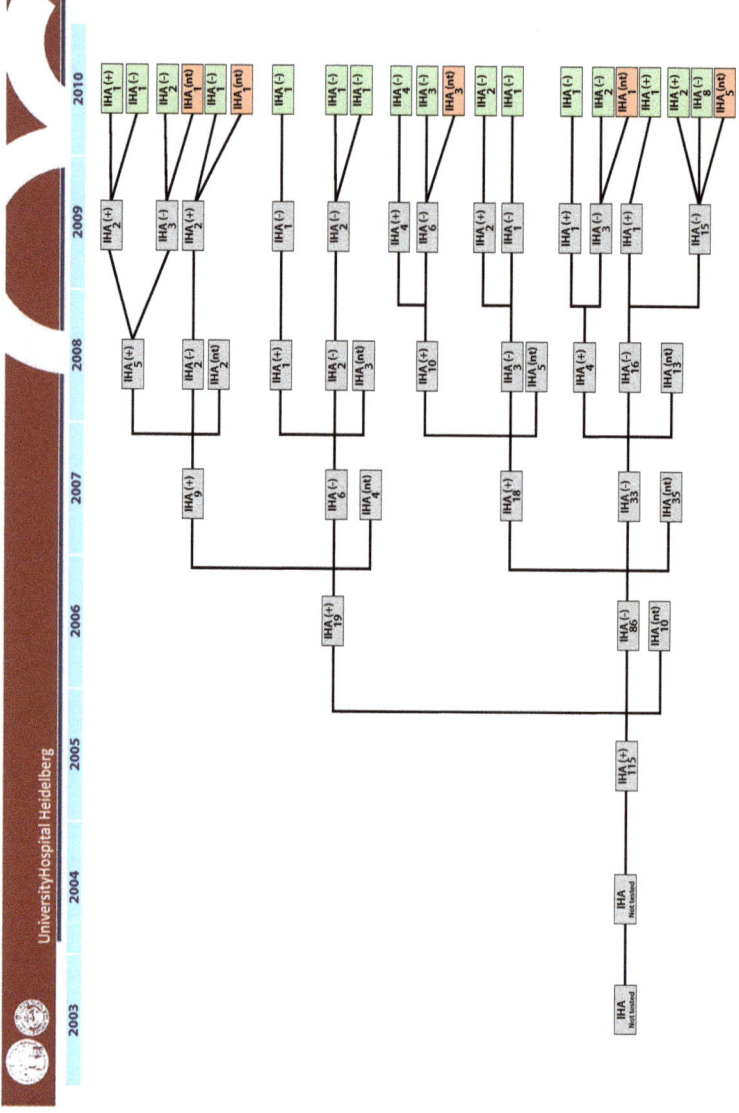

IHA (-): negative IHA test; IHA (+): positive IHA test; IHA (nt): person was not tested (nt) in the respective year. Green: persons tested for 6 consecutive years (2005-2010); red: people tested for 5 consecutive years starting (2005-2009);

Annex 4: Questionnaire for the heads of 12 district level control stations

Assessment of Human Resources in Schistosomiasis Prevention and Control in Wuhan
Questionnaire for 12 district level Schistosomiasis control stations 2

District _____
Town _____
ID number _____

A. General questions about your personal background

A1. Year of birth: _____

A2. Sex: 1. Male ☐   2. Female ☐

A3: Birth place: 1. Wuhan ☐   2. Hubei province (other place than Wuhan) ☐   3. Other province ☐

A4: Marital status? 1. Married ☐   2. Not married ☐

A5: No of children _____

A6: Education: 1. Primary School ☐   2. Middle School ☐   3. High School ☐
4. Higher Education (University, College) ☐

A7. If answer for A6 is 'Higher Education', what is your highest degree?
1. Bachelor ☐   2. Masters ☐   3. MD ☐   4. PhD ☐

A8: If answer for A6 is 'Higher Education', what was your major / field of study?
(If you had a different major for BA and MA study than please write BA or MA after the respective boxes you ticked)

1. Medical Science ☐   2. Economics ☐   3. Natural Sciences ☐
4. Social Sciences ☐   5. Engineering ☐   6. Public Health ☐
7. Other ☐   please specify _____

A9: Name of work facility: _____

A10: Level of your work facility:
1. city level ☐   2. district level ☐   3. town level ☐

A11: Employment status: 1. full time ☐   2. part time ☐   (hours per week: _____)

A12: Monthly income:
1. less than 1,000 RMB ☐   2. 1,000-2,999 RMB ☐
3. 3,000-4,999 RMB ☐   4. 5,000-9,999 RMB ☐
5. 10,000-14,999 RMB ☐   6. 15,000-20,000 RMB ☐
7. over 20,000 RMB ☐

B. Questions related to your work in the field of schistosomiasis

B1. How many years work experience in schistosomiasis control do you have (including previous jobs)?
_____ years

Assessment of Human Resources in Schistosomiasis Prevention and Control in Wuhan
Questionnaire for 12 district level Schistosomiasis control stations

B2. How many years have you been working in your present job as head of the Schistosomiasis department in your district? _____ years

B3. Are you also responsible for the control of diseases other than Schistosomiasis?

    1. yes ☐ which? _____

    2. no ☐

Please answer following questions on the available human resources for schistosomiasis control in your district for the years 2006 and 2011.

B4. How many workers in schistosomiasis control were working in your district in total?

    In 2006 _____ in 2011 _____

    Male _____ Female _____ Male _____ Female _____

    On district level _____ on district level _____

    On town level _____ on town level _____

B5. How many full time employees in schistosomiasis? 2006 _____ 2011 _____

    How many part time employees in schistosomiasis? 2006 _____ 2011 _____

B6: How many clinical doctors?

    In 2006 _____ in 2011 _____

    On district level _____ on district level _____

    On town level _____ on town level _____

B7. How many nurses?

    In 2006 _____ in 2011 _____

    On district level _____ on district level _____

    On town level _____ on town level _____

B8: How many technicians (laboratory technician, X-ray technician)?

    In 2008 _____ in 2011 _____

    On district level _____ on district level _____

    On town level _____ on town level _____

B9. How many public health doctors?

    In 2008 _____ in 2011 _____

    On district level _____ on district level _____

    On town level _____ on town level _____

B10. How many administration workers (secretary, accountant etc.)?

　　　In 2008 _____　　　in 2011 _____

　　　On district level _____　　　on district level _____

　　　On town level _____　　　on town level _____

B11. How many support workers (support staff, driver, cleaner etc.)

　　　In 2008 _____　　　in 2011 _____

　　　On district level _____　　　on district level _____

　　　On town level _____　　　on town level _____

B12: Any other staff, which is not included in the above?

　　　In 2008 _____　　　in 2011 _____

　　　On district level _____　　　on district level _____

　　　On town level _____　　　on town level _____

B13. In the past 12 months how many clinical doctors and nurses were also engaged in control activities outside the hospital (visit to endemic villages and testing people, visits or talks for health education etc.)?

　　Clinical doctors _____　　　nurses _____

B14. In the past 12 months how many health workers were engaged in following activities?

　　1. Diagnosing patients (surveillance in endemic areas, IHA and Kato-Katz tests) _____

　　2. Treatment of chronic patients with praziquantel (in endemic areas) _____

　　3. Treatment of schistosomiasis in-patients in hospitals _____

　　4. Surveying snails _____

　　5. Spraying molluscacide _____

　　6. Overall management (organizing, reports etc.) _____

　　7. Health education activities (going to endemic areas and teach about schistosomiasis, visit schools, compiling information brochures and other material etc.) _____

　　8. Improving sanitation and water supply _____

　　9. Other control activities (please specify) _____

B15. Which of the above mentioned activities are the 3 most labour intensive (people needed)?

　　1. _____　　2. _____　　3. _____

B16. Which of the above mentioned activities are the 3 most time intensive (hours needed, including the planning and preparation phase)?

　　1. _____　　2. _____　　3. _____

B17. Which of the above mentioned activities are the 3 most expensive to carry out (in terms of money)?

1. _____ 2. _____ 3. _____

B18. How many <u>new</u> people did you employ in the past 12 months? _____

B19. How many new people do you employ in average every year? _____

B20. How many people have stopped working in schistosomomiasis control in the past 12 months (retired or changed jobs) ? _____

B21. How many people stop working in Schistosomiasis control in average every year? _____

Please give your opinion on the statements below:

B22. "In my line of work in schistosomiasis control presently there are enough people employed for the current workload."

1. I strongly agree ☐ 2. I agree ☐ 3. I neither agree nor disagree ☐
4. I disagree ☐ 5. I strongly disagree ☐

B23. "Further decrease of schistosomiasis infection rates can only be achieved by employing <u>more</u> people in Schistosomiasis control."

1. I strongly agree ☐ 2. I agree ☐ 3. Neither agree nor disagree ☐
4. I disagree ☐ 5. I strongly disagree ☐

B24. "In my opinion, the amount of work in Schistosomiasis control has steadily increased during the past 10 years."

1. I strongly agree ☐ 2. I agree ☐ 3. Neither agree nor disagree ☐
4. I disagree ☐ 5. I strongly disagree ☐

B 25. "In my opinion the amount of regulations for schistosomiasis control has steadily increased during the past 10 years"

1. I strongly agree ☐ 2. I agree ☐ 3. Neither agree nor disagree ☐
4. I disagree ☐ 5. I strongly disagree ☐

B26. " In my opinion the total number of health workers in Schistosomiasis control has steadily decreased during the past 10 years."

1. I strongly agree ☐ 2. I agree ☐ 3. Neither agree nor disagree ☐
4. I disagree ☐ 5. I strongly disagree ☐

B27. "In my opinion it is difficult to find qualified personnel for the work required in schistosomiasis prevention and control."

1. I strongly agree ☐ 2. I agree ☐ 3. Neither agree nor disagree ☐
4. I disagree ☐ 5. I strongly disagree ☐

Thank you very much for your time and participation in our study!

Annex 5: Questionnaire for non-clinical staff

Assessment of Human Resources in Schistosomiasis Prevention and Control in Wuhan
Questionnaire for non-clinical staff

District _____
Town _____
ID number _____

A. General questions about your personal background

A1. Year of birth: _____

A2. Sex: 1. Male ☐ 2. Female ☐

A3: Birth place: 1. Wuhan ☐ 2. Hubei province (other place than Wuhan) ☐ 3. Other province ☐

A4: Marital status? 1. Married ☐ 2. Not married ☐

A5: No of children _____

A6: Education: 1. Primary School ☐ 2. Middle School ☐ 3. High School ☐
4. Higher Education (University, College) ☐

A7. If answer for A6 is 'Higher Education', what is your highest degree?
1. Bachelor ☐ 2. Masters ☐ 3. MD ☐ 4. PhD ☐

A8: If answer for A6 is 'Higher Education', what was your major / field of study?
(If you had a different major for BA and MA study than please write BA or MA after the respective boxes you ticked)

1. Medical Science ☐ 2. Economics ☐ 3. Natural Sciences ☐

4. Social Sciences ☐ 5. Engineering ☐ 6. Public Health ☐

7. Other ☐ please specify _____

A9: Name of work facility: _____

A10: Level of your work facility:
1. city level ☐ 2. district level ☐ 3. town level ☐

A11: Employment status: 1. full time ☐ 2. part time ☐ (hours per week: _____)

A12: Monthly income:
1. less than 1,000 RMB ☐ 2. 1,000- 2,999 RMB ☐
3. 3,000- 4,999 RMB ☐ 4. 5,000- 9,999 RMB ☐
5. 10,000-14,999 RMB ☐ 6. 15,000-20,000 RMB ☐
7. over 20,000 RMB ☐

B. Questions related to your work in the field of schistosomiasis

B1. How many years work experience in schistosomiasis control do you have (including previous jobs)? _____ years

B2. How many years have you been working in your present job? _____ years

Assessment of Human Resources in Schistosomiasis Prevention and Control in Wuhan
Questionnaire for non-clinical staff

B3. To which of the staff categories below do you belong to?

1. Clinical doctor ☐   2. Nurse ☐   3. Laboratory technician, X-ray technician ☐

4. Others ☐   please specify _____

B4. How much of your total work time do you spend on following activities?

Please read carefully the following explanations before answering the question:

1. If you are involved in several activities please indicate so and tick all the relevant boxes.

2. Please <u>estimate</u> the **days per month** spent on that activity in the Schistosomiasis transmission season (May-September) and non-transmission months (October-April).

ACTIVITY	Estimated time spent (in days per month) during transmission period (May-September)	Estimated time spent (in days per month) during non-transmission months (October-April)
1. Diagnosing patients (including preparation, coordination and planning, performing IHA tests and Kato-Katz tests, laboratory diagnosis, analysis and report of results)	……………days	……………days
2. Treatment of chronic patients with praziquantel (including preparation and planning)	……………days	……………days
3. Treatment of advanced cases in hospitals	……………days	……………days
4. Surveying snails (including preparation and planning, seeking infected snails, laboratory diagnosis, writing reports)	……………days	……………days
5. Spraying molluscacide (including preparation, coordination and planning, writing reports)	……………days	……………days
6. Health education (including preparation and planning, visits, talks, putting up information signs, designing brochures and other informational material)	……………days	……………days
7. Environment modification (including preparation and planning, writing reports)	……………days	……………days
8. Improving sanitation and water supply (including preparation and planning, writing reports)	……………days	……………days
9. Management (supervision, planning overall yearly activities, policy making etc.)	……………days	……………days
10. Administrative and support work (logisticals support, driving)	……………days	……………days
11. Research	……………days	……………days
12. Others Please specify _____	……………days	……………days

Please give your personal opinion on the following statements.

B5. "In my line of work in schistosomiasis control presently there are enough people employed for the current workload."

1. I strongly agree ☐   2. I agree ☐   3. I neither agree nor disagree ☐
4. I disagree ☐   5. I strongly disagree ☐

B6. "Further decrease of schistosomiasis infection rates can only be achieved by employing <u>more</u> people in Schistosomiasis control."

1. I strongly agree ☐   2. I agree ☐   3. I neither agree nor disagree ☐
4. I disagree ☐   5. I strongly disagree ☐

B7. " In my opinion, since I started working in Schistosomiasis, the Schistosomiasis related work load has steadily decreased over time. "

1. I strongly agree ☐   2. I agree ☐   3. I neither agree nor disagree ☐
4. I disagree ☐   5. I strongly disagree ☐

B8. How often do you receive Schistosomiasis related further education or specialised training in average?

1. every year more than once ☐   2. once per year ☐
3. once every two years ☐   4. others ☐

C. Questions related to community participation in schistosomiasis control

C1. During your daily work, do you cooperate with local community participants in schistosomiasis control?

1. Often ☐   2. usually ☐   3. sometimes ☐   4. rarely ☐   5. never ☐

C2. If you do cooperate, how often do you have contact?

1. On a daily basis ☐   2. On a weekly basis ☐
3. On a monthly basis ☐   4. Only a few times a year ☐

C3. Which local community participants are you in contact with?

1. Village authorities ☐   2. Village doctors ☐
3. Villagers, who help with logistics and other support ☐
4. School teachers ☐
5. Others ☐   please specify _____

C4. From your personal experience, how do you rate your cooperation relationship with local community participants in schistosomiasis control?

1. Very good ☐   2. good ☐   3. moderate ☐   4. bad ☐   5. very bad ☐

C5. Please give your <u>personal opinion</u>.

For the success of my <u>personal</u> work activities in schistosomiasis control, local community participation is

1. extremely important ☐   2. very important ☐   3. moderately important ☐

4. slightly important ☐   5. not important ☐

C6. How important is health education on schistosomiasis for the success of your work?

1. extremely important ☐   2. very important ☐   3. moderately important ☐

4. slightly important ☐   5. not important ☐

C7. If you are working 5 or more years in schistosomiasis control, according to your opinion, has the amount of general knowledge of people in the communities you work with about schistosomiasis changed in the past 5 or more years? (Do they know the disease, how they got the disease, what to do to prevent it etc.)

1. No, I see no change in knowledge about schistosomiasis ☐
2. Yes, knowledge about schistosomiasis is less today than 5 years ago ☐
3. Yes, knowledge about schistosomiasis is more today than 5 years ago ☐

C8. In your opinion, how is the knowledge about schistosomiasis among the general population in the area you work?

1. the majority of people (more than 50%) in the area I work has sufficient knowledge about what schistosomiasis is, how it is contracted and how it can be prevented. ☐

2. The majority of people (more than 50%) in the area I work still do not know about what schistosomiasis is, how it is contracted or how it can be prevented. ☐

Thank you very much for your time and participation in our study!

Annex 6: Questionnaire for clinical staff

Assessment of Human Resources in Schistosomiasis Prevention and Control in Wuhan
Questionnaire for clinical staff

A. General questions about your personal background

District _____
Town _____
ID number _____

A1. Year of birth: _____

A2. Sex: 1. Male ☐ 2. Female ☐

A3: Birth place: 1. Wuhan ☐ 2. Hubei province (other place than Wuhan) ☐ 3. Other province ☐

A4: Marital status? 1. Married ☐ 2. Not married ☐

A5: No of children _____

A6: Education: 1. Primary School ☐ 2. Middle School ☐ 3. High School ☐
4. Higher Education (University, College) ☐

A7. If answer for A6 is 'Higher Education', what is your highest degree?
1. Bachelor ☐ 2. Masters ☐ 3. MD ☐ 4. PhD ☐

A8: If answer for A6 is 'Higher Education', what was your major / field of study?
(If you had a different major for BA and MA study than please write BA or MA after the respective boxes you ticked)

1. Medical Science ☐ 2. Economics ☐ 3. Natural Sciences ☐

4. Social Sciences ☐ 5. Engineering ☐ 6. Public Health ☐

7. Other ☐ please specify _____

A9: Name of work facility: _____

A10: Level of your work facility:
1. city level ☐ 2. district level ☐ 3. town level ☐

A11: Employment status: 1. full time ☐ 2. part time ☐ (hours per week: _____)

A12: Monthly income:
1. less than 1,000 RMB ☐
2. 1,000-2,999 RMB ☐
3. 3,000-4,999 RMB ☐
4. 5,000-9,999 RMB ☐
5. 10,000-14,999 RMB ☐
6. 15,000-20,000 RMB ☐
7. over 20,000 RMB ☐

B. Questions related to your work in the field of schistosomiasis

B1. How many years work experience in schistosomiasis control do you have (including previous jobs)? _____ years

B2. How many years have you been working in your present job? _____ years

B3. To which of the staff categories below do you belong to?

1. Clinical doctor ☐   2. Nurse ☐   3. Laboratory technician, X-ray technician ☐

4. Others ☐   please specify _____

B4. How much of your total work time do you spend on following activities?

Please read carefully the following explanations before answering the question:

1. If you are involved in several activities please indicate so and tick all the relevant boxes.

2. Please estimate the days per month spent on that activity in the Schistosomiasis transmission season (May-September) and non-transmission months (October-April)

ACTIVITY	Estimated time spent (in days per month) during transmission period (May-September)	Estimated time spent (in days per month) during non-transmission months (October-April)
1. Laboratory diagnosis for schistosomiasis patients	……………..days	……………..days
2. Treatment of schistosomiasis patients	……………..days	……………..days
3. Schistosomiasis related research	……………..days	……………..days

B5. "In my line of work in schistosomiasis control presently there are enough people employed for the current workload."

1. I strongly agree ☐   2. I agree ☐   3. I neither agree nor disagree ☐

4. I disagree ☐   5. I strongly disagree ☐

B6. "Further decrease of schistosomiasis infection rates can only be achieved by employing more people in Schistosomiasis control."

1. I strongly agree ☐   2. I agree ☐   3. Neither agree nor disagree ☐

4. I disagree ☐   5. I strongly disagree ☐

B7. In 2010, were you involved in any other schistosomiasis related activities outside of the hospital?

1. Yes ☐   2. No ☐

If yes, in which activities are you also involved and how much time did you spend doing them (2010)? Please give a rough personal estimation in <u>days per month</u>.

ACTIVITY	Estimated days per month in transmission period (May – September)	Estimated days per month in non-transmission period (October-April)
Visiting endemic villages / towns and **diagnosing** people for surveillance purposes (collecting blood samples for IHA testing etc.)	……………..days	……………..days

Assessment of Human Resources in Schistosomiasis Prevention and Control in Wuhan
Questionnaire for clinical staff

Laboratory diagnosis of patients tested in the villages/towns for surveillance purposes (IHA tests, Kato-Katz tests)	……………days	……………days
Visiting endemic villages / towns and **treating** schistosomiasis patients	……………days	……………days
Performing **Health education** (for example giving lectures or talks in schools, visit endemic villages to explain about schistosomiasis etc.)	……………days	……………days
Others (please specify)	……………days	……………days

B8. " In my opinion, since I started working in Schistosomiasis, the Schistosomiasis related work load has steadily decreased over time. "

1. I strongly agree ☐ 2. I agree ☐ 3. Neither agree nor disagree ☐

4. I disagree ☐ 5. I strongly disagree ☐

B9. How often do you receive Schistosomiasis related further education or specialised training in average?

1. every year more than once ☐ 2. once per year ☐

3. once every two years ☐ 4. others ☐

C. Questions related to community participation in schistosomiasis control

C1. During your daily work, do you cooperate with local community participants in schistosomiasis control?

1. Often ☐ 2. usually ☐ 3. sometimes ☐ 4. rarely ☐ 5. never ☐

C2. If you do cooperate, how often do you have contact?

1. On a daily basis ☐ 2. On a weekly basis ☐

3. On a monthly basis ☐ 4. Only a few times a year ☐

C3. Which local community participants are you in contact with?

1. Village authorities ☐ 2. Village doctors ☐

3. Villagers, who help with logistics and other support ☐

4. School teachers ☐

5. Others ☐ please specify _____

C4. From your personal experience, how do you rate your cooperation relationship with local community participants in schistosomiasis control?

1. Very good ☐ 2. good ☐ 3. moderate ☐ 4. bad ☐ 5. very bad ☐

C5. Please give your personal opinion.

For the success of my personal work activities in schistosomiasis control, local community participation is

1. extremely important ☐   2. very important ☐   3. moderately important ☐
4. slightly important ☐   5. not important ☐

C6. How important is health education on schistosomiasis for the success of your work?

1. extremely important ☐   2. very important ☐   3. moderately important ☐
4. slightly important ☐   5. not important ☐

C7. If you are working 5 or more years in schistosomiasis control, according to your opinion, has the amount of general knowledge of your patients about schistosomiasis changed in the past 5 or more years? (Do they know the disease, how they got the disease, what to do to prevent it etc.)

1. No, I see no change in knowledge about schistosomiasis ☐
2. Yes, knowledge about schistosomiasis is less today than 5 years ago ☐
3. Yes, knowledge about schistosomiasis is more today than 5 years ago ☐

C8. In your opinion, how is the knowledge about schistosomiasis among the general population in the area you work?

1. the majority of people (more than 50%) in the area I work has sufficient knowledge about what schistosomiasis is, how it is contracted and how it can be prevented. ☐

2. The majority of people (more than 50%) in the area I work still do not know about what schistosomiasis is, how it is contracted or how it can be prevented. ☐

Thank you very much for your time and participation in our study!

Challenges in Public Health

Im Zeitalter der Globalisierung lässt sich *Public Health* nicht mehr allein innerhalb von nationalen Grenzen betreiben: Pandemien, abnehmende Trinkwasservorräte und steigender Tabakkonsum sind nur einige Beispiele für eine Vielzahl von neuen Herausforderungen, die einen weiter reichenden, internationalen Blick erfordern. Zusätzlich trägt eine einseitig an Wirtschaftsinteressen orientierte Globalisierung zu der weltweit zunehmenden gesundheitlichen Ungleichheit bei. Die Globalisierung eröffnet andererseits aber neue Wege, auch über Staatsgrenzen und große Entfernungen hinweg Wissen und Erfahrungen auszutauschen und gemeinschaftlich zu handeln. Kernpunkte für *Public Health* sind dabei die international vergleichende Analyse von Gesundheitsproblemen und möglichen Lösungsansätzen sowie die wissenschaftlich basierte und gerechte Ausgestaltung von Gesundheitssystemen. Hierzu möchte die Buchreihe *Challenges in Public Health* einen Beitrag leisten.

In times of globalisation, Public Health can no longer be practiced within national borders alone. Pandemics, diminishing drinking water supplies and increasing tobacco consumption are examples of the many new challenges that require a cross-border, international approach. In addition, a globalisation that is narrowly focused on economic interests contributes to growing health inequalities worldwide. At the same time, globalisation offers new opportunities to exchange knowledge and experiences and to collaborate across national borders. Key issues for Public Health are an international comparison of health problems and of possible strategies to solve them, as well as an evidence-based and equitable development of health systems. The book series *Challenges in Public Health* aims to contribute to this endeavour.

Medizin in Entwicklungsländern

Herausgegeben von Prof. Hans Jochen Diesfeld

Band 1 Wolfgang Bichmann: Die Problematik der Gesundheitsplanung in Entwicklungsländern. Ein Beitrag zur Geschichte, der Situation und den Perspektiven der Planung des nationalen Gesundheitswesens in den > Least Developed Countries < Afrikas. 1979.

Band 2 Jens Herrmann: Ambition and Reality - Planning for Health and Basic Health Services in the Yemen Arab Republic. 1979.

Band 3 J.M. Pönninghaus: The Cost Benefit of Measles Immunisation. A Study from Southern Zambia. 1979.

Band 4 Hilde Wander (Hrsg.): Bedingungen und Möglichkeiten der Integrierung bevölkerungspolitischer Programme in die nationale und die internationale Entwicklungspolitik. 1980.

Band 5 M. Heidegger/H.J. Diesfeld/A. Selheim: Demographische und soziale Wirkungen von Familienplanung. 1980.

Band 6 H.J. Diesfeld (Hrsg.): Importierte Krankheiten und ärztliche Untersuchungen vor und nach Tropenaufenthalt. Kongreßbericht über die X. Tagung der Deutschen Tropenmedizinischen Gesellschaft vom 22.-24. März 1979 in Heidelberg. 1980.

Band 7 Alexander Boroffka: Benedict Nta Tanka's Commentary and Dramatized Ideas on "Disease and Witchcraft in our Society". A Schreber Case from Cameroon Annotated Autobiographical Notes by an African on his Mental Illness. 1980.

Band 8 Hartmut Brandt: Work Capacity Restraints in Tropical Agricultural Development. 1980.

Band 9 nicht erschienen

Band 10 Tilman Nitzschke / Donata von Lüttwitz: Annehmbarkeit präventiver und promotiver Maßnahmen eines Health Centre für die Bevölkerung. Dargestellt am Beispiel der ländlichen Gesundheitsversorgung der Vereinigten Republik Kamerun. 1981.

Band 11 H.J. Diesfeld (Ed.): Health Research in Developing Countries. Proceedings of the Joint Meeting of the Belgische Vereniging voor Tropische Geneeskunde, Société Belge de Medecine Tropicale, the Nederlandse Vereniging voor Tropische Geneeskunde and the Deutsche Tropenmedizinische Gesellschaft. 1982.

Band 12 Axel Kroeger/Francoise Barbira-Freedman: Cultural Change and Health: The Case of Southamerican Rainforest Indians. With special reference to the Shuar/Achuar of Ecuador. 1982.

Band 13 Dorothea Sich: Mutterschaft und Geburt im Kulturwandel. Ein Beitrag zur transkulturellen Gesundheitsforschung aus Korea. 1982.

Band 14 Uwe K. Brinkmann: Onchozerkose in Westafrika. 1982.

Band 15 Peter Oberender/Hans Jochen Diesfeld/Wolfgang Gitter (Hrsg.): Health and Development in Africa. International, Interdisciplinary Symposium, 2-4 June 1982, University of Bayreuth. 1983.

Band 16 Josef Boch (Hrsg.): Tropenmedizin, Parasitologie, Trypanosomiasis, Malaria, Bilharziose, Onchozerkose, Importierte Virusinfektionen, Lepra, Intermediate Technology, Zecken und durch sie übertragene Krankheiten, Immundiagnostik. 1984.

Band 17 Abdin Hamid Shaddad: Anforderungen an Gesundheitseinrichtungen der Basisversorgung im Sudan. Ein Beitrag zur Gesundheitsversorgung und zu baulichen Maßnahmen für die Gesundheitseinrichtungen unter besonderer Berücksichtigung der vorhandenen Ressourcen, der sozialen Verhältnisse und der klimatischen Bedingungen. 1984.

Band 18 Gerhard Heller: Krankheitskonzepte und Krankheitssymptome. Eine empirische Untersuchung bei den Tamang von Cautara/Nepal zur Frage der kulturspezifischen Prägung von Krankheitserleben. 1985.

Band 19 Hans-Jochen Diesfeld / Sigrid Wolter (Hrsg.): Medizin in Entwicklungsländern. Handbuch zur praxisorientierten Vorbereitung für medizinische Entwicklungshelfer. 5. neubearbeitete Auflage. 1989.

Band 20 Verena Kücholl: Soziokulturelle Wege des Heilens. Eine ethnomedizinische Analyse und Interpretation des Samkhya und der Heiltradition der Navajo. 1985.

Band 21 Frank-Peter Schelp (Ed.): Health Problems in Asia and in the Federal Republic of Germany. How to solve them? Proceedings of a seminar on "Techniques and Problems of Intervention Trials in Developing and Developed Countries". 1985.

Band 22 Rolf Heinmüller, Winfried Kern: Primäre Gesundheitsversorgung im südwestlichen Sudan. Eine Feldforschung bei den südsudanesischen Azande zur Evaluierung der Einflüsse des 'Primary Health Care'-Programms auf gesundheitliche Lage und allgemeine Lebensbedingungen. Detailed English Summary. 1987.

Band 23 Andreas Hahold/Axel Kroeger: Krankheitsbewältigung im Andenhochland Perus. Ergebnisse einer Bevölkerungsbefragung. 1986.

Band 24 Georg Kamm / Peter Witton / Hatibu Lweno: Anaesthesia Notebook for Medical Auxilaries. With special Reference to Anaesthesia Practice in Developing Countries. 1989.

Band 25 Alice S. Kuhn: Heiler und ihre Patienten auf dem Dach der Welt. Ladakh aus ethnomedizinischer Sicht. 1988.

Band 26 Wolfgang Bichmann: Community Involvement in Nepal's Health System. A case study of district health services management and the Community Health Leader scheme in Kaski district. 1989.

Band 27 M. Luisa Vázquez / Renate Lipowsky / Axel Kroeger: Malaria und kutane Leishmaniase in Kolumbien. Vorkommen, Volkskonzepte und traditionelle Behandlungsformen. 1989.

Band 28 Heinrich Berg / Axel Kroeger / Carmen Perez-Samaniego / Fernando Malo: Kranke Menschen – krankes Gesundheitswesen? Eine epidemiologische Untersuchung in Nord-Mexiko. 1989.

Band 29 Emmie Ho-Tsui / Margit Urhahn: Medizin und Gesundheitsforschung in Entwicklungsländern. Bibliographie des Instituts für Tropenhygiene 1984-1988. 1991.

Band 30 Thomas Lux: Gespräche mit afrikanischen Krankenpflegern und Heilern. Bilder von Krankheit im Mikrokosmos von Malanville(Benin), 1991.

Band 31 Christopher Knauth: Arzneimittelgebrauch armer Bevölkerungsschichten in städtischen Elendsvierteln Perus. Möglichkeiten und Grenzen der Gesundheitserziehung zum rationalen Arzneimittelgebrauch. 1991.

Band 32 Erhard Hinz: Geomedizinische und biogeographische Aspekte der Krankheitsverbreitung und Gesundheitsversorgung in Industrie- und Entwicklungsländern. 1991.

Band 33 Klaus Hoffmann: Psychiatrie in Afrika. Eine Einführung für Entwicklungshelfer. 1992.

Band 34 Dorothea Sich / Hans Jochen Diesfeld / Angelika Deigner / Monika Habermann (Hrsg.): Medizin und Kultur. Eine Propädeutik für Studierende der Medizin und der Ethnologie mit 4 Seminaren in Kulturvergleichender Medizinischer Anthropologie (KMA). 1993. 2., unveränd. Aufl. 1995.

Band 35 Annette Wiemann-Michaels: Die verhexte Speise. Eine ethnopsychosomatische Studie über das Depressive Syndrom in Nepal. 1994.

Band 36 Christine Loytved: Hebammen in Ozeanien zwischen traditioneller und westlicher Medizin. Weiterbildung traditioneller Hebammen in Westsamoa und Tonga. 1994.

Band 37 Andrea Materlik: Medizinisch-anthropologische Aspekte von Lepra im Amazonas und ihre Bedeutung für die Gesundheitserziehung. 1994.

Band 38 Oliver Razum: Improving Service Quality through Action Research, as applied in the Expanded Programme on Immunization (EPI). 1994.

Band 39 Ulrich Schramm: Einflußfaktoren auf die Akzeptanz von baulichen Anlagen der ländlichen Gesundheitseinheiten in Ägypten. Fallstudie am Beispiel der staatlichen Einheit in Zebeda unter Verwendung der Post-Occupancy Evaluation. 1995.

Band 40 Rainer Sauerborn / Adrien Nougtara / Hans Jochen Diesfeld (Eds.): Recherche sur les systèmes de santé: Le cas de la zone médicale de Solenzo, Burkina Faso. Auteurs: Rainer Sauerborn, Adrien Nougtara, Hans Jochen Diesfeld, Gaston Sorgho, Joseph Bidiga, Lougousse Tiébélessé, Eric Latimer, Roberto Sallier de La Tour, Uwe Brinkmann, Don Shepard. 1995.

Band 41 Rainer Sauerborn / Adrien Nougtara / Hans Jochen Diesfeld (Eds.): Les Côuts Economiques de la Maladie pour les Ménages au Milieu Rural du Burkina Faso. Avec des contributions de Rainer Sauerborn, Adrien Nougtara, Maurice Hien, Issouf Ibrango, Matthias Borchert, Justus Benzler, Eberhard Koob, Hans Jochen Diesfeld. 1996.

Band 42 Erhard Hinz: Helminthiasen des Menschen in Thailand. 1996.

Band 43 Matthias Perleth: Historical Aspects of American Trypanosomiasis (Chagas' Disease). 1997.

Band 44 Christiane Fischer: Über die Effektivität der Dorfgesundheitsarbeiterinnen innerhalb der Nichtregierungsorganisation ACCORD in Tamil Nadu/Südindien. Aktionsforschung im Rahmen der Gesundheitssystemforschung. 1998.

Band 45 Maureen Dar lang: Assessment of antenatal and obstetric care services in a rural district of Nepal. 1999.

Band 46 Julia Katzan: *sòi mendan* – Die Sache mit dem Wasser... Eine medizinethnologische Untersuchung zum Zusammenhang von Wasser und Krankheit aus indigener Sicht. 2001.

Band 47 Catharina Will: Malaria-Selbstmedikation mit Chloroquin in einem hyperendemischen Gebiet (Mali). 2001.

Band 48 Ansgar Gerhardus: Entscheidungsprozesse im Gesundheitssektor. Der Beitrag der Theorie der politischen Ökonomie. 2001.

Band 49 Sylvie Schuster: Der Schwangerschaftsabbruch im Grasland Kameruns. Medizin, Kultur und Praxis. 2004.

Band 50 Sascha Klotzbücher: Das ländliche Gesundheitswesen der VR China. Strukturen – Akteure – Dynamik. 2006.

Challenges in Public Health

Editor: Prof. Dr. Oliver Razum

Band 51 Ulrich Ronellenfitsch: Cardiovascular Mortality among Ethnic German Immigrants from the Former Soviet Union. 2007.

Band 52 Manuela De Allegri: To Enrol or not to Enrol in Community Health Insurance. Case Study from Burkina Faso. 2007.

Band 53 Catherine Kyobutungi: Ethnic German Immigrants from the Former Soviet Union: Mortality from External Causes and Cancers. 2008.

Band 54 Maren Bredehorst: Information Systems for the Rehabilitation of Landmine Survivors. 2007.

Band 55 Sven Voigtländer / Gabriele Berg-Beckhoff / Oliver Razum: Gesundheitliche Ungleichheit. Der Beitrag kontextueller Merkmale. 2008.

Band 56 Oliver Razum / Jürgen Breckenkamp / Pitt Reitmaier (Hrsg.): Kindergesundheit in Entwicklungsländern. 2008.

Band 57 Steffen Fleßa: Costing of Health Care Services in Developing Countries. A Prerequisite for Affordability, Sustainability and Efficiency. 2009.

Band 58 Patrick Brzoska / Oliver Razum: Validity Issues in Quantitative Migrant Health Research. The Example of Illness Perceptions. 2010.

Band 59 Oliver Razum / Anna Reeske / Jacob Spallek (Hrsg.): Gesundheit von Schwangeren und Säuglingen mit Migrationshintergrund. 2011.

Band 60 Olaf Müller: Malaria in Africa. Challenges for Control and Elimination in the 21st Century. 2011.

Band 61 Walter Bruchhausen / Helmut Görgen / Oliver Razum (Hrsg.): Entwicklungsziel Gesundheit. Zeitzeugen der Entwicklungszusammenarbeit blicken zurück. 2011.

Band 62 Oliver Razum / Jacob Spallek / Anna Reeske / Melina Arnold (eds.): Migration-sensitive Cancer Registration in Europe. Challenges and Potentials. 2011.

Band 63 Martin Kohls: Demographie von Migranten in Deutschland. 2012.

Band 64 Patrick Brzoska: Psychometrically Relevant Differences between Source and Migrant Populations. 2014.

Band 65 Pauline Grys: Schistosomiasis Control in China. Diagnostics and Control Strategies Leading to Success. 2016.

www.peterlang.com